Educational Thoughts of Sri Aurobindo

Educational Thoughts of Sri Aurobindo

Dr. Sudharma Joshi

CRESCENT
PUBLISHING CORPORATION

Educational Thoughts of Sri Aurobindo

Edition 2025

ISBN 978-81-8342-160-7

Published by
CRESCENT PUBLISHING CORPORATION
4806/24, Mathur Lane,
Ansari Road, Darya Ganj,
New Delhi - 110 002
Ph.: 011 - 23244131
Mob.: + 91 - 9711991838, 9999021668
E-mail: crescentbook@gmail.com
Website: www.crescentpublishingcorp.weebly.com

Printed at:
Balaji Digital
Delhi

Preface

Sri Aurobindo today is often hailed as one of the most important modern seer and Vedic scholar of India, whose speeches, writings and actions were characterised by his insistance on complete Independence of India from colonial rule, assuring him a place in history as a freedom fighter too. As a philosopher and a poet, he also embodied a social visionary who was to encompass within his purview relevant issues, including that of education. Revered as a Yogi, he incorporated within the framework of his educational ideology a unique blend of intellectual, spiritual and physical pursuits meant to make educations a wholesome and fulfilling experience.

This book on the educational thoughts of great Indians focuses its attention on to unravelling the philosophy of Sri Aurobindo. He once articulated 'The first principle of teaching is that nothing can be taught', thus condensing his educational philosophy of self-pursuit and self-discovery in nutshell. The book explores in detail this philosophy. With its stress on 'Integral education', which looked into the integrated education of body, soul and mind, as well as its emphasis on unearthing the social and psychological aspects of education. In addition, the book compares his ideology with those of his contemporaries, and also analyses its relevance in the present context.

It is hoped that the book's insight serves well for educationists in India.

Dr. Sudharma Joshi

Contents

1

Lifescketch of Sri Aurobindo

Although Sri Aurobindo's first biography in English was published, obviously without his knowledge in 1910, the year Sri Aurobindo came over to Pondicherry in his late thirties. Later when a scholar proposed to write a biography with his knowledge, Sri Aurobindo discouraged him, saying that no one could write about his life because it had not been on the surface for man to see.

Sri Aurobindo's reluctance would surprise many, for his life, even the first thirtyseven years of it, which, he mostly spent in England, Baroda (Vadodara) and Calcutta, had been marked by tumultuous events and most significant ones in relation to the recent history of the nation. How does he belittle them ?

The fact is, Sri Aurobindo considered his most worthwhile actions as those which were not on the surface, but deep in the ocean of consciousness—actions which were too profound for any factual narration. Whatever we know of them, we know through the persistent queries of his disciples and, of course, much can be surmised from his writings.

However, so many have violated his suggestions against writing his biography and we too, following the academic traditions, give below a chronological account of his life—a bare outline of it.

Sri Aurobindo's father, Dr. K. D. Ghose, who had received a post-graduate medical degree from the West, was totally Westernized in his life-style and sense of values. On the other hand Sri Aurobindo's mother, Swarnalata Devi was the daughter of Rajnarayan Bose, known as "the grandfather of Indian Nationalism", a great patriot and visionary.

Sri Aurobindo, the third son in the family, was born on August 15, 1872. Neither the mother nor the grandfather had much opportunity to mould Sri Aurobindo's outlook, for Dr. Ghose left all his three sons, the elder two being Benoy Bhushan and Man Mohan respectively, at Loretto Convent, Darjeeling, in the company of European children. Sri Aurobindo was then aged five.

Two years later, in 1875, Dr. Ghose and Swarnalata Devi led their children to England and left them at Manchester, under the care of Latin scholar, Mr. Drewett.

In 1884 the three boys shifted to London, with Mrs. Drewett, a devout Christian, as their guardian. Sri Aurobindo was admitted to St. Paul's School, where he continued for five years, shining as a brilliant student, securing all the top prizes for literature and history. His elder brother, Man Mohan, grew into a poet and as a friend of Oscar Wilde and Lawrence Binyon. Sri Aurobindo's poetic genius began to bloom at this stage though very little of his writing of this period has survived the vicissitudes of time. Mrs. Drewett left them before long and the boys had to live through great hardship because Dr. Ghose, a legendary philanthrope at home, neglected to send his sons even the minimum amount of money they needed. Recollects Sri Aurobindo : "During a whole year a slice or two of sandwich, bread and butter and a cup of tea in the morning and in the evening a penny saveloy formed the only food."

A scholarship from St. Paul's enabled Sri Aurobindo to go to King's College, Cambridge, in 1889. He practically bagged all the prizes in Greek and Latin. He passed the first part of the classical Tripos in the first class in 1892. The same year he successfully passed his I.C.S. examination. But he did not report for the riding test and thereby got himself disqualified for the Civil Services.

His well-wishers, who did not know that Sri Aurobindo had secured his disqualification deliberately, tried to persuade the authorities to admit Sri Aurobindo into the Service ignoring the technical lacuna in his performance. G.W. Prothero, a Senior Fellow of King's College, wrote to James Cotton, Sir Henry Cotton's brother :

"He performed his part of the bargain as regards the college most honourably and took a high place in the first class of the classical Tripos, part one, at the end of the second year of his residence. He also obtained certain college prizes, showing command of English and literary ability. That a man should have been able to do this (which alone is quite enough for most under-graduates) and at the same time to keep up his I.C.S. work, proves very unusual industry and capacity. Besides his classical scholarship, he possessed knowledge of English literature far beyond the average of under-graduates, and wrote much better English than most young Englishmen."

The authorities would have probably considered the submission made on Sri Aurobindo's behalf (though without his consent) sympathetically, but by then they had received the intelligence that Sri Aurobindo was a member of a secret Society called the "Lotus and Dagger", dedicated to fighting for India's freedom. His speeches at the Indian Majlis at Cambridge, attacking the British rule in India, had been reported too.

It was a relief to Sri Aurobindo that the I.C.S. mercifully left him unclaimed. He had, needless to say, no call for that kind of a career.

Just then, Maharaja Sayaji Rao, the Gaekwad of Baroda was on a visit to London. James Cotton arranged a meeting between him and Sri Aurobindo and the Maharaja recruited Sri Aurobindo to his government. After an absence of fourteen years, Sri Aurobindo returned to India in February 1893. It was a quiet homecoming, preceded by a tragedy unknown to him. The ship by which he was to reach Mumbai sank off the coast of Lisbon—and the shocking news reached Dr. K. D. Ghosh who had no knowledge of his son having changed his plan at the last moment and of having boarded another ship. Dr. Ghosh died of a heart-attack.

Sri Aurobindo was overwhelmed by a vast peace that descended on him the moment he set foot on the soil of India at Apollo Bunder, Mumbai. That seems to be the way the soul of India received him. Years later he wrote to a disciple :

"My own life and my yoga have always been, since my coming to India, both this-worldly and other-worldly without any exclusiveness on either side....Since I set foot on the Indian soil on the Apollo Bunder in Bombay, I began to have spiritual experiences, but these were not divorced from this world but had an inner and infinite bearing on it, such as a feeling of the Infinite pervading material space and the Immanent inhabiting material objects and bodies. At the same time I found myself entering supraphysical worlds and planes with influences and an effect from them upon the material plane, so I could make no sharp divorce or irreconcilable opposition between what I have called the two ends of existence and all that lies between them."

We do not know who informed him of his father's demise. He proceeded straight to Vadodara and joined the Gaekwad's administration as Professor of English and French at the Maharaja's College. During his thirteen years of stay there, he also worked in several departments of the Maharaja's Secretariat at different times, apart from working as the Vice-Principal and Acting Principal of the College.

Simultaneously, he delved deep into the ancient Indian lore, mastering Sanskrit, Bengali and several other Indian languages. He translated parts of the epics and works of Kalidasa and Bhartrihari into English, wrote original poetry and plays and began practising Yoga.

All those who were in contact with him knew about these activities of his, but very few people knew that he had become the source of inspiration for groups of dedicated youths, scattered in different parts of India, ready to sacrifice their lives for the cause of the motherland's freedom. Through some of his trusted lieutenants including his younger brother Barindra, he channelised their spirit along a certain line of preparatory action.

The Indian National Congress, formed in 1885, was pursuing a policy that was nowhere nearer the goal of freedom for the country. In a periodical named the *Indu Prakash* published at Mumbai and edited by his Cambridge friend K. G. Despande, Sri Aurobindo wrote a series of articles under the title "New Lamps for Old" which created a stir in the political circle of the time.

Interesting glimpses of Sri Aurobindo's Vadodara days are left by Direndra Kumar Roy, a well-known Bengali writer, who lived with Sri Aurobindo for a while to help him learn Bengali. Roy was amazed at the fact that Sri Aurobindo would at times refuse an invitation from the Maharaja himself for joining him for breakfast or dinner, under the pretext that he had no time, while so many Europeans and members of the Indian nobility waited for days together for an appointment with the Maharaja!

Sri Aurobindo did not care for status or money and he lived the life of an ascetic. There was no change in this even after his marriage to Mrinalini Devi in 1901, at Calcutta. Roy sums up his impression of him with these words : "Sri Aurobindo was not a man of this earth; he was a god descended from heavens, probably under a curse."

One of his private letters to Mrinalini Devi, written from Vadodara which became famous because the prosecution produced it in the Court in the course of the historic Alipore Conspiracy Case, gives an intimate picture of his mind (translated from Bengali by an early biographer) :

"I have three madnesses. Firstly, it is my firm faith that whatever virtue, talent, higher education and knowledge and wealth, which God has given me, belongs to Him. I have the right to spend only as much as is needed for the maintenance of the family and on what is absolutely necessary. Whatever remains should be returned to the Divine. If I spend all of it on myself, for personal comfort, for enjoyment, then I am a thief. According to Hindu Scriptures one who accepts money from the Divine and does not return it to Him is a thief. Till now I have been giving only a small fraction of my money to God and have been spending nine-tenths of it for my personal happiness—thus have I settled the account and have remained immersed in worldly happiness. Half of the life has already been wasted; even an animal feels gratified in feeding itself and its family.....

"I have no regrets for the money that I gave to Sarojini or to Usha, because assisting others is Dharma, to protect those who depend on you is a great Dharma, but the account is not settled if one gives only to one's brothers and sisters. In these hard days, the whole country is like a dependent at our doors. I have thirty crores of brothers and sisters in this country—many of them die of starvation, most of them are weakened by suffering and troubles and are somehow dragging on their existence. They must be helped. What do you say, will you be my wife sharing this Dharma with me ? We will eat and dress like ordinary people and buy what is really essential, and give the rest to the Divine. That is what I would do. If you agree to it, and accept the principle of sacrifice then my resolution can be fulfilled. You were complaining that you have made no progress. This is a path to progress that I point out to you. Would you like to take that path ?

"The second folly has recently taken hold of me. It is this : by whatever means, I must get the direct realisation of the Lord. The religion of today consists in repeating the name of God every now and then, in praying to Him in the presence of everybody and in showing to people how religious one is; I do not want it. If the Divine is there, then there must be a way of experiencing His existence, of realising His presence; however hard the path, I have taken a firm irresolution to follow it. Hindu Dharma asserts that the path is to be found in one's own self, in one's mind. The rule that enables one to follow the path is also given to me; I have begun to observe all the rules and within a month I have been able to ascertain that the words of the Hindu Dharma are not false, I have had the experience of all the signs that have been mentioned by it. I would like to take you also along that path; you would not be able to keep up with me as you have not yet had the knowledge, but there is nothing to prevent your following me. Anybody can reach perfection by following the path. But it depends upon one's choice to enter the path. Nobody can force you to enter it. If you are willing, I will write more about this subject.

"The third folly is this : whereas others regard the country as an inert object, and know it as the plains, the fields, the forests, the mountains and rivers, I look upon my country as the mother, I worship her and adore her as the mother. What would a son do when a demon sitting on the breast of his mother is drinking her blood? Would he sit down content to take his meals, and go on enjoying himself in the company of his wife and children, or would he, rather, run to the rescue of his mother? I know I have the strength to uplift this fallen race; it is not physical strength, I am not going to fight with the sword or with the gun, but with the power of knowledge. The power of warrior is not the only kind of force, there is also the power of the 'Brahman' which is founded on knowledge. This is not a new feeling with me, it is not of a recent origin, I was born with it, it is in my very marrow, God sent me to the earth to accomplish this great mission. At the age of fourteen the seed of it had begun to sprout and at eighteen it had been firmly rooted and become unshakable."

That was the time when Curzon's move to partition Bengal inspired a determined protest from all nationalists. "Never had India seen such popular demonstration", wrote Valentine Chirol, the correspondent of *The Times* of London.

At the request of friends who founded the National Council of Education in Calcutta, Sri Aurobindo came over to Calcutta in 1906 to head a college that would be a bold alternative to the system of clerk-making education imposed on India by its colonial masters.

Sri Aurobindo had already developed a distinct educational vision by then. In his article entitled 'A system of National Education' published in 1907, he wrote :

"Every one has in him something divine, something his own, a chance of perfection and strength in however small a sphere which God offers him to take or refuse. The task is to find it, develop it and use it. The chief aim of education should be to help the growing soul to draw out that in itself which is best and make it perfect for a noble use."

In 1910 was published the article containing the line which has by now become famous as an epigram : "The first principle of true teaching is that nothing can be taught."

Almost simultaneously Bipin Chandra Pal, a leading public figure of the time, launched a newspaper, the *Bande Mataram*, and invited Sri Aurobindo to edit it. Sri Aurobindo acceded to the request and in no time the newspaper, "full of leading and special articles written in English with brilliance and pungency not hitherto attained in the Indian Press", as S. K. Ratcliffe, the then editor of *The Statesman*, recollected later, became "the most effective voice of what was then called nationalist extremism."

The enthusiasm with which Sri Aurobindo and the *Bande Mataram* were greeted, can be imagined from a comment in *Sandhya* edited by the veteran, Brahmabandhav Upadhyay : "Have you ever seen the spotless all-white Aurobindo (lotus), the hundred-petalled Aurobindo in full bloom in India's Manasarovara?... Our Aurobindo is a rare phenomenon in the world. In him can be marked the splendour of the *Sattvik*, snow-white and resplendent. Great and vast—vast in his heart, great in his personal glory—his *Swadharma*... Pure and complete a man, a fire-charged thunder yet tender and delicate as the lotus-petal.... The words of *Bande Mataram* will drive out your fear; steel your arms with the might of thunder; fire will course through your veins; death will put on a face of a spring-time joy... True, Aurobindo has had his education in England, but he has not succumbed to its bewitching spell. An efflorescence of the glory of his country's *Swadharma* and culture, Aurobindo is now at the feet of the Motherland, as a fresh-blown lotus of the autumn, luminous with the spirit of his self-offering... There, bow down to the Mother, with the Mantra of *Bande Mataram*. Freedom is not far." (Translated from Bengali).

M. R. Jayakar, a young delegate to the Calcutta Session of the Congress (1906), records in his autobiography, *The Story of My Life* (Vol. 1) :

"I then had any first opportunity of observing from close quarters the Congress leaders of those times with some of whom my contact increased later. I then saw Aurobindo Ghose and his associates. What struck me were his great earnestness and dignified appearance. He had not then developed, so far as outside appearance could show, into a complete Yogi, but I got, from a distance, an indication that his political philosophy was different from that of those who surrounded him."

In 1907 the Government prosecuted the *Bande Mataram* and Sri Aurobindo as its editor for spreading sedition. It was a nationwide sensation. Tagore wrote his famous poem, "Aurobindo, Accept the Salutations of Rabindra", during this period.

The government's case failed in the court. Towards the end of the same year the historic Surat Congress took place where the nationalists and moderates clashed and the former assembled in a separate conference. As author and journalist Henry Nevinson who was present as a correspondent of *The Daily News* of London records in his *New Spirit in India* : "Grave and silent, I think without saying a single word, Mr. Aurobindo Ghose took the chair and sat unmoved, with far-off eyes, as one who gazes at futurity. In clear, short sentences, without eloquence or passion, Mr. Tilak spoke till the stars shone out and someone kindled a lantern at his side."

This was a turning in the history of India's fight for freedom. *Swaraj,* complete freedom, became the specific target to be achieved and Sri Aurobindo had spelt out the methods: Boycott of British goods, national education, organisation of a volunteer force to fight for the cause, etc.

Sri Aurobindo toured several parts of Gujarat and Maharashtra and received ovations the like of which were not known till then. Prosecution Counsel North complained during the Alipore trial : "Aurobindo was treated with the reverence due to a king wherever he went. As a matter of fact, he was regarded as the leader not merely of Bengal but of the whole country."

On May 2, 1908, Sri Aurobindo was arrested, implicated in several militant activities conducted under the leadership of his younger brother, Barindra. From May 5, 1908 till the May 6 of the next year, he was lodged in the Alipore Central Jail, Calcutta.

In his solitary cell, he turned his ordeal into a unique opportunity, realising what he had already known—the Cosmic Consciousness and the Divine in every being and thing. He said in his speech upon his acquittal :

"I looked at the jail that secluded me from men and it was not longer by its high walls that I was imprisoned; no, it was Vasudeva, who surrounded me. I walked under the branches of the tree in front of my cell but it was not the tree, I knew it was Vasudeva, it was Sri Krishna whom I saw standing there and holding over me His shade.... I looked and it was not the Magistrate whom I saw, it was Vasudeva, it was Narayana who was sitting there on the bench. I looked at the Prosecuting Counsel and it was not the counsel for the prosecution that I saw; it was Sri Krishna who sat there... and smiled."

The exciting trial continued for a full year, Sri Aurobindo refusing to say or do anything to protect himself. But the young legal genius who stepped forward to defend him—later famous as Deshbandhu Chittaranjan Das—proved prophetic when he concluded his final submission with these words:

"My appeal to you therefore is that a man like this who is being charged with the offences imputed to him stands not only before the bar in this Court but stands before the bar of the High Court of History and my appeal to you is this : That long after this controversy is hushed in silence, long after this turmoil, this agitation ceases, long after he is dead and gone, he will be looked upon as the poet of patriotism, as the prophet of nationalism and the lover of humanity. Long after he is dead and gone his words will be echoed and re-echoed not only in India, but across distant seas and lands. Therefore I say that the man in his position is not only standing before the bar of this Court but before the bar of the High Court of History."

Sri Aurobindo was acquitted. The *Bande Mataram* had ceased publication. He launched an English weekly, the '*Karmayogin*', followed by a Bengali weekly, the '*Dharma*'. The government, however, could never rest in peace with Sri Aurobindo at large. They drew up several strategies to justify his deportation. Lord Minto, the Viceroy and Governor-General of India, would have liked this action very much, but Lord Morley, the Secretary of State for India, was inclined to weigh the question on the scales of pragmatism and not exigencies. "As for deportation, I will not listen to it", he asserted.

As the news of a warrant being issued against Sri Aurobindo for a so-called seditious article by him in the *Karmayogin*, flashed in *The Times*, London, Sir Ramsay MacDonald, leader of the newly formed Labour Party, demanded that the article be produced in the House. When the Secretary of State for India could not oblige him, Sir Ramsay himself produced the magazine and read out passages from it and said, "Surely, to any man who reads this article as it was meant to be read the meaning of that sentence is perfectly clear, and Mr. Aurobindo Ghose, as is perfectly well known by those who have followed his actions and his writings, sincerely believes that the nationalist movement of which he is the head for the time being at any rate, or was still quite recently, is the one guarantee that there shall be no violence done in India and he blames the officials who have suppressed the free expression of Nationalist sentiment for the unfortunate circumstances which have led to murder and death and executions which everyone deplores."

It may be of interest here to refer to a brief dialogue A Member of the House, Mr. J. King, asked in a friendly way "whether this article is published in Bengali and whether Mr. Aurobindo Ghose is not a Bengali !"

Replied Sir Ramsay : "The article is in the most excellent English. There is not a line of Bengali in the whole of it except the date of this Issue and its own title Mr. Aurobindo Ghose could no more write an article in Bengali than I could."

While they were confidently debating on the issue, Sri Aurobindo, obeying an inner inspiration, suddenly left Calcutta for the French pocket Chandernagore and later sailed for Pondicherry where he arrived in April, 1910. Even then, in his last but one letter concerning Sri Aurobindo, Minto wrote to Morley (May 26, 1910) : "As to the celebrated Aurobindo,... I can only repeat what I said to you in my letter of April 14th that he is the most dangerous man we now have to reckon with... and has an unfortunate influence on the student class and Indians who know him quite well have told me he is quite beyond redemption."

But, for Sri Aurobindo, now the issue was the redemption of humanity from its present ignorant state and at Pondicherry he plunged into an exploration of the realms of consciousness, determined to unravel the destiny of man. He saw :

"The earliest preoccupation of man in his awakened thoughts and, as it seems, his inevitable and ultimate preoccupation, for it survives the longest periods of scepticism and returns after every banishment, is also the highest which his thought can envisage. It manifests itself in the divination of Godhead, the impulse towards perfection, the search after pure Truth and unmixed Bliss, the sense of a secret Immortality. The ancient dawns of human knowledge have left us their witness to this constant aspiration; today we see a humanity satiated but not satisfied by victorious analysis of the externalities of Nature preparing to return to its primeval longings. The earliest formula of Wisdom promises to be the last,—God, Light, Freedom, Immortality."—(*The Life Divine*)

Can this primeval quest of man find fulfilment ? For ages, seekers have continued to escape from the so-called mundane life so that they could dwell in an isolated bliss. Was the world then doomed to remain only a field of travails or an illusion as any number of wise mystics would look upon it—without any spiritual culmination?

Sri Aurobindo saw :

"If a spiritual unfolding on earth is the hidden truth of our birth into Matter, if it is fundamentally an evolution of consciousness that has been taking place in Nature, then man as he is cannot be the last term of that evolution: he is too imperfect an expression of the spirit,

Mind itself is a too limited form and instrumentation; Mind is only a middle term of consciousness, the mental being can only be a transitional being. If, then, man is incapable of exceeding mentality, he must be surpassed and Supermind and Superman must manifest and take the lead of the creation. But if his mind is capable of opening to what exceeds it, then there is no reason why man himself should not arrive at Supermind and Supermanhood or at least lend his mentality, life and body to an evolution of that greater term of the spirit manifesting in Nature."

According to Sri Aurobindo, "At present mankind is undergoing an evolutionary crisis in which is concealed a choice of its destiny; for a stage has been reached in which the human mind has achieved in certain directions an enormous development while in others it stands arrested and bewildered and can no longer find its way."

Sri Aurobindo visualised the next stage of human evolution possible with the descent of a gnostic power, the Supramental, capable of transforming the present man.

The Mother, French by birth, though of Middle-Eastern ancestry, first met Sri Aurobindo in 1914. The 'Arya', a monthly, was launched under her initiative. Many of Sri Aurobindo's major works were first serialised in this magazine. The Mother had to leave for France about a year later, but the magazine continued to be published. The Mother returned to Pondicherry in 1920 and the Ashram took shape under her loving care. Sri Aurobindo's works now began to be published in an organised way, first by the Arya Publishing House, Calcutta and later by the Ashram.

Sri Aurobindo, who had started writing at an early age, even during his stay at Manchester (1879-1884), had continued with his creativity through all the turbulent phases of his life, even during his incarceration.

His first book, a collection of poems, entitled *Songs to Myrtilla*, was published in 1895. Between that and the last work to be published during his lifetime, Savitri (1950), he had written extensively on Yoga, culture, sociology, in addition to his poetry and plays. He also answered numerous letters from seekers most of which are compiled as books. His major works are *The Life Divine, The Synthesis of Yoga, Essays on the Gita, The Foundations of Indian Culture, The Future Poetry, The Human Cycle, The Ideal of Human Unity, Collected Poems and Plays* and the epic *Savitri*. All this and his translations, letters and minor works were compiled and published in a systematic manner, after his passing away on the December 5, 1950, and a new edition of them, in 30 volumes, was brought out on the occasion of his first birth centenary in 1972.

It is not possible to say in brief about the Mother. Her spiritual vision, her conviction about the destiny of man, were the same as those of Sri Aurobindo, from her childhood. She was the collaborator in Sri Aurobindo's Yoga of Tansformation. She affirmed that what Sri Aurobindo represents in earth's history is not a teaching, not even a revelation, but a decisive action direct from the Supreme.

On January 6, 1952, the Mother inaugurated the Sri Aurobindo International University Centre—later to be known as Sri Aurobindo International Centre of Education.

Writes Dr. K. R. Srinivasa Iyengar :

"The key to knowledge is within, for it is the awakened soul within that observes, records, sorts out, omits, unites, transmutes, and turns facts and information into knowledge, knowledge into wisdom, and wisdom into the dynamo of right aspiration and action. The spark is indeed within, albeit often obscured by the thick fog of the egoistic prison-house. It is the true task of education to provide the atmosphere, the friendly help or guidance, the leverage that will release the spark and make it flame forth into a blaze of consciousness characterised by an ever increasing intensity and wideness. The physical, the vital, the mental, all will be drafted into this adventure of consciousness, but still the soul will be the rider of the chariot that is the body, with the vital and the mind as the twin horses of the race. Sri Aurobindo has defined Yoga as 'a methodised effort towards self-perfection by the expression of the potentialities latent in the being, and a union of the human individual with the universal and transcendent Existence.' In its far aims as also in its essential processes, education coalesces with Yoga, and it is thus no mystery at all that the Centre of Education is an inseparable part of the Yogashram at Pondicherry.

"Since education is viewed essentially as a field conducive to soul-awakening and soul-growth, the Centre has no use for the artificial distinction between education for boys and education for girls. The Centre of Education accordingly provides the same programme—including physical education—for boys and girls. There is still room for plenty of choice, but the options are made by the inner preference and not by the fact of sex and the compulsion of traditional taboos.

Again, what brings pupils and teachers together in the general run of educational institutions is a system of market-place attitudes and monetary objectives. At the Centre of Education, on the contrary, pupils pay no fees—once admitted, the education is free. As for the teachers, although fully qualified for the work they have to do, they are only maintained by the Ashram like the other 'sadhaks' and receive no salaries or other monetary awards. This elimination of the rancour of the market-place and the lure of mere monetary incentive makes for better pupils and better teachers who are brought together, not as buyers or sellers of knowledge, but as fellow-seekers and pilgrims on the march owing an unswerving allegiance to Sri Aurobindo and the Mother as the embodiments of Truth and Love. Academic and hierarchic differentiations have a functional use only, and are not meant to invade the deeper unity that derives from the common spirit of dedication and self-consecration. The Centre of Education is a community, almost a single consciousness, that is trying to realise to the full its evolutionary possibility."

Through her continuous guidance in every matter, the Mother had seen to it that the Centre of Education had found firm roots by the time she left her body on November 17, 1973. But the institution has never believed that it had as though arrived at its destination. It continues to experiment with ideas emerging from Sri Aurobindo's vision, applying them to the process of learning and teaching to the best of its ability.

The Mother, in 1968, also launched Auroville, an epochmaking experiment in collective living, residents of the township trying to rise above their religious, communal and racial limitations and aspiring to look for a greater future. "Auroville wants to be a new creation expressing a new Consciousness in a new way and according to new methods", said the Mother.

In a wider sense the Auroville experiment is an educational experiment. It is an assertion of faith in the future of man and an effort to evolve a new pattern of living, keeping in mind Sri Aurobindo's vision of a new humanity.

2

Aurobindo's Vision of Education

An explorer and adventurer in consciousness, a visionary of evolution, Sri Aurobindo, had disclosed 'No one can write about my life because it has not been on the surface for man to see' finds echo in Rabindranath Tagore, the fellow Bengali poet-artist and a Nobel laureate with whom Aurobindo felt a deep mutuality, who too had warned that one should not look for the poet in his biography. In fact, McDermott felt that 'interpreting the life of a great spiritual personality is always a treacherous enterprise, and the life of Sri Aurobindo is peculiarly inscrutable'.

Born in Calcutta, then the capital of British India on 15 August 1872, Aurobindo Ackroyd Ghose-the Western middle name was given to by his father at birth-was the third son of his parents-Dr.Krishnadhan Ghose and Swarnalata Devi. The honorific 'Sri' was traditionally used as a mark of respect or worship forming an integral part of his name. In Sanskrit, the word Aurobindo means lotus. Aurobindo's father chose this name for him, thinking that it was unique, but he little suspected that, in the language of occultism, the lotus is the symbol of divine consciousness.

Aurobindo received his early education in a convent school intended for European children and in 1879 was taken by his father to England for schooling in

Manchester and later at St. Paul's School, London. A scholarship from St. Paul's enabled Aurobindo to go to King's College, Cambridge, in 1889. He practically won all the prizes in Greek and Latin. He passed the first part of the classical Tripos in the first class in 1892. The same year he successfully passed his Indian Civil Service Examination. But he did not report for the riding test and thereby was disqualified for the civil service.

Sri Aurobindo, who had started writing at an early age, even during his study at Manchester, had continued with his creativity through all the turbulent phases of his life, even during his incarcertation. His first book, a collection of poems, entitled Songs to Myrtilla, was published in 1895. Between that and the last work to be published during his lifetime, Savitri, he had written extensively on Yoga, culture, sociology, in addition to his poetry and plays-contributions of far-reaching and multi-faceted importance to human thought and in action.

He has given a new cosmology and a new metaphysics in his Life divine 'considered as the philosophical masterpiece of the century' which has revolutionised our very conception of psychology and gave it a new basis in Life divine and in his letters. He formulated a profoundly new approach to sociology in his The human cycle and showed through a searching analysis of past and current systems of social and political thought how a truly spiritual attitude is essential as a foundation of a new and lasting social order. He extended the application of this very approach to the sphere of international politics in his The ideal of human unity.

In his writings on education, he formulated a theory that could, with some variations, be adapted to all the nations of the world, fostering the growth of the integral consciousness in every pupil and bringing back to legitimate authority of the Sprit over a matter fully developed and utilised. He showed in his The synthesis of Yoga how all the systems of Yoga combine and converge on the path to Supermind. In his The secret of the Vedas, The essays on the Gita and writings on Upanishads, he opened up new and epoch-making ways of studying the ancient Indian texts, throwing new light on philosophy and reducing both anthropology and anthropomorphology to their proper place in a balanced scheme of knowledge. He offered an illuminating interpretation of Indian culture down the centuries in his The foundations of Indian culture.

Sri Aurobindo's elaborated epic, Savitri reveals the consummation of the many poetic styles that he attempted in all his works. Written in nearly 24,000 lines in blank verse, Sri Aurobindo's Savitri has been estimated to be the largest poem in the English language. In The future poetry, Sri Aurobindo worked out a literary theory considered as an original contribution to aesthetics in its concept of poetry. All this and his translations, letters and minor works were compiled and published in a systematic manner after his passing away on the 5 December 1950. A new edition of them, in thirty volumes, was brought out on the occasion of the centenary of his birth in 1972. The Swedish Academy considered him for the nomination for the Nobel Prize of 1950, the last year of Sri Aurobindo's life.

There are many ways of approaching Sri Aurobindo, but the light that one can gain from him, as Joshi noted, will depend upon the height and breadth of one's own quest. It is in raising most comprehensive questions in their profundity relating to the world and its future possibilities and the role that we are required to play as also how we should prepare ourselves to fulfil that role that we shall find the real relevance of Sri Aurobindo and find ourselves truly equipped to study him and the supra-mental consciousness that he has discovered and brought down on the earth.

Three fundamental problems which gave direction to the spiritual quest and philosophical thinking and helped to fashion Sri Aurobindo's major theories, relate to the paradox of the national life of India, the supposed conflict between spirituality and action, and the evolution of man. The search for solutions to these problems relates to the unique and creative tension in his own experience between spirituality and politics, both during his years of political activity and during his four decades of sadhana (spiritual discipline) at Pondicherry. Aurobindo's writings provide the needed force for action, realisation and transformation which is reflected in his philosophy arrived at through inner experience. He wrote 'in fact I was never satisfied till experience came and it was on this experience that later on I founded my philosophy'. His integral philosophy grew out of his Yoga-not the other way round.

Two phrases that surge out of Sri Aurobindo's writings that sum up his message are: 'Integral perfection' and 'Spiritual religion of humanity'. His call for integrality and synthesis is most distinctively reflected in his statements: 'We of the coming day stand at the head of a new age of development which must lead to such a new and larger synthesis. [...] We do not belong to the past dawns, but to the noons of the future'. To attain integral perfection, Sri Aurobindo has found education to be critical.

Integral Education

Originally a poet and a politician, not a philosopher, Sri Aurobindo engaged himself for forty-five years out of his seventy-eight years in the practice of Yoga, and developed a philosophy of complete affirmation, affirming the reality of the world from the ultimate standpoint and the meaningfulness of socio-political action from the spiritual standpoint. He was sovereignly aware of the significance of variations in the concept of man, his life and destiny, of the nation and of humanity and the life of human race, which get reflected in the respective philosophies of education, and developed his scheme of integral education rooted in 'the developing soul of India, to her future need, to the greatness of her coming self creation, to her eternal spirit'.

India, according to Sri Aurobindo, has seen always in man the individual a soul, a portion of the Divinity enwrapped in mind and body, a conscious manifestation in Nature of the universal self and spirit. In his educational philosophy, Sri Aurobindo upheld the basic but commonly forgotten principle that 'it is the spirit, the living and vital issue that we have to do with, and there the question is not between modernism and antiquity, but between an imported civilisation and the greater possibilities of the Indian mind and nature, not between the present and the past, but between the present and the future'. In devising a true and living education, three things according to Sri Aurobindo-the man, the individual in his commonness and his uniqueness, the nation or people and universal humanity-should be taken into account.

Accordingly, Aurobindo conceived of education as an instrument for the real working of the spirit in the mind and body of the individual and the nation. He thought of education that for the individual will make its one central object the growth of the soul and its powers and possibilities, for the nation will keep first in view the preservation, strengthening and enrichment of the nation-soul and its Dharma (virtue) and raise both into powers of the life and ascending mind and soul of humanity. And at no time will it lose sight of man's highest object, the awakening and development of his spiritual being. A concept underlying the true and living integral education.

Integrality of education is conceived as a process of organic growth, and the way in which various faculties could be developed and integrated is dependent upon each child's inclination, rhythm of progression and law of development, Swabhava (inherent disposition) and Swadharma (inner nature). Integral education is not conceived as a juxtaposition of a number of subjects and even juxtaposition of varieties of faculties. The idea is to provide facilities for varieties of faculties, varieties of subjects and various combinations of pursuits of Knowledge, Power, Harmony and Skill in works. These faculties are so provided that they could be made use of by each student and the teacher so that a natural process of harmonious development could be encouraged.

Antahkarna

According to Sri Aurobindo, mind or antahkarana which consists of four layers is the instrument of the educationist. 'The reservoir of past mental impressions, the citta or storehouse of memory, which must be distinguished from the specific act of memory, is the foundation on which all the other layers stand. The passive memory or citta needs no training, it is automatic and naturally sufficient to its task; there is not the slightest object of knowledge coming within its field which is not secured, placed and faultlessly preserved in that admirable receptacle. It is the active memory, a higher but less perfectly developed function, which is in need of improvement'.

Manas or mind proper, the sixth sense of Indian psychology, is the second layer. Its function is to receive the images of things translated into sight, sound, smell, taste and touch, the five senses and translate these again into thought-sensations. Therefore right use of the six senses is vital to see that they are not stunted or injured by disuse, but trained by the child himself under the teacher's direction to that perfect accuracy and keen subtle sensitiveness of which they are capable. In addition, whatever assistance can be gained by the organs of action, should be thoroughly employed.

The hand, for instance, should be trained to reproduce what the eye sees and the mind senses. The speech should be trained to a perfect expression of the knowledge which the whole antahkarna possesses. The real instrument of thought which forms the third layer is the intellect or buddhi. It orders and disposes of the knowledge acquired by the other parts of the machine. Infinitely the most important of the three thus far named for education, Sri Aurobindo considers intellect as an organ composed of several groups of functions, divisible into two important classes, the functions and faculties of the right hand, the functions and faculties of the left hand.

> 'The faculties of the right-hand are comprehensive, creative and synthetic; the faculties of the left-hand critical and analytic. To the right-hand belong judgement, imagination, memory, observation; to the left-hand comparison and reasoning. The critical faculties distinguish, compare, classify, generalise, deduce, infer, conclude; they are the component parts of the logical reason. The right-hand faculties comprehend, command, judge in their own right, grasp, hold and manipulate. The right-hand mind is the master of the knowledge, the left-hand its servant. The left-hand touches only the body of knowledge, the right-hand penetrates its soul. The left-hand limits itself to ascertained truth, the right-hand grasps that which is still elusive or unascertained. Both are essential to the completeness of the human reason. These important functions of the machine have all to be raised to their highest and finest working-power, if the education of the child is not to be imperfect and onesided'.

Sri Aurobindo adds that there is another layer of faculty which, not as yet entirely developed in man, is attaining gradually to a wider development and more perfect evolution. 'The powers peculiar to this highest stratum of knowledge are chiefly known to us from the phenomena of genius, -- sovereign discernment, intuitive perception of truth, plenary inspiration of speech, direct vision of knowledge to an extent often amounting to revelation, making a man a prophet of truth. These powers are rare in their higher development, though many possess them imperfectly or by flashes. They are still greatly distrusted by the critical reason of mankind because of the admixture of error, caprice and a biased imagination which obstructs and distorts their perfect workings. Yet it is clear that humanity could not have advanced to its present stage if it had not been for the help of these faculties, and it is a question with which educationists have not yet grappled, what is to be done with this mighty and baffling element, the element of genius in the pupil. The mere instructor does his best to discourage and stifle genius, the more liberal teacher welcomes it'.

Physical and Moral Education

Seeking to effect a synthesis of the values of the East and the West in the contemporary philosophy of education, Sri Aurobindo insisted that a healthy body is a necessary condition for intellectual or spiritual attainment. For him physical education means not only the proper functioning of the various organs of the body but also the development of strength, balance, and a sense of beauty. According to him, beauty is the ideal which physical life has to realise. ' If our seeking is for a total perfection of the being', says Aurobindo, 'the physical part of it cannot be left aside; for the body is the material basis, the body is the instrument which we have to use. [...] The perfection of the body, as great a perfection as we can bring about by means at our disposal' must be the ultimate aim of physical culture'. Therefore, 'a development of the physical consciousness must always be a considerable part of our aim, but for that the right development of the body itself is an essential element; health, strength, fitness are the first needs, but the physical frame itself must be the best possible'.

The education of the intellect, says Aurobindo, divorced from the perfection of the moral and emotional nature, is injurious to human progress. He admits the difficulties involved in providing a suitable moral training for the school and college. He distinguishes the heart from the mind, and says, that to instruct the mind is not to instruct the heart. He senses the danger of moral textbooks being used for the purpose, in that they make the thinking of high things mechanical and artificial, and whatever is mechanical and artificial is inoperative for good. Further, he points out pertinently that 'the attempt to make boys moral and religious by the teaching of moral and religious text-books is a vanity and a delusion, precisely because the heart is not the mind and to instruct the mind does not necessarily improve the heart.

The best kind of moral training for a man, that Sri Aurobindo conceives of is, 'to habituate himself to the right emotions, the noblest associations, the best mental, emotional and physical habits and the following out in right action of the fundamental impulses of his essential nature'. By way of moral and religious education, any attempt at imposition of a certain discipline on children, dressing them into a certain mould, lashing them into a desired path is essentially hypocritical and heartless. Only what the man admires and accepts, becomes part of himself; the rest is a mask. On the other hand, to neglect moral and religious education is to corrupt the race. In moral training, Sri Aurobindo stresses the value of suggestion and deprecates imposition.

'The first rule of moral training', he says, 'is to suggest and invite, not command or impose. The best method of suggestion is by personal example daily converse and the books read from day to day'. 'Every boy should', says Aurobindo, 'therefore be given practical opportunity as well as intellectual encouragement to develop all that is best in the nature. If he has bad qualities, bad habits, bad samaskaras (behaviour patterns), whether of mind or body, he should not be treated harshly as a delinquent, but encouraged to get rid of them by the Rajayogic (a type of yoga) method of samyama (self-control), rejection and substitution'. Instead of discouraging such people, Aurobindo would like them to be rather encouraged to think such bad traits, 'not as sins or offences, but as symptoms of a curable disease, alterable by a steady and sustained effort of the will-falsehood being rejected [..] and replaced by truth, fear by courage, selfishness by sacrifice and renunciation, malice by love'. Unformed virtues may not be rejected as faults.

No religious teaching, according to Aurobindo is of any value 'unless it is lived, and the use of various kinds of sadhana, (spiritual self-training and exercise) is the only effective preparation for religious living. The ritual of prayer, homage, ceremony is carved for by many minds as an essential preparation and, if not made an end itself, is a great help to spiritual progress; if it is withheld, some other forms of meditation, devotion or religious duty must be put in its place. Otherwise, religious teaching is of little use and would almost be better ungiven'.

Principles of Teaching and Training

In a series of articles that Sri Aurobindo wrote in 1909-10, he enunciated three fundamental principles of teaching. 'The first principle of true teaching is that nothing can be taught. The teacher is not an instructor or task master; he is a helper and a guide. His business is to suggest and not to impose'. The second principle according to Sri Aurobindo, is that 'the mind has to be consulted in its growth'. He pointed out that the idea of hammering the child into the shape desired by the parents or teacher is a barbarous and ignorant superstition. He warned that to force the nature to abandon its own dharma is to do it permanent harm, mutilate its growth and deform its perfection, and that there can be no greater error than for the parents or the teachers to arrange beforehand that the given student shall develop particular qualities, capacities, ideas, virtues or be prepared for a pre-arranged career. And the third principle of education that Sri Aurobindo laid down is to work from near to the far, from that which is to that which shall be.

In other words, Sri Aurobindo underlined that education must proceed from direct experience and that even that which is abstract and remote from experience should be brought to the ken of experience. Knowledge has to be a growth from personal experience to larger and intenser and higher experience. There are several other guidelines that we find in Sri Aurobindo. While explaining the instruments of the work of the teacher, he writes 'Teaching, example, influence-these are the three instruments of the guru (teacher or guide). But the wise teacher will not seek to impose himself or his opinions on the passive acceptance of the receptive mind; he will throw in only what is productive and sure as a seed that will grow under the divine fostering within. He will seek to awaken much more than to instruct; he will aim at the growth of faculties and the experiences by a natural process and free expansion. He will give a method as an aid, as a utilisable device, not as an imperative formula or a fixed routine. And he will be on his guard against any turning of the means into a limitation, against the mechanising of process'.

'What is his method and his system?' asks Sri Aurobindo and answers, 'He has no method and every method. His system is a natural organisation of the highest processes and movements of which the nature is capable. Applying themselves even to the pettiest details and to actions the most insignificant in their appearance with as much care and thoroughness as to the greatest, they in the end lift all into the Light and transform all'. 'This imperfect nature of ours,' 'explains Sri Aurobindo', 'contains the materials of our perfection, but inchoate, distorted, mis-placed, thrown together in disorder or a poor imperfect order. All this material has to be patiently perfected, purified, reorganised, new-moulded and transformed, not hacked and hewn and slain or mutilated, not obliterated by simple coercion and denial'.

These principles, it will be observed, are subtle and complex, and no rigid formula of practice can be derived from them. They impose a great responsibility on the teacher and demand from him extraordinary qualities of a profound psychologist. In the matter of the training of the senses, Aurobindo aims at nothing less than perfection. This, he says, must be one of the first cares of the teacher. The two important things that are needed of the senses, he points out are "accuracy and sensitiveness".

The senses depend for their accuracy and sensitiveness on the unobstructed activity of the nerves which are the channels of their information and the passive acceptance of the mind, the recipient. In case of any obstruction, the remedy lies in the purification of the nerve system. 'This process inevitably restores the perfect and unobstructed activity of the channels and, if well and thoroughly done, leads to a high activity of the senses. The process is called in yogic discipline nadi-suddhi or nerve—purification'. Six senses which minister to knowledge, sight, learning, smell, touch and taste, mind or manas (the sixth sense of the Indian psychology) can be developed through the physical nerves and their end-organs, but manas could be developed through yogic discipline suksmadristi or subtle reception of images. Aurobindo wrote :

> Telepathy, clairvoyance, clairaudience, presentiment, thought-reading, character-reading and many other modern discoveries are very ancient powers of the mind which have been left undeveloped, and they all belong to the manas. The development of the sixth sense has never formed part of human training. In a future age it will undoubtedly take a place in the necessary preliminary training of the human instrument. Meanwhile there is no reason why the mind should not be trained to give a correct report to the intellect so that our thought may start with absolutely correct if not with full impressions.

Sri Aurobindo while analysing the causes of inefficiency of the senses, as gatherers of knowledge, attributes it to 'insufficient use'. Students, he suggests, should overcome tamasic(optuseness of the mind and the senses) inertia and ought to be accustomed to catch the sights, sounds, etc., around them, distinguish them, mark their nature, properties and sources and fix them in the citta so that they may be always ready to respond when called for by the memory. 'Attention' according to him, is the chief factor in knowledge and considers it the first condition of right memory and accuracy. Besides attention 'concentration on several things at a time' says Aurobindo is often indispensable. He holds the view that it is quite possible to develop the power of double concentration, triple concentration, multiple concentration, which is a matter of abhyasa or steady natural practice.

Along with faculties of memory, judgement, observation, comparing and contrasting and analogy which are indispensable aids in the acquisition of knowledge, Aurobindo emphasizes Imagination as the most important and indispensable instrument. It has been divided into three functions, the forming of mental images, the power of creating thoughts, images and imitations or new combinations of existing thoughts and images,the appreciation of the soul in things, beauty, charm, greatness, hidden suggestiveness, the emotion and spiritual life that pervades the world. 'This is in every way as important as the training of the faculties which observe and compare outward things'. These mental faculties, as Aurobindo suggests, should first be exercised on things, afterwards on words and ideas.... All this should be done informally, drawing on the curiosity and interest, avoiding set teaching and memorising of rules.

Sri Aurobindo is critical of the practice of teaching by snippets which is in practice in the existing system of education. Teaching by snippets, says Aurobindo, must be relegated to the lumber-room of dead sorrows. He is critical since:

> A subject is taught a little at a time, in conjunction with a host of others, with the result that what might be well learnt in a single year is badly learned in seven and the boy goes out ill-equipped, served with imperfect parcels of knowledges, master of none of the great departments of human knowledge.

He characterizes such a system of education as one attempting to 'heighten this practice of teaching by snippets at the bottom and the middle and suddenly change it to a grandiose specialism at the top. This is to base the triangle on its apex and hope that it will stand'. Aurobindo has, therefore, found some meaning in the old system which was more rational than the modern: 'If it did not impart so much varied information, it built up a deeper, nobler and much more real culture. Much of the shallowness, discursive lightness and fickle mutability of the average modern mind is due to the vicious principle of teaching by snippets'.

However, Aurobindo is clear that in the future education we need not bind ourselves either by the ancient or the modern system but select only the most perfect and rapid means of mastering knowlege. For him, every child is an inquirer, an investigator, analyser, a merciless anatomist. Appeal to these qualities in him and let him acquire without knowing it the right temper and the necessary fundamental knowledge of the scientist. Every child has an insatiable intellectual curiosity and turn for metaphysical enquiring. Use it to draw him on slowly to an understanding of the world and himself.

Every child has the gift of imitation and a touch of imaginative power. Use it to give him the ground work of the faculty of the artist. It is by allowing Nature to work that we get the benefit of the gifts she has bestowed on us Aurobindo is particular that the first attention of the teacher must be given to the medium and the instruments and, until these are perfected, to multiply subjects of regular instruction is to waste time and energy. 'The mother tongue', he says 'is the proper medium of education and therefore the first energies of the child should be directed to the thorough mastering of the medium'.

In connection with language teaching he advocates that when the mental instruments are sufficiently developed to acquire a language easily and swiftly, that is the time to introduce him to many languages, not when he can partially understand what he is taught and masters it laboriously and imperfectly. He believes in the disciplinary value of learning one language, especially one's own language, which he says, prepares one for mastering another. He maintains that with the facility developed in one's own language, to master others in easier.

Psychic and Spiritual Education

Aurobindo also speaks of mental and psychic education, but his real interest is in a still higher stage, which according to him is spiritual or supra-mental education.

This does not imply the annihilation of the individual but his enrichment through contact with the Absolute. The spiritual stage transcends the mental and the psychic stage. The justification for psychic and spiritual education rests upon three important considerations:

- education should provide to the individual a steady exploration of something that is inmost in the psychological complexity of human consciousness;
- the most important question of human life is to consider the aim of human life and the aim of one's own life and one's own position and the role in the society; and this question can best be answered only when the psychic and spiritual domains are explored and when one is enabled to develop psychic and spiritual faculties of knowledge; and
- the contemporary crisis of humanity has arisen because of the disbalancement between the material advancement on the one hand and inadequate spiritual progression.

If, therefore, this crisis has to be met, development of psychic and spiritual consciousness should be fostered. Aurobindo tries to draw a distinction between psychic and spiritual in the following terms. At the life of psychic life, the individual feels an unbroken continuity in the world of forms and sees level as an immortal function in endless time and limitless space. The spiritual consciousness goes beyond time and space and is an identification with the infinite and the eternal. Aurobindo is expressing the same idea when he says that in psychic life selfishness must be discarded, but in the spiritual life there is no sense of the separate self. Aurobindo insists that it is not annihilation of the individual but its transformation which is the end of integral education. When man attains such education there is total transformation of matter. He calls it supramental education as it will work, not only upon the consciousness of individual beings, but upon the very substance of which they are built and even upon the physical environment in which they live.

An unprecedented kind of experiment in education was launched by Sri Aurobindo and the Mother, when in 1943, a school came to be established at Sri Aurobindo Ashram at Pondicherry with merely 20 students on its rolls, soon it began to grow, and in 1951, when the number of students had increased, and studies in Higher Education had to be organized, it was expanded into Sri Aurobindo International University Centre. The Centre was conceived as one of the best means of preparing humanity for future that would be marked by the manifestation of a new light and power-the supra-mental light and power. It was launched so that the elite of the humanity may be made ready who would be able to work for the progressive unification of the race and who at the same time would be prepared to embody the new force descending upon the earth to transform it.

The Centre conducted a programme of experimental research under the direct guidance of the Mother, and it became a laboratory of education for tomorrow (for details see Tewari, 1998). The educational doctrine of Sri Aurobindo is closely linked with his futuristic vision of human destiny which is reflected in his statement: They should be children of the past, possessors of the present, creators of the future. The past is our foundation, the present our material, the future our aim and summit. Aurobindo's visionary mystic mind articulated a concept of life which was unique since he conceived of it as a lavish and manifold opportunity given us to discover, realize, express the Divine and accordingly, visualized a system of education which would help expression of unrealized potentialities, in line with his concept of life. This called for a creative vision and an extraordinary adventure. For him human destiny is an ascent towards the supermind, towards realization of the Godhead and his philosophy of education provides a forceful and resilient framework to attain this goal.

3

Aurobindo on Human Development

There are several angles to look at man and to conclude that he is indeed different from all his fellow-species on this earth — far more different than the birds are from the beasts or, among the beasts themselves, the elephant is from the rodent. But the difference that strikes us immediate is the fact that he is capable of marvelling at himself, he knows that he is a riddle unto himself. "Apart from man, no being wonders at its own existence", said Schopenhaur.

Sri Aurobindo says in *The Life Divine* : "The animal is satisfied with a modicum of necessity; the gods are content with their splendours. But man cannot rest permanently until he reaches some highest good. He is the greatest of living beings because he is the most discontented, because he feels most the pressure of limitations. He alone, perhaps, is capable of being seized by the divine frenzy for a remote ideal."

Mankind, thus different from all the other species, is again marked by difference within itself — depending on factors such as culture, religion, nationality, wealth, education, temperament, refinement and much more. But the most remarkable difference between man and man, it may be said, is determined by the degree of the aforesaid "divine frenzy for a remote ideal."

Indeed, while all the other creatures live in the present, man alone lives in three modes of time simultaneously, be he conscious of it or unconscious of it. He has to drag along his past as memory, he has to struggle through the present; and the future—be it near or be it far—is always a factor to mould his thoughts and actions. In most people this position may not mean anything more than experience (past) in the process of use (present) for a better future, better in the sense of a happier living, but this leads at least a few to raise several basic questions: Why is man what he is ? Why was he created at all ? To live, to enjoy, to suffer, to occasionally reflect, but ultimately to die—are they all we have to 'life'? Aristotle defining man as a political animal or Spinoza seeing him as a social animal are well-pronounced statements of fact, each carrying a certain truth, but they do not satisfy the fundamental queries. At the same time, man cannot leave these stubborn far behind him.

Aurobindo says in *The Life Divine* : "We speak of the evolution of Life in Matter, the evolution of Mind in Matter; but evolution is a word which merely states the phenomenon without explaining it. For there seems to be no reason why Life should evolve out of material elements or Mind out of living form, unless we accept the Vedantic solution that Life is already involved in Matter and Mind in Life because in essence Matter is a form of veiled Life, Life a form of veiled Consciousness. And then there seems to be little objection to a farther step in the series and the admission that mental consciousness may itself be only a form and a veil of higher states which are beyond mind."

This observation of Sri Aurobindo precisely links the past with the present and the present with the future, for, despite all the progress made by mankind, it cannot rest content until this basic quest has been satisfied.

It seems that there was a time when this basic quest of man, which can be termed as his inner quest, because response to this could come only from an exploration of his consciousness, went hand in hand with his external explorations of the environment, Nature, in search of better living conditions. In the Indian tradition we come across that remarkable phenomenon, the Rishi, who was at once an explorer of these inner mysteries of life and an architect of life in its social context, capable of leading a seeker along the spiritual path and guiding a king through his pragmatic political crisis; he could author an esoteric hymn and also be a poet of the splendours of life. For him life was a field of experience embracing both the Physical World and the Spirit, but with a goal—and that was the conquest of the former by the latter.

This knowledge, at a certain phase of human development, resulted in the formation of two different paths: the path of the Spirit and the path of the Mundane World. The first meant a total preoccupation with the spirit, ignoring the worldly affairs and the second meant a total absorption in the worldly affairs at the cost of the Spirit—albeit giving some concessions to the latter in the way of taking interest in religion or leading a so-called 'God-fearing' life.

But what the Rishis intended in their aspirations for the conquest of the mundane world by the spirit was not ignoring the mundane nor by its relegation to a position of unreality. Their concept of the conquest was a kind of elevation of the mundane by the spirit—an enlightenment of those elements of our being which are most active in the mundane affairs (namely, our physical existence, our passions and emotions, our thoughts and knowledge) by the alchemy of our soul.

In fact, the Rishis had hit upon the truth that until one had discovered this inner-most aspect of one's being, the Soul, one will never know oneself, nor will one be oneself.

The knowledge and realisation of the soul not only put life on a new pedestal, but also changed its definition. Life could no longer be seen as a mere prisoner in the body, its duration measured by birth and death. In its true nature, it was immortal.

While we find this knowledge of the soul, its immortality in the lores of great antiquity in India (in the Upanishadic story of Nachiketa for example), it was wrapped up in an allegorical myth in another ancient civilisation, as a mere story for the people in general but as a revelation for the initiate.

After wrecking havoc in Thebes, a strange, winged creature with face of a woman, the body of a dog, the tail of serpent and the paws of a lion stationed itself atop a hillock along a desert road. It would throw this riddle at any unsuspecting traveller. "Who is the being to walk on four legs at morn, on two as the day grows and on three in the evening?" The traveller is given time till the sundown. Should he be able to answer, he could pass. If not, the creature pounced upon him and killed him. No traveller escaped death until the day Oedipus happened to reach the spot. "I am the answer", he said when confronted by the terrible creature, and explained, "Man the infant crawls on all fours at the dawn of his life; then he walks normally on two legs; in the evening of his life he takes recourse to a walking stick, his third leg." No sooner had the hero answered the riddle than the enigmatic examiner, the Sphinx, jumped to its own death.

Unmistakable is the wisdom sealed in this famous Grecian-Roman myth, a version of the Upanishadic doctrine: Man dies because he does not know himself. The day he has known himself, it is death that would die!

(The bizare composition of Sphinx, according to one symbolism, indicated its own unreality).

Since it is the Spirit which is at the root of creation and the soul in man is that mode of the Spirit which remains pure and self-conscious whereas the other faculties constituting him, namely his body, life and mind, though essentially modes of the same Spirit, are diluted and self-oblivious, it is through discovering his soul alone that man can discover the truth of himself and, consequently, find answers to all the basic riddles of life.

If was necessary, in the process of evolution, for the mind to get the full opportunity for its thorough exercise, for a demonstration of its marvellous possibilities. Without this exercise of mind's power of exploration, observation and its capacity for progress by utilisation of its experience and knowledge, we will have neither science nor philosophy, neither technology nor diplomacy.

The irony is, all these achievements of mind have not yielded to man what he had been seeking since the dawn of his consciousness. What is more, those who are capable of reviewing the situation, in regard to man vis-a-vis his fundamental quest, nurture no illusion that the efficacy of mind can ever do justice to that quest. On the other hand, there looms large a fear that the mind, ungoverned by something more enlightened, can be unpredictable in the direction it will take, can wreck havoc on the totality (the being) of which it is only a part.

As Sri Aurobindo diagnoses the situation; at present mankind is going through an evolutionary crisis. It is only through a decisive transcendence of the mind and an emergence into a higher stage of consciousness that man can come face to face with the realisation of all that has remained his dream and his aspiration through the ages.

The Yoga of Sri Aurobindo and the Mother was directed towards paving the way for such a transcendence—through the transforming intervention of a power of the Divine Consciousness they termed the Supramental. The riddle of Sphinx is the Riddle of our life, but the future awaits not only the man who knows himself, but also the man who is capable of applying that knowledge to fulfil his destiny—by welcoming the advent of a greater Self :

> "And when that greater Self comes sea-like down
> To fill this image of our transience,
> All shall be captured by delight, transformed :
> In waves of undreamed ecstasy shall roll
> Our mind and life and sense and laugh in a light
> Other than this hard limited human day,
> The body's tissues thrill apotheosised,
> Its cells sustain bright metamorphosis........"
>
> —*Savitri*

Never in history has there been an age of paradox like ours. Today man builds magnificent cities, and also makes bombs capable of destroying them totally, man has produced great wealth, yet the deadly sting of poverty keep many limbs of humanity paralysed. Those who are in a position to enjoy the fruits of technological progress are haunted by an overwhelming sense of insecurity. Man has developed the greatest ever awareness of human rights and dignity, yet his ego—individual and collective—turns tyrant to others at the earliest opportunity.

Can such broadening gulfs on so many fronts be bridged? Not until man has climbed to a new state of consciousness, a higher one than hitherto realised, where mentally irreconcilable situations can be reconciled. According to Sri Aurobindo's diagnosis of the situation, it can be said that we are passing through the greatest-ever transition. This does not mean that a sweeping social, educational, political or cultural change is called for. Changes in these spheres will of course come—but not through any kind of constitutional reform. They will be the outcome of a mighty upliftment in human consciousness.

The promise of such a stride in consciousness, Sri Aurobindo says, is inherent in the natural scheme of things and is evident in man's perennial urge to exceed himself, in his age-old quest for perfection.

Is the progress visualised by Sri Aurobindo spiritual in nature? Indeed, it is, but in the highest sense of the term true spirituality does not admit any dichotomy between the material world and the spirit. In his *Life Divine,* Sri Aurobindo shows how man's earliest formula of wisdom also promises to be his last — his quest after God, Light, Freedom, Bliss and Immortality. All his endeavours in the way of improving his life and his environment and giving expression to his diverse inner urges—scientific, artistic, et al—can fall into one of these categories. Even the destructive instincts and emotions are not independent realities by themselves, but are either the pulls of an inconscient state from which the process of our emancipation is continuing, or are the distortions and perversions of some of our positive qualities. Truth's relation to falsehood can be compared with light's relation to shadow. "A shadow depends on light for its existence, but light does not depend for its existence on the shadow."

For long man has tried to get rid of the evil in life through the means of rejection or destruction. He has not succeeded. Rejection only keeps the evil in waiting; destruction is just not possible—for in a sense nothing can be truly destroyed. Besides, good and evil are intricately interwoven. Even man's noblest inspirations such as love and religion can be corroded with lust and violence ingrained in him. Sri Aurobindo envisages the transformation of the evil. The transforming power, the Supermind, is in fact involved in the evolutionary process. Time has come for man to aspire for its emergence. We are passing through an evolutionary crisis and nothing short of this can really take us out of it.

No simpler summary of Sri Aurobindo's vision and Yoga can be made than the one by the Mother :

"There is an ascending evolution in Nature which goes from the stone to the plant, from the plant to the animal, from the animal to man. Because man is, for the moment, the last rung at the summit of the ascending evolution, he considers himself as the final stage in this ascension and believes there can be nothing on earth superior to him. In that he is mistaken. In his physical nature he is yet almost wholly an animal, a thinking and speaking animal, but still an animal in his material habits and instincts. Undoubtedly, nature cannot be satisfied with such an imperfect result; she endeavours to bring out a being who will be to man what man is to the animal, a being who will remain a man in its external form, and yet whose consciousness will rise far above the mental and its slavery to ignorance.

"Sri Aurobindo came upon earth to teach this truth to men. He told them that man is only a transitional being living in a mental consciousness, but with the possibility of acquiring a new consciousness, the Truth-consciousness, and capable of living a life perfectly harmonious, good and beautiful, happy and fully conscious. During the whole of his life upon earth, Sri Aurobindo gave all his time to establish in himself this consciousness he called supramental, and to help those gathered around him to realise it."

The educational doctrine of Sri Aurobindo, needless to say, has to be closely linked with this futuristic vision of human destiny. Sri Aurobindo startles us by saying that the first thing a teacher must know is that nothing can be taught. The paradox is not meant to be an enigma. He emphasises the need for a natural and spontaneous growth of the child—each being unique—according to its own inherent capacity, its *Swadharama*. The real wisdom lies imbedded in the child. No teacher need tell a child that the flower is beautiful.

Apart from the well-known principles of taking care to see that the education was integral, all the parts of the being, physical, vital or life-element, mind and the spirit within got equal chance to develop simultaneously, Sri Aurobindo's vision of man will oblige us to treat every child as a unique being, a special joy of the creative power in its manifestation of variety. This element of joy is of vital importance and the process of education must be a process of inspiring joy in the child.

Once we accept that man is an evolving being, we have to allow many of our stock ideas to change—ideas which have been formulated taking man as he is for granted. Take, for example, the case of the very discipline which deals with human consciousness—psychology. Once we remember that there is something in man that is in the process of a transformation or an evolution, we will lose our enthusiasm to apply a principle to it which was formulated on the basis of a more or less static proposition.

We have taken the idea for granted that it is the past which determines the present and that the past and present will determine the future. But, in the light of Sri Aurobindo we may very well revise the idea and wonder if it is not the future which has made the past and the present. That is to say, there is a destiny which is in the process of realising itself and all that has happened and all that is happening are a part of that process. Our interpretation of events will then be quite different.

Unlike the American biologist Euston who proposes a solution of human problems by reducing the future generations to pocket-size men and women so that, among other things, food problems will be solved, our attention will go over to a radical change inevitable in human consciousness, for basically all problems concern consciousness.

Let us recall a one-page story by Oscar Wilde. As we know, among the several miracles Jesus had performed, one was to restore sight to a man grown blind, another was to cure a leper and yet another was to resurrect a dead man. Once Jesus comes down from the heavens and enters a locality. It is night. From inside a house comes the sound of music. He enters it and sees a man holding a cup of wine in his hand, enjoying a lusty dance. Jesus touches him on his shoulder. The man gives a start and looks. "I know who you are. Once I was blind. You restored to me my sight. What am I to do with my sight if not enjoy this?"

Jesus sighed and went out into the street. He saw another man chasing a coy damsel. He stood between them. The man stopped, stared at him and said, "I know who you are. Once I had a rotten body. You restored it to its health. How am I going to use it if not in this way?" Jesus sighed and moved away. On the outskirts of the locality, beside a lake, there sat a man shedding tears. Jesus patted him on the back. He looked back and said, "I know who you are. Once I was dead and you revived me. What am I to do with my life if not to weep it away!" Jesus sighed and returned to his abode.

The story leaves in our mind a formidable question. What if all our desires were fulfilled? With the quality of our consciousness remaining what it is, is mere fulfilment of desires going to give us a greater satisfaction in living, a greater sense of fulfilment? Doesn't affluence and a sense of futility often go together? Even the expectations which the intelligentsia in the 18th and 19th century had—that science and socialism will usher in a new and happy civilisation—were belied in the 20th century.

Nevertheless if Huxley thought of applying a principle of positive eugenics to check the quality of the future population and Russell wondered if Providence made such an elaborate backdrop for a puny and transitory result like man, Sri Aurobindo brings a certain assurance about the future of man and in his light we find a solid ground for developing a new optimism for the future, despite some deplorable signs to the contrary and if this faith in the future can be infused into the process of education and the message of a new consciousness can replace the stock notions of human nature, we can then hope for a qualitative turn in our philosophy of education.

Education would then embrace, to quote from *The Human Cycle* by Sri Aurobindo, "all knowledge in its scope, but would make the whole trend and aim and the permeating spirit not mere worldly efficiency, but this self-developing and self-finding. It would pursue physical and psychical science not in order merely to know the world and Nature in her processes and to use them for material human ends, but to know through and in and under and over all things the Divine in the world and the ways of the Spirit in its masks and behind them.

It would make it the aim of ethics not to establish a rule of action whether supplementary to the social law or partially corrective of it, the social law that is after all only the rule, often clumsy and ignorant, of the biped pack, the human herd, but to develop the divine nature in the human being. It would make it the aim of Art not merely to present images of the subjective and objective worlds, but to see them with the significant and creative vision that goes behind their appearances and to reveal the Truth and Beauty of which things visible to us and invisible are the forms, the masks or the symbols and significant figures."

The greatest help we can give to the future is to arm the young with an unshakable faith in the future.

THE SCIENCE OF LIVING

An aimless life is always a miserable life. Every one of you should have an aim. But do not forget that on the quality of your aim will depend the quality of your life. Your aim should be high and wide, generous and disinterested; this will make your life precious to yourself and to others. But whatever your ideal, it can not be perfectly realised unless you have realised perfection in yourself.

To work for your perfection, the first step is to become conscious of yourself, of the different parts of your being and their respective activities. You must learn to distinguish these different parts one from another, so that you may become clearly aware of the origin of the movements that occur in you, the many impulses, reactions and the conflicting wills that drive you to action. It is an assiduous study which demands much perseverance and sincerity. For man's nature, especially his mental nature, has a spontaneous tendency to give a favourable explanation for everything he thinks, feels, says and does.

It is only by observing these movements with great care, by bringing them, as it were, before the tribunal of our highest ideal, with a sincere will to submit to its judgement, that we can hope to form in ourselves a discernment that never errs. For if we truly want to progress and acquire the capacity of knowing the truth of our being, that is to say what we are truly created for, what we can call our mission upon earth, then we must, in a very regular and constant manner, reject from us or eliminate in us whatever contradicts the truth of our existence, whatever is opposed to it. In this way, little by little, all the parts, all the elements of our being can be organised into a homogeneous whole around our psychic centre. This work of unification requires much time to be brought to some degree of perfection. Therefore, in order to accomplish it, we must arm ourselves with patience and endurance with a determination to prolong our life as long as necessary for the success of our endeavour.

As you pursue this labour of purification and unification, you must at the same time take great care to perfect the external and instrumental part of your being. When the higher truth manifests, it must find in you a mind that is supple and rich enough to be able to give the idea that seeks to express itself a form of thought which preserves its force and clarity. This thought, again, when it seeks to clothe itself in words, must find in you a sufficient power of expression so that the words reveal the thought and do not deform it. And the formula in which you embody the truth should be manifested in all your feelings, all your acts of will, all your actions, in all the movements of your being. Finally, these movements themselves should, by constant effort, attain their highest perfection.

All this can be realised by means of fourfold discipline, the general outline of which is given here. The four aspects of the discipline do not exclude each other, and can be followed at the same time; indeed, this is preferable. The starting-point is what can be called the psychic discipline. We give the name "psychic" to the psychological centre of our being, the seat within us of the highest truth of our existence, that which can know this truth and set it in movement. It is therefore of capital importance to become conscious of its presence in us, to concentrate on this presence until it become a living fact for us and we can identify ourselves with it.

In various times and places many methods have been prescribed for attaining this perception and ultimately achieving this identification. Some methods are psychological, some religious, some even mechanical. In reality, everyone has to find the one which suits him best, and if one has an ardent and steadfast aspiration, a persistent and dynamic will, one is sure to meet, in one way or the another—outwardly through reading and study, inwardly through concentration, meditation, revelation and experience—the help one needs to reach the goal. Only one thing is absolutely indispensable: the will to discover and realise. This discovery and realisation should be the primary preoccupation of our being, the pearl of great price which we must acquire at any cost. Whatever you do, whatever your occupations and activities, the will to find the truth of your being and to unite with it must be always living and present behind all that you do, all that you feel, all that you think.

To complement this movement of inner discovery, it would be good not to neglect the development of the mind. For the mental instrument can equally be a great help or a great hindrance. In its natural state the human mind is always limited in its vision, narrow in its understanding, rigid in its conceptions, and a constant effort is therefore needed to widen it, to make it more supple and profound. So it is very necessary to consider everything from as many points of view as possible. Towards this end, there is an exercise which gives great suppleness and elevation to the thought. It is as follows; a clearly formulated thesis is set; against it is opposed its antithesis, formulated with the same precision. Then by careful reflection the problem must be widened or transcended until a synthesis is found which unites the two contraries in a larger, higher and more comprehensive idea.

Many other exercises of the same kind can be undertaken; some have a beneficial effect on the character and so possess a double advantage: that of educating the mind and that of establishing control over the feelings and their consequences. For example, you must never allow your mind to judge things and people, for the mind is not an instrument of knowledge; it is incapable of finding knowledge, but it must be moved by the knowledge. Knowledge belongs to a much higher domain than that of the human mind, far above the region of pure ideas. The mind has to be silent and attentive to receive knowledge from above and manifest it. For it is an instrument of formation, of organisation and action, and it is in this function that it attains its full value and real usefulness.

There is another practice which can be very helpful to the progress of the consciousness. Whenever there is a disagreement on any matter, such as a decision to be taken, or an action to be carried out, one must never remain closed up in one's own conception or point of view. On the contrary, one must make an effort to understand the other's point of view, to put oneself in his place and, instead of quarrelling or even fighting, find the solution which can reasonably satisfy both parties; there always is one for men of goodwill.

Here we must mention the discipline of the vital. The vital being in us is the seat of impulses and desires, of enthusiasm and violence, of dynamic energy and desperate depressions, of passions and revolts. It can set everything in motion, build and realise; but it can also destroy and mar everything. Thus it may be the most difficult part to discipline in the human being. It is a long and exacting labour requiring great patience and perfect sincerity, for without sincerity you will deceive yourself from the very outset, and all endeavour for progress will be in vain. With the collaboration of the vital no realisation seems impossible, no transformation impracticable. But the difficulty lies in securing this constant collaboration.

The vital is a good worker, but most often it seeks its own satisfaction. If that is refused, totally or even partially, the vital gets vexed, sulks and goes on strike. Its energy disappears more or less completely and in its place leaves disgust for people and things, discouragement or revolt, depression and dissatisfaction. At such moments it is good to remain quiet and refuse to act; for these are the times when one does stupid things and in a few moments one can destroy or spoil the progress that has been made during months of regular effort. These crises are shorter and less dangerous for those who has established a contact with their psychic being which is sufficient to keep alive in them the flame of aspiration and the consciousness of the ideal to be realised. They can, with the help of this consciousness, deal with their vital as one deals with a rebellious child, with patience and perseverance, showing it the truth and light, endeavouring to convince it and awaken in it the goodwill which has been veiled for a time. By means of such patient intervention each crises can be turned into a new progress, into one more step towards the goal. Progress may be slow, relapses may be frequent but if a courageous will is maintained, one is sure to triumph one day and see all difficulties melt and vanish before the radiance of the truth-consciousness.

Lastly, by means of a rational and discerning physical education, we must make our body strong and supple enough to become a fit instrument in the material world for the truth-force which wants to manifest through us.

In fact, the body must not rule, it must obey. By its very nature it is a docile and faithful servant. Unfortunately, it rarely has the capacity of discernment it ought to have with regard to its masters, the mind and the vital. It obeys them blindly, at the cost of its own well-being. The mind with its dogmas, its rigid and arbitrary principles, the vital with its passions, its excesses and dissipations soon destroy the natural balance of the body and create in it fatigue, exhaustion and disease. It must be freed from this tyranny and this can be done only through a constant union with the psychic centre of the being.

The body has a wonderful capacity of adaptation and endurance. It is able to do so many more things than one usually imagines. If, instead of the ignorant and despotic masters that now govern it, it is ruled by the central truth of the being, you will be amazed at what it is capable of doing. Calm and quiet, strong and poised, at every minute it will be able to put forth the effort that is demanded of it, for it will have learnt to find rest in action and to recuperate, through contact with the universal forces, the energies it expends consciously and usefully.

In this sound and balanced life a new harmony will manifest in the body, reflecting the harmony of the higher regions, which will give it perfect proportions and ideal beauty of form. And this harmony will be progressive, for the truth of the being is never static; it is a perpetual unfolding of a growing perfection that is more and more total and comprehensive. As soon as the body has learnt to follow this movement of progressive harmony, it will be possible for it to escape, through a continuous process of transformation, from the necessity of disintegration and destruction. Thus the irrevocable law of death will no longer have any reason to exist.

When we reach this degree of perfection which is our goal, we shall perceive that the truth we seek is made up of four major aspects:

— Love,

— Knowledge,

— Power and

— Beauty.

These four attributes of the Truth will express themselves spontaneously in our being. The psychic will be the vehicle of true and pure love, the mind will be the vehicle of infallible knowledge, the vital will manifest an invincible power and strength and the body will be the expression of a perfect beauty and harmony.

4

Concept of Integral Education

It was Sri Aurobindo's influence on the Indian National Congress, in the first decade of the century which made the organisation include Swadeshi, Boycott and National Education in its programme. He wrote editorial in the *Bande Mataram*, more than once, urging the party to give sufficient attention to education, which was divided in two groups. One favoured running a chain of national schools, parallel with the government schools and the other group was much more ambitious. It wanted its ideas to infiltrate all the government schools!

The grotesque defects in the system of education that prevailed in India pained not only patriotic Indians, but also some Englishmen. For example, wrote W. W. Hunter, "Your State education is producing a revolt against three principles which, although they were pushed too far in ancient India, represent the deepest wants of human nature—the principle of discipline, the principle of religion, the principle of contentment." He said further, "What are you to do with this great clever class, forced up under a foreign system, without discipline, without contentment and without God ?" In his well-known work, *Indian Unrest*, Valentine Chirol observed :

"The fundamental weakness of our Indian educational system is that the average Indian student cannot bring his education into any direct relation with the world in which, outside the class or lecture room, he continues to live. For that world is still the old Indian world of his forefathers, and it is as far removed as the poles asunder from the Western world which claims his education."

Hemendra Prasad reviews the situation in his foreword to *A Phase of the Swadeshi Movement : National Education* by Prof. Haridas Mukherjee and Prof. Uma Mukherjee, thus :

"But they had to encounter immense difficulty in introducing a system of national education chiefly because the alien Government stood in the way. The Government would not recognise any system of education which was not stamped with their approval and, consequently, was not likely to serve their end. The door to the professions was barred for those who were not the products of the system which had a denationalising effect on the people. It created a huge hiatus between the educated and the masses; for, the educated considered themselves a separate class and developed what may be called superiority-complex. As an inevitable result the desire to diffuse the fertilising waters of intellectual knowledge from their great and copious fountainheads at the Universities by a thousand irrigating channels over the whole length and breadth of the land—deteriorated and learning was not connected with the living forces of society—the masses were not made a sharer in the classic traditions of the lettered world."

"In 1906, the National Council of Education was founded in Calcutta. The Bengal National College and School started its working career since August 15 at a rented house at 191/1, Bowbazar Street, with Aurobindo Ghose as its first Principal and Satis Chandra Mukherjee as its first Executive Head or the Superintendent.... Aurobindo's name alone proved a very valuable asset to the Bengal National College and added enormously to the prestige of the institution in public eyes. But as he soon became,—particularly since October 1906,—more and more involved in active politics and in the conduct of the famous *Bande Mataram*,—he could not turn up regularly in the college whose life-force was, in fact, Satis Chandra Mukherjee, the silent inspirer of Young Bengal."

That was a turbulent time. The freedom movement was gathering momentum. The character of the Indian National Congress was to undergo a radical change at its historic Surat session in 1907, the nationalists meeting under the Presidentship of Sri Aurobindo and the government bringing the charge of sedition against the *Bande Mataram* and then arresting him in connection with the Alipore Conspiracy Case.

But the need for a greater experiment in national education continued to be felt by him. In the *Bande Mataram* of 24 February 1908 he wrote, under the title 'A National University':

"The idea of a National University is one of the ideas which have formulated themselves in the national consciousness and become part of the immediate destiny of a people. It is a seed which is sown and must come to its fruition, because the future demands it and the heart of the nation is in accord with the demand. The processes of its increase may be rapid or it may be slow, and when the first beginnings are made, there may be many errors and false starts, but like a stream gathering volume as it flows, the movement will grow in force and certainty, the vision of those responsible for its execution will grow clearer, and their hands will be helped in unexpected ways until the purpose of God is worked out and the idea shapes itself into an accomplished reality. But it is necessary that those who are the custodians of the precious trust, should guard it with a jealous care and protect its purity and first high aim from being sullied or lowered."

Sri Aurobindo, no wonder, could not give his time to the educational movement and the functioning of the College founded by the National Council seems to have deteriorated because of the people managing it trying to dissociate it from the general national fervour sweeping the country and making it purely academic in character. The anguish Sri Aurobindo felt found expression in an article entitled 'National Education', published in the *Karmayogin* (January 1, 1910), the weekly he edited after his acquittal in the Alipore Conspiracy Case and before leaving for Pondicherry :

"National Education languishes because the active force has been withdrawn from it; it does not absolutely perish because a certain amount of Nationalist self-devotion has entrenched itself in this last stronghold and holds it against great odds and under the most discouraging circumstances. A certain amount only,—because part of the active enthusiasm and self-sacrifice which created the movement, has been deliberately extruded from it in obedience to fear or even baser motives, part has abandoned in disgust at the degeneration of the system in incapable hands and the rest is now finding its self-devotion baffled and deprived of the change of success by the same incapacity and weakness at headquaters.

"The National Council of Education, as it is at present composed, has convicted itself of entire incapacity whether to grasp the meaning of the movement or to preserve or create the conditions of its success. To the majority of the members it is merely an interesting academic experiment in which they can embody some of their pet hobbies or satisfy a general vague dissatisfaction with the established University system. To others the only valuable part of it is the technical instruction given in its workshops. The two or three who at all regard it as part of a great national movement, are unnerved by fear, scepticism and distrust... It is folly to expect that the nation at large will either pay heavily or make great sacrifices merely to support an interesting academic experiment, still less to allow a few learned men to spoil the intellectual development of the race by indulging their hobbies at the public expense... Unless this movement is carried on, as it was undertaken, as part of a great movement of national resurgence, unless it is made, visibly to all, a nursery of patriotism and a mighty instrument of national culture, it cannot succeed. It is foolish to expect men to make great sacrifices while discouraging their hope and enthusiasm. It is not intellectual recognition of duty that compels sustained self-sacrifice in masses of men; it is hope, it is the lofty ardour of a great cause, it is the enthusiasm of a noble and courageous effort. It is amazing that men calling themselves educated and presuming to dabble with public movements should be blind to the fact that the success or failure of National Education is intimately bound up with and, indeed, entirely depends upon the fortunes of the great resurgence which gave it birth. They seem to labour under the delusion that it was an academic and not a national impulse which induced men to support this great effort, and they seek to save the institution from a premature death by exiling from it the enthusiasm that made it possible. They cannot ignore the service done by that enthusiasm, but they regard it merely as the ladder by which they climbed and are busy trying to kick it down. They are really shutting off the steam, yet expect the locomotive to go on."

At Pondicherry, with the appearance of the monthly *Arya*, Sri Aurobindo's vision and reflections on all the great issues of life and of Yoga and spirituality found a distinct medium for their serialised presentation. He wrote "A Preface on National Education" (1920-1921) in which he clearly analysed, in the backdrop of the 20th century, how a national outlook of education can be synthesised with the modern development. He says "National education was not a mere change of control of the educational institutions, the authority passing from the hands of the Westerners to Indians. "I presume that it is something more profound, great and searching that we have in mind and that, whatever the difficulty of giving it shape, it is an education proper to the Indian soul and need and temperament and culture that we are in quest of, not indeed something faithful merely to the past, but to the developing soul of India, to her future need, to the greatness of her coming self-creation, to her eternal spirit."

"There could be questions on the idea of a national education. Is it not true that the training of good citizenship is the same in the East or the West? Is it not true that man is same everywhere and his needs are common? Education should have a universal character and not limited by any concept. No nation can reject the discoveries or inventions in science because they were possible in another country. We cannot dismiss Galileo and Newton and stop with Bhaskara, Aryabhatta and Varahamihira. We cannot revive the syllabus followed at Takshashila or Nalanda. After all we live in the twentieth century and cannot revive the India of Chandragupta or Akbar; we must keep abreast with the march of truth and knowledge, fit ourselves for existence under actual circumstances, and our education must be therefore upto date in form and substance and modern in life and spirit."

To such possible observations, Sri Aurobindo's answer was:

"All these objections are only pertinent if directed against the travesty of the idea of national education which would make of it a means of an obscurantist retrogression to the past forms that were once a living frame of our culture but are now dead or dying things; but that is not the idea nor the endeavour. The living spirit of the demand for national education no more requires a return to the astronomy and mathematics of Bhaskara or the forms of the system of Nalanda than the living spirit of Swadeshi a return from railway and motor traction to the ancient chariot and the bullockcart. There is no doubt plenty of retrogressive sentimentalism about and there have been some queer violences on common sense and reason and disconcerting freaks that prejudice the real issue, but these inconsequent streaks of fantasy give a false hue to the matter. It is the spirit, the living and vital issue that we have to do with, and there the question is not between modernism and antiquity, but between an imported civilization and the greater possibilities of the Indian mind and nature, not between the present and the past, but between the present and the future. It is not a return to the fifth century but an initiation of the centuries to come, not a reversion but a break forward away from a present artificial falsity to her own greater innate potentialities that is demanded by the soul, by the Shakti of India."

That a policy of national education did not mean merely infusing in the student the spirit of the nation's culture, aspirations and other qualities peculiar to it, but something more, to make the student a worthy unit of humanity, was emphasised in the next part of the essay :

"It follows that that alone will be a true and living education which helps to bring out to full advantage, makes ready for the full purpose and scope of human life all that is in the individual man, and which at the same time helps him to enter into his right relation with the life, mind and soul of the people to which he belongs and with that great total life, mind and soul of humanity of which he himself is a unit and his people or nation a living, a separate and yet inseparable member. It is by considering the whole question in the light of this large and entire principle that we can best arrive at a clear idea of what we would have our education to be and what we shall strive to accomplish by a national education. Most is this largeness of view and foundation needed here and now in India, the whole energy of whose life purpose must be at this critical turning of her destinies directed to her one great need, to find and rebuild her true self in individual and in people and to take again, thus repossessed of her inner greatness, her due and natural portion and station in the life of the human race."

If this were all—though this is profoundly ideal—then this could apply to the ideal system of education emanating from any culturally advanced country of the world. But making a good individual, a good citizen of the country and an ideal citizen of the world could not be the end for the perfect Indian vision of education. Since times immemorial India has discovered as the final goal of life a point beyond the visible horizon of life. It has defined life not as a span of existence bracketed by birth and death, but as a spirit launched into the infinity, at the same time capable of experiencing the infinity in this world of finites assigned to him. A Nachiketa who demanded of the God of Death the power to unravel the mystery of death, a Markandeya who could totally identify himself with the Eternity so that the appointed time for his death came and passed without the powers concerned being able to locate him as a mortal individual, a Savitri who could alter the destiny of her husband by the dint of her love sharpened by askesis, an Arjuna taught to view things and happenings through his inner eye, from the point of view of his soul and thereby look upon as gross a situation as a battle as an opportunity for Yoga—are examples testifying to this attitude of ushering in the alchemy of infinity into the finite life.

It is this aspiration to know the hidden realities which gives the spirit of India, as reflected in its literature, philosophy and traditions, often distorted though, an exclusive feature. An education to be truly Indian must light in the consciousness of the student the flame of this quest.

Hence, said Sri Aurobindo:

"India has seen always in man the individual a soul, a portion of the Divinity enwrapped in mind and body, a conscious manifestation in Nature of the universal self and spirit. Always she has distinguished and cultivated in him a mental, an intellectual, an ethical, dynamic and practical, an aesthetic and hedonistic, a vital and physical being, but all these have been seen as powers of a soul that manifests through them and grows with their growth, and yet they are not all the soul, because at the summit of its ascent it arises to something greater than them all, into a spiritual being, and it is in this fact that she has found the supreme manifestation of the soul of man and his ultimate divine manhood, his *paramartha* and highest *purusartha*. And similarly India has not been understood by the nation or people as an organised State or an armed and efficient community well prepared for the struggle of life and putting all at the service of the national ego,—that is only the disguise of iron armour which masks and encumbers the national *purusha*,—but a great communal soul and life that has appeared in the whole and has manifested a nature of its own and a law of that nature, a *Swabhava* and *Swadharma*, and embodied it in its intellectual, aesthetic, ethical, dynamic, social and political forms and culture. And equally then our cultural conception of humanity must be in accordance with her ancient vision of the universal manifesting in the human race, evolving through life and mind but with a high ultimate spiritual aim,—it must be the idea of the spirit, the soul of humanity advancing through struggle and concert towards oneness, increasing its experience and maintaining a needed diversity through the varied culture and life motives of its many people, searching for perfection through the development of the powers of the individual and his progress towards a diviner being and life, but feeling out too though more slowly after a similar perfectability in the life of the race."

Integral Education Theory

The primary purpose of education, if not forgotten, had remained ignored for long. Way back in 1909, Sri Aurobindo wrote in the *Karmayogin*. The first necessity for the building up of a great intellectual superstructure is to provide a foundation strong enough to bear it. Those systems of education which start from an insufficient knowledge of man, think they have provided a satisfactory foundation when they have supplied the student with a large or well-selected mass of information on the various subjects which comprise the best part of human culture at the time.

The school gives the materials, it is for the student to use them—this is the formula. But the error here is fundamental. Information cannot be the foundation of intelligence, it can only be part of the material out of which the knower builds knowledge, the starting-point, the nucleus of fresh discovery and enlarged creation. An education that confines itself to imparting knowledge, is not education. The various faculties of memory, judgement, imagination, perception, reasoning, which build the edifice of the thought and knowledge for the knower, must not only be equipped with their fit and sufficient tools and materials, but trained to bring fresh materials and use more skillfully those of which they are in possession. And the foundation of the structure they have to build, can only be the provision of a fund of force and energy sufficient to bear the demands of a continually growing activity of the memory, judgement and creative power.

We find his concept of an 'integral education' already inherent in this passage, although the phrase was used much later by the Mother. In a series of articles published in the *Arya* in the second decade of the 20th century (subsequently compiled under the title *War and Self-Determination*), we find him laying emphasis on the child as a soul—a truth which any sound system of education must recognise, first and foremost, and then proceed to help its other faculties to develop.

"The child was in the ancient patriarchal idea the live property of the father; he was his creation, his production, his own reproduction of himself; the father, rather than God or the universal Life in place of God, stood as the author of the child's being; and the creator has every right over his creation, the producer over his manufacture. He had the right to make of him what he willed, and not what the being of the child really was within, to train and shape and cut him according to the parental ideas and not rear him according to his own nature's deepest needs, to bind him to the paternal career or the career chosen by the parent and not that to which his nature and capacity and inclination pointed, to fix for him all the critical turning-points of his life even after he had reached maturity. In education the child was regarded not as a soul meant to grow, but as brute psychological stuff to be shaped into a fixed mould by the teacher. We have travelled to another conception of the child as a soul with a being, a nature and capacities of his own who must be helped to find them, to find himself, to grow into their maturity, into a fullness of physical and vital energy and the utmost breadth, depth, and height of his emotional, his intellectual and his spiritual being."

Between the twenties and the thirties of the 20th century, Sri Aurobindo's seer-vision encompassed the entire range of human life—with all its activities, social, political, cultural, educational, etc., so much so that we do not know of any other savant in recorded history to have tackled so many subjects at so very lofty planes. His return to the issue of education again and again was unavoidable and again and again, in different contexts, he highlighted the unique role of the soul. Reflecting on the possible contribution of education to a divine life on earth, he says :

"But it has not been found in experience, whatever might have once been hoped, that education and intellectual training by itself can change man; it only provides the human individual and collective ego with better information and a more efficient machinery for its self-affirmation, but leaves it the same unchanged human ego. Nor can human mind and life be cut into perfection,—even into what is thought to be perfection, a constructed substitute,—by any kind of social machinery; matter can be so cut, thought can be so cut, but in our human existence matter and thought are only instruments for the soul and the life-force. Machinery cannot form the soul and life-force into standardised shapes; it can at best coerce them, make soul and mind inert and stationary and regulate the life's outward action; but if this is to be effectively done, coercion and compression of the mind and life are indispensable and that again spells either unprogressive stability or decadence. The reasoning mind with its logical practicality has no other way of getting the better of Nature's ambiguous and complex movements than a regulation and mechanisation of mind and life. If that is done, the soul of humanity will either have to recover its freedom and growth by a revolt and a destruction of the machine into whose grip it has been cast or escape by a withdrawal into itself and a rejection of life. Man's true way-out is to discover his soul and its self-force and instrumentation and replace by it both the mechanisation of mind and the ignorance and disorder of life-nature. But there would be little room and freedom for such a movement of self-discovery and self-effectuation in a closely regulated and mechanised social existence."

Since Sri Aurobindo made this observation, mankind has witnessed several instances to corroborate it. Among many tumultuous events of the twentieth century is the World War II—revealing how fragile an assurance education and all the trappings of so-called civilized societies were against an upsurge of dark elements in man or against a hostile force taking possession of him—showing him as he is in his utter nakedness.

But when we meditate on the issue, we are most likely to arrive at an impasse. We stand convinced that the awakening of soul in man is the answer to the state of human predicament, but how to bring about the fulfilment of that condition?

There comes the relevance of Yoga.

But what is Yoga? While Yoga means union, union with the source of our being, people often understand by Yoga Hathayoga, practice of a system of physical postures, breath-control etc. to arrive at certain experience or to achieve certain powers. There are also other distinguished schools of Yoga: Rajayoga, which leads the seeker to various states of trance, Jnanayoga, a discipline to grow closer to the goal through Knowledge, Karmayoga and Bhaktiyoga which lead the seeker to the same goal through Action and Devotion respectively.

But Sri Aurobindo presents Yoga in a far more natural perspective. "In the right view of both life and Yoga, all life is either consciously or sub-consciously a Yoga", he says and proceeds thus :

"For we mean by this term a methodised effort towards self-perfection by the expression of the potentialities latent in the being and a union of the human individual with the universal and transcendent Existence we see partially expressed in man and in the Cosmos. But all life, when we look behind its appearances, is a vast Yoga of Nature attempting to realise her perfection in an ever increasing expression of her potentialities and to unite herself with her own divine reality. In man, her thinker, she for the first time upon this Earth devises self-conscious means and willed arrangements of activity by which this great purpose may be more swiftly and puissantly attained. Yoga, as Swami Vivekananda has said, may be regarded as a means of compressing one's evolution into a single life or a few years or even a few months of bodily existence."

Sri Aurobindo saw that since the different schools of Yoga aimed at one goal, one union, a synthesis could be achieved among them :

"By the very nature of the principal Yogic schools each covering in its operations a part of the complex human integer and attempting to bring out its highest possibilities, it will appear that a synthesis of all of them largely conceived and applied might well result in an integral Yoga. But they are so disparate in their tendencies, so highly specialised and elaborated in their forms, so long confirmed in the mutual opposition of their ideas and methods that we do not easily find how we can arrive at their right union."

Again, those who got a taste of the Infinite through Yoga looked upon the finite world as something almost superfluous. Since everything in this phenomenal world was subject to death and other sorts of impermanence, Yogis who grew acquainted with the indescribable glory of the Power that was beyond the universe (transcendent), developed an attitude of contempt for the things that were phenomenal.

But Yoga cannot be integral unless it found both the finite and the infinite as aspects of the same Power—call it Divine or Godhead or Brahman or the Supreme Reality. "The ultimate knowledge is that which perceives and accepts God in the universe as well as beyond the universe and the integral Yoga is that which, having found the Transcendent, can return upon the universe and possess it, retaining the power freely to descend as well as ascend the great stair of existence."

Needless to say, a concept of Integral Education is in line with the Integral Yoga, both the disciplines pointing at a progress in the direction of realising the best qualities inherent in man, an urge for perfection and thirst for knowledge and truth. Like Integral Yoga visualising not only a realisation of the soul, but also a transformation of the gross physical, vital and mental aspects of man into Divine instruments, the Integral Education intends at preparing all aspects of the students through a creative cultivation of their potentialities, to become, with full awareness and a sense of joy, vehicles of a higher consciousness. Since there is always the fear of the meaning of the phrase 'Integral Education' being diluted—for much will depend on the capacity and understanding of those who are trying to put the idea into practice and the opportunities available to them—it is necessary that those concerned do not forget its sublime goal. The Mother expects the process of integral education to help ushering in the next phase of human evolution, when man would have crossed his mind to step into the Supramental. She says, "To pursue the integral education that leads to the Supramental realisation a four fold austerity is necessary and also a four fold liberation.

The Mother makes it transparently clear that by austerity she does not mean asceticism or self-mortification. Far more difficult than the practice of such external methods is mastering power over one's self, "to maintain the consciousness always on the peak of its capacity and never allow the body to act under the influence of a lower impulse."

The gradation, she says, is from above downward and they need not be followed in that order mechanically—each one formulating his own system according to his capacity and personal needs.

She explains the austerities from the bottom of the list. The discipline of Beauty requires to form a programme following which one can build a body beautiful in form, harmonious in posture, supple and agile in its movements, powerful in its activities and resistant in its health and organic function.

The body, to prepare itself for receiving a higher consciousness, must follow a sound routine regarding sleep, food, physical exercise and other activities. "To reach this ideal goal one must strictly shun all excess, all vice small or big, one must deny onself the use of such slow poisons as tobacco, alcohol, etc. which men have the habit of developing into indispensable needs that gradually demolish their will and memory."

The Mother gives more importance on the quality of sleep than the length of the period of sleep and advises to go to bed keeping the mind clear and calm. A brief meditation may help.

Exercise should be chosen keeping in mind the body's capacity and need. And then comes the question of work. "For the man who wishes to perfect himself, there is nothing like small and big work, important work or unimportant." One can cultivate the secret of finding interest in any work one is required to do.

The result of this discipline is liberation in action. The body and the actions thereof would no longer remain in bondage to Nature's dictates, to impulses and lower desires. Then comes the 'tapasya' of Power—observing emotional austerities. 'Vital' means the seat of life-force. "It is in the vital that thought changes into will and become a dynamism of action. It is also true that the vital is the seat of desires and passions, of violent impulses and equally violent reactions, of revolt and depression."

Generally those who do not wish to be the victims of their vital desires completely suppress them, starve them. But that is not austerity. True 'tapasya' in this aspect of our being is to utilise the senses with discrimination and discernment. "The senses should be able to bear everything without disgust or displeasure.... the senses should be utilised as instruments to approach and study the physical and vital world in all their complexity... It is by enlightening, strengthening and purifying the vital and not by weakening it that one can help towards the progress of the being."

The vital, when properly taught, can become a flame of aspiration for the higher life. Liberation from desire will obtain for the seeker peace, serenity and power.

Coming to the *tapasya* of Knowledge, the Mother lays great emphasis on the need for right speech. "Man is the first animal upon earth to be able to use the articulate sound. He is indeed proud of it and exercises this capacity without measure or discrimination. The world is deafened with the noise of his speech and at times you almost seem to miss the harmonious silence of the vegetable kingdom", she says.

True knowledge can be gathered in silence, not through arguments and assertion. There prevails a general impression that those belonging to the academic or intellectual fraternity are more reasonable than the average man in their speech. The Mother says, "It is nothing of the kind, however; for even here, into this home of ideas and knowledge, man has introduced violence of his convictions, sectarian intolerance, passion of preference."

Mental austerity is a great discipline; control over one's speech is far more important than keeping mum. Often people pass judgement over others. But how much does one know oneself that he should judge someone else?

"Be silent in your mind, keep steady in the true attitude, that of constant aspiration towards the All-Wisdom, the All-Knowledge and the All-Consciousness. Then, if your aspiration is sincere, if it is not a mere cover for your ambition to do things well and to be successful, if it is pure, spontaneous and integral, then you will speak simply, you will utter the words that should be uttered, neither more nor less, and they will possess a creative power," she answers.

This discipline will liberate one from ignorance. Last is the *tapasya* of Love. This emotion or passion is generally looked upon as irresistible. Through so many social and moral rules and laws man has tried to keep this emotion under control, but in vain.

But, the true love, the Divine Love, of which the human passion of love is only a caricature, a distortion, alone can bring about man's ultimate union with his source, the Divine. "One who has known Divine Love, finds all other love obscure, mixed with smallness and egoism and darkness. It looks like a bargain or a struggle for superiority and authority: and even in the best of men, it is full of misunderstanding and sensitiveness, frictions and misgivings."

"Besides, it is a well-known fact that you grow into the likeness of that which you love. If therefore you want to be like the Divine, love Him alone. One who has experienced the ecstasy of the communion of love with the Divine can alone know how insipid, dull and feeble all other love is, in comparison. And even if the most austere discipline is needed to arrive at this communion, nothing is too hard, too long, too severe, provided it takes you there; for it surpasses all expression."

An integral education will recognise the individual not as a vague combination of matter (body) and spirit, but a personality having four distinct aspects: (a) Physical, (b) Vital, (c) Mental and (d) Psychic. An ideal system of education must open up avenues for the best possible development of each of these faculties of the student.

In a right environment, the inner being of the student, the soul, the psychic, must dominate the other aspects of his being. That will ensure harmonious growth of the person. Each child is unique. Creation finds a delight in variety and multiplicity. Hence, clubbing a group of students together and judging them applying a common, mechanical yardstick is wrong. Each one has a possibility, a hidden capacity, a talent. Environment and opportunity must be created for that latent quality to blossom.

Man as he is, is not the final product of Evolution. Sri Aurobindo visualises the advent of a new man. The mental man must prepare to pave the way for the advent of the Supramental man. The mental man will be transformed into or evolve into the new being.

The syllabus for Integral Education is all life—and promises that are there beyond the present conditions of life—and behind the appearances of life. For it neither matter nor spirit is unreal, but the traditional dichotomy between them is unreal.

Experiments in Integral Education

One of the most recent forms under which Sri Aurobindo

conceived of the development of his work was to establish at Pondicherry an International University Centre open to students from all over the world.

"It is considered that the most fitting memorial to his name would be to found this University now so as to give concrete expression to the fact that his work continues with unabated vigour", said the Mother in 1951 and on the 6th of January 1952 the Sri Aurobindo International University Centre was inaugurated—its name changed, in 1959, in order to keep itself free from the conventional ideas which go with a University, to Sri Aurobindo International Centre of Education.

The Centre of Education consists of sections from Kindergarten till the Higher Course—which approximates to the graduation level in other colleges. But the system of learning and teaching here being very flexible, in principle a student can qualify himself much more than a graduate, if he is sincere and of the right aptitude.

Flexibility, indeed, is one of the cardinal virtues of this institution. There are no mechanical promotions taking into consideration a certain average performance of the student. If a student is observed to be better in a particular subject than expected at his level, he can very well be in a higher class in that particular subject.

The Centre of Education has these faculties : Humanities, Languages, Science and Engineering Technology. There are well-organised provisions for learning painting, music and dance (both Indian and Western), dramatics, crafts, practical ecology etc. Libraries and laboratories are well-equipped.

Physical education is given great importance. Facilities are there for athletics, gymnastics, exercises, combatives, aquatics and field games. A daily routine of activities is formulated for all the students.

Contests and tournaments continue throughout the year, but in a spirit of progress and not in the conventional sense of competition. Playground, sports ground, swimming pool etc. are maintained with great care.

The objectives of the Centre of Education are :

1. to evolve and realise a system of integral education and to make it a dynamic ideal for society;
2. to organise an environment and an atmosphere affording inspiration and facilities for the exercise and development of the five essential aspects of personality: the physical, the vital, the mental, the psychic and the spiritual;
3. to emphasise the unity of all knowledge and to attempt to bring Humanities and Science closer together into a real sense of unity for the benefit of both;
4. to develop the sense of the oneness of mankind and international collaboration; and
5. to prepare for the role that India has to play in the formation of the new international harmony.

The Centre of Education does not award degrees. The Mother explains why it is so :

"For the last hundred years or so mankind has been suffering from a disease which seems to be spreading more and more and which has reached a climax in our times; it is what we may call 'utilitarianism'. People and things, circumstances and activities seem to be viewed and appreciated exclusively from this angle. Nothing has any value unless it is useful. Certainly something that is useful is better than something that is not. But first we must agree on what we describe as useful—useful to whom, to what, for what ?"

"For, more and more, the races who consider themselves civilised describe as useful whatever can attract, procure or produce money. Everything is judged and evaluated from a monetary angle. That is what I call utilitarianism. And this disease is highly contagious, for even children are not immune to it."

"At an age when they should be dreaming of beauty, greatness and perfection, dreams that may be too sublime for ordinary common sense, but which are nevertheless far superior to this dull good sense, children now dream of money and worry about how to earn it."

"So when they think of their studies, they think above all about what can be useful to them, so that later on when they grow up they can earn a lot of money."

And the thing that becomes most important for them is to prepare themselves to pass examinations with success, for with diplomas, certificates and titles they will be able to find good position and earn a lot of money.

For them study has no other purpose, no other interest. To learn for the sake of knowledge, to study in order to know the secrets of Nature and life, to educate oneself in order to grow in consciousness, to discipline oneself in order to become master of oneself, to overcome one's weaknesses, incapacities and ignorance, to prepare oneself to advance in life towards a goal that is nobler and vaster, more generous and more true... they hardly give it a thought and consider it all very utopian. The only thing that matters is to be practical, to prepare themselves and learn how to earn money.

Children who are infected with this disease are out of place at the Centre of Education of the Ashram. And it is to make this quite clear to them that we do not prepare them for any official examination or competition and do not give them any diplomas or titles which they can use in the outside world.

We want here only those who aspire for a higher and better life, who thirst for knowledge and perfection, who look forward eagerly to a future that will be more totally true.

"There is plenty of room in the world for all the others."

Pavitra, a French savant whose original name was P. B. Saint-Hilaire, who was the Director of the Centre of Education, wrote :

"It is quite clear that, according to Sri Aurobindo, the current idea that the teacher should impart his knowledge—what he knows about a subject—to a child is fundamentally wrong. He must show the child how to learn that subject by himself, help him in devising his own methods of learning and of organizing the knowledge which he gathers or discovers.

"We can understand this better if we observe how a young child gains spontaneously the knowledge of his surroundings. He does it through a ceaseless activity which is natural to him whenever he finds interest in the objects at his disposal. He examines, touches, manipulates every object he can lay his hand upon, studies how he can use it for his own purposes (often very different from his parents' ends and views). He explores every nook and corner of the room, of the house, of the garden, sees how he can make use of them for his activities, his games (with little care for the purpose and the tranquility of the grown-ups).

All this is done and pursued in conformity with the needs of his stage of growth. It is the learning by doing, as named by Dewey. When we say that a child is amusing himself or playing (alone or with playmates), it is almost always the purposeful activity (alone or with playmates), it is almost always the purposeful activity (solitary or collective) of a growing being deeply engaged in the process of building up and perfecting his instruments of knowledge and action. We are indeed in presence of a genuine education, leading to discovery and invention—discovery of the world around and of its meaning (for the child's mentality), invention of the usage he can put it to (for the child's aims and interests)—and it is a self-education as it does not require lectures or books. An adult's intervention is in most cases not sought for, nor is it effective, as the adult's understanding is too remote from the child's mentality.

"But the adult has an important part to fulfil. When a child is idle, restless or mischievous, it is either that his natural activity has been hampered or distorted, or that he had exhausted the opportunities given to him by his surroundings and his activity has no outlet. It is for the adult—parent or teacher—to keep the environment supplied with elements of interest. These objects should act by their presence, not by their purpose. Their aim is to satisfy an immediate and actual need of the child, not a future need as anticipated by the parent or teacher (pass an exam, get a good job, raise a family). The purpose of a child is always immediate : the satisfaction of an actual need, which is one of the forms taken by the deep fundamental urge in him to grow physically, emotionally and mentally. He does not paint with the aim of becoming an artist (such an aim belongs to the adult mentality, but it is often unwisely and untimely instilled into a child's receptive mind), but for the satisfaction of the creative impulse in him. He does not try to solve a problem of mathematics to become a mathematician or a good engineer, or even to know geometry and algebra, but for the satisfaction of the discovery, the lightning that suddenly flashes into his mind when he gets it, for the inner joy of having overcome a difficulty and succeeded. He does not play the mouth organ to have a large audience and be recognized as a musician (if he has these ambitions, he got them by the praises bestowed upon him by elders), but for the joy of self-expression and the pleasure he gives to his nearest mates and friends."

A salient feature of the educational methods followed here is known as the Free Progress stream. The Mother says, "Free Progress is progress guided by the soul and not subjected to habits, conventions and preconceived ideas."

According to the Centre's brochure :

"All education aims at the progress of the individual."

But the basic question is : What is progress ? For the word 'progress' can and does have many meanings and implications widely differing in their content and scope.

The view the Centre takes is that progress is essentially a growth of consciousness, discovery and increasing awareness of an inner power and principle of guidance, which holds in it the light and truth of the development, harmony and perfection of our body, life and mind. It could be said that true progress is an ever-open step towards a total evolution of our entire being and consciousness so as to transcend and transform all the limitations to which man as an evolutionary being is at present subject. And this can only be done by a constant living contact with man's true self, the soul.

And once we accept this view, it would then be irrational to set a standard of progress which is uniform for all. It would be wiser although more difficult, to consider each individual as a special centre having his own unique rhythms and modes of progress and thus to assess each individual's progress by standards appropriate to him. Moreover, "If the individual can progress at his maximum, the group will necessarily benefit by it. If the individual is submitted to the possibility and capacity of the group, he loses his chance to total progress", says the Mother.

On this basis, education would become a process of free growth and not a rigid system. For, if man is not the last term of evolution, if reason is not the true or highest governor of life, if the aim of human life is to discover one's inmost and highest principles and to transform by their light and power the entire mode of one's present embodied mental life, and if the specific aim of each individual is to be a special or unique centre of a higher action, then education must be a process of Free Progress.

Some features of the Free Progress approach are :

1. The structure is oriented towards the meeting of the varied needs of the students, each one of whom has his own special pace and process of development.
2. It is not merely the 'subjects' of study that should count in education; the aspiration, the need for growth, the experience of freedom, the possibility of educating oneself, of self-experimentation, the discovery of the inner needs and their relation with the programme of studies, and the discovery of the aim of life and the art of life—these are much more important and the structure of the organisation must provide for them.
3. As he grows older, the student has an increasing freedom in the choice of his subjects and the organisation of his time; but his freedom has to be luminously *guided*. The student should experience freedom but it might be *misused;* the student has therefore to be watched with care, sympathy and wisdom.
4. A great stress falls upon the *individual work* of the students. This individual work may be the result of the student's own choice to follow a particular topic

of interest; or it may be the result of a suggestion from the teacher but accepted by the student. It may be a follow-up of something explained by the teacher or it may be an original line of inquiry. The essential aim is to encourage and stimulate the student to find genuine interest and joy in work.

5. This individual work may be pursued in several ways:

a. quiet reflection or meditation;

b. referring to books or relevant portions of books suggested by the teacher;

c. working on specific exercises/texts prepared for the student by the teacher;

d. consultation or interviews; and

e. carrying out experiments.

6. Apart from individual work, the student participates in group classes as these also have their value. In addition, lectures are organised; such lectures seek appeal to the sense of discovery, imagination and creativity in the student, and not merely burden him with information.

7. There are also periods of discussion between teachers and students and between students and students. However, the discussions need not pertain merely to academic subjects; they can centre round the individual needs of growth and thus provide an opportunity for guiding the students in their inner search.

8. There are topics which more easily yield to the project system. Teachers therefore announce a number of projects in these subjects and students according to their individual or group choice select a few on which they work individually or collectively

and produce charts, monographs, designs, etc. which are periodically exhibited for the benefit of others.

9. The role of the teacher in this process of education may be summarised as follows :

   a. to aid the student in uncovering the inner will to grow and to progress—that needs to be the constant endeavour of the teacher,

   b. to evolve a programme of education for each student in accordance with the felt needs of the student's growth,

   c. to watch the students with deep sympathy, understanding and patience, ready to intervene and guide as and when necessary,

   d. to stimulate the student with striking words, ideas, questions, stories, projects and programmes—this should be the main work of the teacher. The teacher must be a friend and a guide, must not impose himself, but may intervene when necessary. The wastage of opportunities given should not be allowed indefinitely. But when and how to intervene depends on the discretion of the teacher. To radiate inner calm and cheerful dynamism so as to create an atmosphere conducive to the development of higher faculties of inner knowledge and institution—that may be regarded as the heart of the work of the teacher.

10. An adequate organisation for the proper working of the free progress approach would need the following:

    a. A room or rooms of silence to which students who like to do uninterrupted work or would like to reflect or meditate in silence can go as and when they like ;

b. Rooms of documentation where students can find the required materials to seek answers to their questions;

c. Rooms for study, group discussion, consultation.

11. In this view of education, there is no rivalry amongst various branches or disciplines of knowledge, or any stress of their relative importance. In the study of each subject, the aim and attempt is so directed that it leads towards a discovery of the fundamental truths underlying the subject and progressively towards a larger discovery of the unity underlying these truths and the truths of other branches of knowledge, thus helping in the progressive growth of the consciousness of the student.

This sense of the unity of the truths would contribute to the reconciliation of the various branches of knowledge, thus leading to the harmony of Science, Philosophy, Technology and Fine Arts.

This evidently demands a certain maturity and a sense of responsibility. Though the training of the mental faculties begins much earlier, it is only after the age of fourteen that a child is in a position to derive the full benefit from the free progress approach.

In its essence, the free progress approach is endlessly open and innovative and the foregoing should not be taken as rigidly binding.

Experiments and adventures in education in the light of Sri Aurobindo's thoughts are carried out at several other places, within their limitations.

A major field of such experiments is Auroville, not far from Pondicherry. To a question what system of education Auroville proposes to follow, a teacher, Yvonne Artand says: "It is less a system than an environment. We want to give everyone, and especially our children, the possibility of living in an environment which constantly helps them to evolve and to become that which they can become when there is no difference between school and home or between study and play.

"The learning process will no longer be something which is turned on from 7.30 to 11.30 a.m., but the natural attitude of a normally developed mind in this universe during its whole life, an attitude of inquiry, a joy of knowing, and a joy of being and of being able to do."

To another question on the nature of their syllabus, she says, "Our syllabus is the same as that of evolution. Evolution has deposited in the DNA chains of each of us a syllabus, a programme, and given us the possibility of becoming more than our parents were. We intend to help our children to find this programming in themselves, and then to realize it. Like evolution, we want them to become more than man—'Afterman'."

5

Aurobindo on Spirituality and Education

Among the intellectual and spiritual giants born in this land, Sri Aurobindo has a special standing. Here's Sri Aurobindo on Indian spirituality:

Spirituality is the master key of the Indian mind. It is this dominant inclination of India which gives character to all the expressions of her culture. In fact, they have grown out of her inborn spiritual tendency of which her religion is a natural out flowering. The Indian mind has always realized that the Supreme is the Infinite and perceived that to the soul in Nature the Infinite must always present itself in an infinite variety of aspeets. The aggressive and quite illogical idea of a single religion for all mankind, a religion universal by the very force of its narrowness, one set of dogmas, one cult, one system of ceremonies, one ecclesiastical ordinance, one array of prohibitions and injunctions which all minds must accept on peril of persecution by men and spiritual rejection or eternal punishment by God, that grotesque creation of human unreason which has been the parent of so much intolerance, cruelty and obscurantism and aggressive fanaticism, has never been able to take firm hold of the Indian mentality.

We in India have become so barbarous that we send our children to school with the grossest utilitarian motive unmixed with any disinterested desire for knowledge; but the education we receive is itself responsible for this... The easy assumption of our educationists that we have only to supply the mind with a smattering of facts in each department of knowledge and the mind can be trusted to develop itself and take its own suitable road is contrary to science, contrary to human experience... Much as we have lost as a nation, we have always preserved our intellectual alertness, quickness and originality; but even this last gift is threatened by our University system, and if it goes, it will be the beginning of irretrievable degradation and final extinction. The very first step in reform must therefore be to revolutionise the whole aim and method of our education.

In India ...we have been cut off by a mercenary and soulless education from all our ancient roots of culture and tradition... The value attached by ancients to music, art and poetry has become almost unintelligible to an age bent on depriving life of its meaning by turning earth into a sort of glorified ant-heap or beehive.

National education cannot be defined briefly in one or two sentences, but we may describe it tentatively as the education which starting with the past and making full use of the present builds up a great nation. Whoever wishes to cut off the nation from its past is no friend of our national growth. Whoever fails to take advantage of the present is losing us the battle of life. We must therefore save for India all that she has stored up of knowledge, character and noble thought in her immemorial past. We must acquire for her the best knowledge that Europe can give her and assimilate it to her own peculiar type of national temperament. We must introduce the best methods of teaching humanity has developed, whether modern or ancient. And all these we must harmonise into a system which will be impregnated with the spirit of self-reliance so as to build up men and not machines.

The greatest knowledge and the greatest riches man can possess are [India's] by inheritance; she has that for which all mankind is waiting... But the full soul rich with the inheritance of the past, the widening gains of the present, and the large potentiality of the future, can come only by a system of National Education. It cannot come by any extension or imitation of the system of the existing universities with its radically false principles, its vicious and mechanical methods, its dead-alive routine tradition and its narrow and sightless spirit. Only a new spirit and a new body born from the heart of the Nation and full of the light and hope of its resurgence can create it... The new education will open careers which will be at once ways of honourable sufficiency, dignity and affluence to the individual, and paths of service to the country. For the men who come out equipped in every way from its institutions will be those who will give that impetus to the economic life and effort of the country without which it cannot survive in the press of the world, much less attain its high legitimate position. Individual interest and National interest are the same and call in the same direction.

The living spirit of the demand for national education no more requires a return to the astronomy and mathematics of Bhaskara or the forms of the system of Nalanda than the living spirit of Swadeshi a return from railway and motor traction to the ancient chariot and the bullock-cart... It is the spirit, the living and vital issue that we have to do with, and there the question is not between modernism and antiquity, but between an imported civilisation and the greater possibilities of the Indian mind and nature, not between the present and the past, but between the present and the future. It is not a return to the fifth century but an initiation of the centuries to come, not a reversion but a break forward away from a present artificial falsity to her own greater innate potentialities that is demanded by the soul, by the Shakti of India.

Aurobindo on Spirituality

There are two misconceptions about the term 'Spiritual' and both are too stubborn to give way to an objective explanation of the word. First, 'spiritual' and 'spirituality' are understood as synonyms of religious and religion. Second, 'Spiritual' is taken to be the opposite of material, pragmatic or practical, an idea that inspires in our minds the picture of other-worldliness and asceticism.

To confuse spirituality with religion, of course, is not always wrong, for much depends on what one understands by religion. Says Sri Aurobindo, "There are two aspects of religion—true religion and religionism. True religion is spiritual religion, that which seeks to live in the spirit, in what is beyond the intellect, beyond the aesthetic and ethical and practical being of man, and to inform and govern these members of our being by the higher light and law of the spirit.

Religionism, on the contrary, entrenches itself in some narrow pietistic exaltation of the lower members or lays exclusive stress on intellectual dogmas, forms and ceremonies, on some fixed and rigid moral code, on some religio-political or religio-social system. Not that these things are altogether negligible or that they must be unworthy or unnecessary or that a spiritual religion need disdain the aid of forms, ceremonies, creeds or systems. On the contrary, they are needed by man because the lower members have to be exalted and raised before they can be fully spiritualised, before they can directly feel the spirit and obey its law. An intellectual formula is often needed by the thinking and reasoning mind, form or ceremony by the aesthetic temperament or other parts of the infrarational being, a set moral code by man's vital nature in their turn towards the inner life. But these things are aids and supports, not the essence; precisely because they belong to the rational and infrarational parts, they can be nothing more and, if too blindly insisted on, may even hamper the suprarational light. Such as they are, they have to be offered to man and used by him, but not to be imposed on him as his sole law by a forced and inflexible domination. In the use of them toleration and free permission of variation is the first rule which should be observed. The spiritual essence of religion is alone the one thing supremely needful, the thing to which we have always to hold and subordinate to it every other element or motive."

Viewed in a comprehensive perspective, Materialism, the material science in particular, by exploring the mysteries of Nature and harnessing her powers for welfare and progress, has made man more and more conscious of his own potential capacity on the one hand, and, on the other hand, of the infinite possibilities and promises that are there in Nature. This increase or expansion of man's knowledge of himself and of his environment can never be opposed to his spiritual quest.

If spiritual quest leads man inward, makes him look for the inner splendours of his consciousness, the material quest helps him to understand the phenomenon outside and around him. It is the poverty of human mind and human perception which fails to recognise the harmony between Spirit and Matter, their secret intimacy and the fact that both owe their existence to a common source.

Matter itself is a form of Spirit in which consciousness remains asleep and involved. "Matter means the involution of the conscious delight of existence in self-oblivious force and in self-dividing, infinitesimally disaggregated form of substance", says Sri Aurobindo.

It is our ignorance which does not allow us to get over the dichotomy between Matter and Spirit. But, says Sri Aurobindo, "The affirmation of a divine life upon earth and an immortal sense in mortal existence can have no base unless we recognise not only eternal Spirit as the inhabitant of this bodily mansion, the wearer of this mutable robe, but accept Matter of which it is made, as a fit and noble material out of which He weaves constantly His garbs, builds recurrently the unending series of His mansions."

A spiritual education, in the light of Sri Aurobindo, would naturally help the seeker to view both Spirit and Matter in a new light. For him Spirituality is an adventure with matter for its basis. For him the material or the so-called mundane world is neither false, nor illusory, but a truth, a reality though shrouded in falsehood and illusion.

One seeking for Truth must change one's attitude to matter, "For this is the monstrous thing, the terrible and pitiless miracle of the material universe that out of this no-Mind a mind or, at least, minds emerge and find themselves struggling feebly for light, helpless individually, only less helpless when in self-defence they associate their individual feeblenesses in the midst of the giant Ignorance which is the law of the universe.

Out of this heartless Inconscience and within its rigorous jurisdiction hearts have been born and aspire and are tortured and bleed under the weight of the blind and insentient cruelty of this iron existence, a cruelty which lays its law upon them and becomes sentient in their sentience, brutal, ferocious, horrible. But what after all, behind appearances, is this seeming mystery? We can see that it is the Consciousness which had lost itself returning again to itself, emerging out of its giant self-forgetfulness, slowly, painfully, as a Life that is would be sentient, half sentient, dimly sentient, wholly sentient and finally struggles to be more than sentient, to be again divinely self-conscious, free, infinite, immortal. But it works towards this under a law that is the opposite of all these things. Under the conditions of Matter, that is to say, against the grasp of the Ignorance. The movements it has to follow, the instruments it has to use are set and made for it by this brute and divided Matter and impose on it at every step ignorance and limitation."

True Spiritual Education

A true spiritual education has to teach the students to recognise this relationship between Spirit and Matter, so that one neither looks down upon Matter and all the problems the material life presents, nor shuns Spirituality as a lesson in escapism. A spiritual education would prepare the student to face life armed with a greater faith and face with an outlook which is integral. His recognition of the problems of life will not depend entirely on their appearances; he will be able to delve deep into them and see the play of hidden forces behind them. He will be able to grow spiritually through tackling the hurdles, presented by life.

"All life is Yoga", says Sri Aurobindo, giving a radically expansive definition to the concept of Yoga. The same can be said of education; all life is education. So far as the body is concerned, at least the present human body, it grows mechanically and grows old; so far as the growth of consciousness is concerned, it waits for man's conscious aspiration and it never grows old!

In reply to a seeker's query, the Mother said, "India has or rather had the knowledge of the Spirit, but she neglected matter and suffered for it. "

"The West has the knowledge of matter but rejected the Spirit and suffered badly for it.

"An integral education which could, with some variations, be adapted to all the nations of the world, must bring back the legitimate authority of the Spirit over a matter fully developed and utilised."

Spirit, in a positive form, remained in man as the soul.

"........each human being is a self-developing soul and....... the business of both parent and teacher is to enable and to help the child to educate himself, to develop his own intellectual, moral, aesthetic and practical capacities and to grow freely as an organic being, not to be kneaded and pressured into form like an inert plastic material. It is not yet realised what this soul is or that the true secret, whether with child or man, is to help him to find his deeper self, the real psychic entity within. That, if we ever give it a chance to come forward, and still more if we call it into the foreground as 'the leader of the march set in our front', will itself take up most of the business of education out of our hands and develop the capacity of the psychological being towards a realisation of its potentialities of what our present mechanical view of life and man and external routine methods of dealing with them prevent us from having any experience or forming any conception."

Commenting on this passage, Dr. K. R. Srinivasa Iyengar says in his *Re-thinking on Ends and Means in Education* (A lecture delivered on the occasion of the Silver Jubilee Celebrations of the British Council Library, Chennai) : "In education, therefore, it is of the utmost importance to awaken this veiled and withdrawn soul within—as Ramakrishna awakened the inner self of Vivekananda—and make it 'the leader of the march'. Population explosion, knowledge explosion, and the threat of nuclear explosion, all seem to indicate a crisis in human civilisation. Life, knowledge, power—all threaten to destroy by their very surfeit. For what is lacking is Love, and Love fails us because our understanding is partial and defective. But for such a fuller understanding a new education centered in the soul or the psychic entity can alone have the key."

No wonder that at a certain phase in Indian history, the greatest emphasis the educational system laid was on making the student conscious of his soul. The process of learning, from this point of view, began from within.

What the teacher—who was often a Rishi or a seer—wished to see was, all the faculties, all the parts of the pupil's personality, must be governed by his soul, instead of by his crude physical desires, mental preferences or impulses. A great doctrine to which they subscribed was the doctrine of *Swadharma*. In the phenomenal world marked by multiplicity, each human being had a specific inner nature, apart from his share of the common stock of desires, emotions and passions, constituting his superficial personality, his ego-self. To transcend the ego-self and to illumine the consciousness in the splendour of the soul was looked upon as the true goal of education.

But what was most significant, this process of discovering one's *Swadharma* or inner nature and probing the soul did not mean a breaking away from the world, the trial and tribulations, challenges and risks offered by the normal life. In fact, the art of developing one's consciousness lay in one's ability to decipher numerous secret lessons which even apparently most ordinary situations in life could offer. The Upanishads and the Epics present several illustrations of this truth. The most astounding of them is the use of the battlefield by Lord Krishna to reveal the supreme spiritual secret to his dear disciple, Arjuna, on the eve of a terrible war. Another significant incident concerns the childhood of Aruni, an illustrious sage. Aruni had satisfied his guru with his mastery over the scriptures and the different lores he was required to study. Yet the master did not tell him that he had completed his course.

Then came a rainy night. The Gurukul or the Ashram school owned a plot of paddy field. The guru feared that the nearby tank might overflow into the field, submerging the tender crop to its detriment. He asked Aruni to go and ensure that the embankment between the field and the tank stood intact. Reaching the site, Aruni saw a breach in the embankment, already causing a steady flow of water into the paddy field. He tried to fill up the breach with handfuls of earth, but in vain. Without a moment's hesitation he lay down against the breach, stopping the flow. He fainted and was found by his guru and his fellow-students when the weather improved at dawn. That day, when he had fully recovered from his exhaustion, the guru told him, "Today I am satisfied that your education has been completed."

The incident illustrates how theoretical knowledge alone was not enough for one to be deemed educated. We see some distinct undercurrents beneath Aruni's action: his was an enlightened pragmatism. That is to say, not that he did not know that it was not proper to risk one's life for a temporary material gain. But he took the risk because his zeal belonged to another plane where to defy the odds and to stand up to a commitment was an ideal worth achieving, its utilitarian worth or worthlessness notwithstanding. He had conquered his ego; even though he was a scholar, he did not look upon the action he took as something inferior to his status. Education had taught him humility.

But how far is this spirit of education relevant to our time? "Education must have an end in view, for it is not an end in itself," said Sybil Marshall in *An Experiment in*

Education. And if we recognise that goal to be at least helping to student to become a better human being, then the spirit in question is absolutely relevant.

The spiritual education is not a specific subject like history, geography or mathematics. It begins with the very formation of an individual's consciousness. Today the proliferation of educational institutions and the phenomenal growth in student-population have made a personal relationship between the teacher and the pupil very difficult. The students feel harassed and they don't mind harassing their educators in return.

"When the expanding youth generation comes to the academy, we expect it to master in a few years what the entire evolutionary adventure has accomplished so laboriously over all past ages. If the tasks of education were never easy, today they are bewilderingly more difficult than ever before. Too many students, alas: and too many loads of knowledge: and too meagre resources: and too little time at our disposal: and too much distraction to permit us to make really profitable use of even the available time! The aggregating situation is plainly impossible. Expansion seems already to have gone past the stage of profitable returns, and yet we feel helpless to arrest this growth, this madness, this headlong run towards racial suicide."

Added to this situation are a hundred other factors, politics (by no means in a theoretical sense) making inroads into the campus, the influence of the irresponsible and anarchic explosion of vulgar entertainments through electronic and other media, etc. Where is the opportunity for spiritual education to claim their attention?

But, luckily, the key to ignite in the children a spiritual outlook is in the hands of those who have the sole monopoly of the child's attention and the sole hold on the child's time at the most important stage of the child's growth. Needless to say, they are the parents.

Next in importance, no doubt, is the teacher. Discussing with the teachers of Sri Aurobindo International Centre of Education the issue of teacher-student relationship and how a teacher can really exercise his or her influence on the students, the Mother said, "Teachers who are not perfectly calm, who do not have an endurance that never fails and a quietude which nothing can disturb, who have no self-respect... will get nowhere. One must be a saint and a hero to be a good teacher. One must have a perfect attitude to demand a perfect attitude from the students. You cannot ask anyone to do what you don't do yourself. That is a rule....

"... I have never asked anyone educated here to give lessons without seeing that this would be for him the best way of disciplining himself, of learning better what he is to teach and of reaching an inner perfection he would never have if he were not a teacher and had not this opportunity of disciplining himself, which is *exceptionally* severe. Those who succeed as teachers here—I don't mean an outer, artificial and superficial success, but becoming truly good teachers—this means that they are capable of making an inner progress of impersonalisation, of eliminating their egoism, controlling their movement, capable of a clear-sightedness, an understanding of others and a never-failing patience".

In a true system of education it is not the student alone who makes progress, but the teacher too does the same.

6

Principles of True Teaching

The present conditions of our world are not the result of an inadequate government system, an impotent and corrupt bureaucracy or a deficient economic structure; it is simply and directly the outcome and expression of our state of consciousness (what we are within). An inner change must precede the outer if it must be lasting and meaningful. An integral education is the key to this inner change on a larger collective basis; it is the key to true world-progress and a better future for all mankind.

Meaning and Purpose of Education

We must therefore understand education in its widest and deepest sense. Education is meant to bring out the best in Man, to develop his potentialities to the maximum, to integrate him with himself, his surroundings, his society, his country and humanity to make him the "complete man", the "integrated man". In Sri Aurobindo's words :

"That alone will be a true and living education which helps to bring out to full advantage, makes ready for the full purpose and scope of human life all that is in the individual man, and which at the same time helps him to enter into his right relation with the life, mind and soul of the people to which he belongs and with that great total life, mind and soul of humanity of which he himself is a unit and his people or nation a living, a separate yet inseparable member."

If this is the meaning of education, then what passes in its name today in our educational institutions, is obviously very far from the mark. The purpose of education cannot be, even at its best, to merely create a literate individual, or a highly informed person crammed with information and facts, or to prepare an individual to find a job, or to create a good worker, a skilled technician and scientist, or an efficient doctor or lawyer, or a capable industrialist or politician, even to create a good and law abiding citizen. These may be needed but they are not sufficient in themselves. Nor do they create the whole man or a great nation.

They do not take into account the even more important aspects of the individual—his character, his personality, his values. Would we not like our children to be truthful, courageous, generous and benevolent? The question is what is meant by bringing out the best in man. India has always seen in him not merely a body, an emotional and aesthetic being, a rational and thinking mind, but much more fundamentally a soul, evolving gradually into a higher consciousness, towards truth, light, freedom, harmony and immortality. It is this concept which has made India a nation apart and our education too must reflect this attitude. It must lay stress on the emergence of the spirit, not rejecting but embracing and perfecting matter and life.

Approach

We have put before ourselves an integral goal, so also the process of education must be integral. According to the Indian yogic psychology, the personality of an individual has four main aspects:

— The Physical, formed of our body and all its inner and outer functionings.

— The Vital, the seat of our impulses and desires, of enthusiasm and violence, of dynamic energy, passions and will.

— The Mind, formed of our thinking and reasoning parts.

— The `Psychic', or soul which is "the psychological centre of our being, the seat within of the highest truth of our existence, that which can know and manifest the truth."

Up to now our education has been mostly confined to developing a very small part of our mental being. Recently, with the increase of interest in sports, the development of the physical has begun to gain in importance. Conscious work on the vital is very limited and confined to the kindergarten. As for the psychic we are not even aware of its presence.

But our education, to be integral, must help all these four aspects of our personality to grow to the fullest. New methods and processes have to be found which will enable us to first become conscious of these different parts of our being, to develop them, and to integrate them fully with one another.

Learning Society

Such a gigantic and difficult work cannot be the sole responsibility of the teachers or confined to the schools and educational institutions. The entire society must participate in it and its structure should be so designed that every aspect of social life and every experience of the child becomes a means and an opportunity for learning and progressing. The process of learning should expand into the homes and outside. The classroom should only be an occasion for a concentrated and systematic working on a specific topic.

Finally this process of learning and education should not be confined to a short period in the early stages of the life of a child but should continue throughout life. The student must develop this constant thirst for knowledge and perfection, and the society should create educational institutions which can help him at each and every stage of his life and growth.

Another important aspect of education should be to develop a love for our Motherland, an understanding of our culture and the values which have given it birth. In the words of the Mother:

"Each nation has a psychic being which is its true being and moulds its destiny from behind the veil : It is the soul of the country, the national genius, the spirit of the people, the centre of national aspiration, the fountainhead of all that is beautiful, noble, great and generous in the life of the country. True patriots feel its presence as a tangible reality."

Family of Man

But our nationalism is not a narrow, fanatical self-assertion. We must also inculcate in the children the feeling of human unity, of the brotherhood of man, of the common destiny of mankind, enriched by the diversity and uniqueness of each individual and nation.

Integral Education

Sri Aurobindo says : "The children should be helped to grow up into straightforward, frank, upright and honourable human beings ready to develop into divine nature."

Education must prepare us for life in the widest sense. It must help blossom the very best in an individual, the unique and exquisite something which every individual is born to offer to the world.

Integral Education based on the Indian yogic science aims at the total and complete development of the individual: a strong, supple, well formed and healthy body; a sensitive unselfish and mature emotional nature, a positively energetic vital, an enlightened mind, a wide-ranging and vibrant intelligence, a strong will, a balanced and pleasant personality; and the subtler spiritual qualities that can channelise, harmonise and direct all the different parts of an individual into a life that is beneficial to the individual and to his fellow-men.

Importance of Spritual Education

An important question with which we have to deal immediately concerns the meaning of "spiritual education" and its place in our system of education.

Today, because of the situation which prevails in India, there is a very strong emphasis on "secularising" education. On the other hand it is interesting to observe that all those who were the leaders of Indian Renaissance, who are revered by the country and who helped India to come out of the darkness into which she had sunk, nearly all of them affirmed categorically that the fountain-head of India's greatness is her spirituality. It is this, they insisted, which had to permeate every aspect of life, including education, if India had to rise again.

We find ourselves in front of a paradox. How do we reconcile the need for "secularism" with the need for "spirituality"? But this is not a real contradiction. The difficulty arises because we are confusing "morality" and "religion" with "spirituality". Spirituality is something much deeper and higher than religion, where all divisions, fanaticism, exclusiveness, ritualism and religiosity fall away. Spirituality is the aspiration to find and express the Reality behind all existence, the unity behind the diversity of creation. Spirituality can embrace in its scope not only all religions, morality, and ethics, but even science and technology.

In fact this apparent contradiction may have become acute at present, but the problem is not new. This is what the Radhakrishnan Commission had to say on this point, as early as 1949 :

"To be a secular is not to be religiously illiterate. It is to be deeply spiritual and not narrowly religious."

In ancient India the seats of learning were the Ashrams of the Rishis. The son of the king and the son of the labourer went to the same Ashram and lived together and followed the same discipline. The stress was not on studying subjects but on Brahmavidya, the knowledged of Self and the knowledge of the Reality. Without this basis all other knowledges were considered limited and insufficient.

But they too had their importance and place in life. The Rishis also imparted training in state-craft, in the use of weapons and the art of war, in the 64 arts or kalas, even in the rearing of elephants and horses. There was no division between spiritual and secular.

It was because of such an outlook that ancient India was great in every field. In the words of Sri Aurobindo, India created "abundantly and incessantly, lavishly, with an inexhaustible many-sidedness, republics and kingdoms and empires, philosophies and cosmogonies, and sciences and creeds and arts and poems and all kinds of monuments, palaces and temples, and public works, communities and religious orders, laws and codes and rituals, physical sciences, psychic sciences, systems of yoga, systems of politics and administration, arts spiritual and arts worldly, trades, industries, fine crafts—the list is endless and in each item there is almost a plethora of activity."

We see therefore that it is essential that we understand the true meaning of spirituality and yoga, their importance for India and the role they have to play in a truly national education. Because, without this understanding, we will continue to merely imitate, and that too poorly, some often discarded values and structures of a purely western education and culture. And we may then be able to contribute more meaningfully to a greater perfection in the world also.

SAFIER ACTIVITIES

Activities relating to Children

Research has determined that people complete most of their physical, emotional and mental growth by the age of 12 and that it is important that these early years be accorded appropriate attention.

The Society has established some schools for children, as centres of integral education and continues to establish relations with existing educational establishments for the purpose of incorporating principles of integral education in nurseries, kindergartens, primary and secondary schools in various parts of India. Simultaneously the Society has started Children's Corners which are centres of non-formal, unstructured and free education which complement the existing educational institutions.

Children need well-written and well-illustrated books to inspire, interest and mould their development and character. The Society plans to issue a series of such books on the development of values like truth, courage and generosity based on stories collected from all over the world.

Educational Games and Toys to be effective, education should stimulate interest, awaken enthusiasm and encourage discovery (including self-discovery) and the feeling of mutuality with others. Educational games and toys can be useful means to the idea of education as discovery, but their supply is limited, especially in developing countries.

The Society has a project to collect, develop, manufacture and distribute educational games and toys of high educational quality but within the economic reach of teachers and families in India and other developing countries. The Society also plans to organise a permanent exhibition and Internet Web site of the best educational games and toys available globally.

At the same time we are carrying out research in order to develop new games for the growth of faculties like concentration, imagination, creativity, memory etc.

Teacher Training Programmes

Capable and dedicated teachers are the most important requirement for true education. Incremental programmes are planned to :

Establish an infrastructure in Pondicherry for holding regional, national and international conferences, seminars and workshops for teachers and educators; Organise short education camps and workshops in Pondicherry and, later, in other locations in India to orient teachers to the concept of integral education;

Find ways of incorporating new ideals of education and teacher training in existing teacher training institutions, and to encourage syllabus and pedagogic change in this direction; Develop a teachers training institute based on integral education.

Digital Education

The Society's children and teacher training programmes, while powerful methods of direct inter-personal contact, can reach only a limited number of people. "Digital education", properly supported by trained teachers, can reach a wider range and number of children, teachers and educators.

The following incremental programmes are planned : Audio-visual programming (through television broadcast and video cassettes) that is both engaging to young minds and inspiring in terms of values portrayed.

A permanent library of the best videos suitable for children and adults, and to make the catalogue of this library accessible by electronic mail. The establishment of facilities for the professional production of such audio-visual programming. The establishment of a dedicated television channel with programming containing high values of entertainment, education and motivation.

7

The Four Austerities and the Four Liberations

An integral education that leads to the supramental realisation, four austerities are necessary, and with them four liberations.

Austerity is usually confused with self-mortification, and when someone speaks of austerities, we think of the discipline of the ascetic who, in order to avoid the arduous task of spiritualising the physical, vital and mental life, declares it incapable of transformation and casts it away ruthlessly as a useless encumbrance, as a bondage and an impediment to all spiritual progress, in any case as something incorrigible, as a load that has to be borne more or less cheerfully until Nature, or divine Grace, delivers you from it by death. At best, life on earth is a field for progress and one should take advantage of it as best one can in order to reach as soon as possible the degree of perfection which will put an end to the ordeal by making it unnecessary.

For us the problem is quite different. Life on earth is not a passage or a means; by transformation it must become a goal and a realisation. Consequently, when we speak of austerities, it is not out of contempt for the body nor to detach ourselves from it, but because of the need for control and mastery. For there is an austerity which is far greater, far more complete and far more difficult than all the austerities of the ascetic: it is the austerity which is necessary for the integral transformation, the fourfold austerity which prepares the individual for the manifestation of the supramental truth. For example, one can say that few austerities are as strict as those which physical culture demands for the perfection of the body. But we shall return to this point in due time.

Before starting to describe the four kinds of austerity required, it is necessary to clarify one question which is a source of much misunderstanding and confusion in the minds of most people. It is the question of ascetic practices, which they mistake for spiritual disciplines. These practices, which consist of ill-treating the body in order so they say, to liberate the spirit from it, are in fact a sensuous distortion of spiritual discipline; it is a kind of perverse need for suffering which drives the ascetic to self-mortification.

The sadhu's recourse to the bed of nails or the Christian anchorite's resort to the whip and the hair-shirt are the result of a more or less veiled sadistic tendency, unavowed and unavowable; it is an unhealthy seeking or a subconscious need for violent sensations. In reality, these things are very far removed from all spiritual life, for they are ugly and base, dark and diseased; whereas spiritual life, on the contrary, is a life of light and balance, beauty and joy. They are invented and extolled by a sort of mental and vital cruelty towards the body. But cruelty, even with regard to one's own body, is nonetheless cruelty, and all cruelty is a sign of great unconsciousness. Unconscious natures need very strong sensations, for without them they can feel nothing; and cruelty, which is one form of sadism, brings very strong sensations.

The avowed purpose of such practices is to abolish all sensation so that the body may no longer stand in the way of one's flight towards the spirit; but the effectiveness of this method is open to doubt. It is a recognised fact that in order to progress rapidly, one must not be afraid of difficulties; on the contrary, by choosing to do the difficult thing at every opportunity, one increases the will-power and strengthens the nerves. Now, it is much more difficult to lead a life of moderation and balance, in equanimity and serenity, than to try to contend with over-indulgence in pleasure and the obscuration it entails, by over-indulgence in asceticism and the disintegration it causes.

It is much more difficult to achieve the harmonious and progressive development of one's physical being in calm and simplicity than to ill-treat it to the point of annihilation. It is much more difficult to live soberly and without desire than to deprive the body of its indispensable nourishment and cleanliness and boast proudly of one's abstinence. It is much more difficult to avoid or to surmount and conquer illness by an inner and outer harmony, purity and balance, than to disregard and ignore it and leave it free to do its work of destruction. And the most difficult thing of all is to maintain the consciousness constantly at the height of its capacity, never allowing the body to act under the influence of a lower impulse.

This is why we shall have recourse to the four austerities which will result in four liberations within us. The practice of these austerities will constitute a fourfold discipline or tapasya which can be defined as follows:

— Tapasya of love

— Tapasya of knowledge

— Tapasya of power

— Tapasya of beauty

These terms have been listed from top to bottom, so to say, but their order should not be taken to indicate anything superior or inferior, or more or less difficult, or the order in which these disciplines can and ought to be practised. The order, importance and difficulty vary with each individual and no absolute rule can be formulated. Each one must find and work out his own system according to his personal needs and capacities.

Accordingly, only an overall view will be given here, presenting an ideal procedure that is as complete as possible. Each one will then have to apply as much of it as he can in the best possible way.

The tapasya or discipline of beauty will lead us, through austerity in physical life, to freedom in action. Its basic programme will be to build a body that is beautiful in form, harmonious in posture, supple and agile in its movements, powerful in its activities and robust in its health and organic functioning.

To achieve these results, it will be good, as a general rule, to make use of habit as a help in organising one's material life, for the body functions more easily within the framework of a regular routine. But one must know how to avoid becoming a slave to one's habits, however good they may be; the greatest flexibility must be maintained so that one may change them each time it becomes necessary to do so.

One must build up nerves of steel in powerful and elastic muscles in order to be able to endure anything whenever it is indispensable. But at the same time great care must be taken not to demand more from the body than the effort which is strictly necessary, the expenditure of energy that fosters growth and progress, while categorically excluding everything that causes exhaustion and leads in the end to physical decline and disintegration.

A physical culture which aims at building a body capable of serving as a fit instrument for a higher consciousness demands very austere habits: a great regularity in sleep, food, exercise and every activity. By a scrupulous study of one's own bodily needs—for they vary with each individual—a general programme will be established; and once this has been done well, it must be followed rigorously, without any fantasy or slackness. There must be no little exceptions to the rule that are indulged in "just for once" but which are repeated very often—for as soon as one yields to temptation, even "just for once", one lessens the resistance of the will-power and opens the door to every failure.

One must therefore forgo all weakness: no more nightly escapades from which one comes back exhausted, no more feasting and carousing which upset the normal functioning of the stomach, no more distractions, amusements and pleasures that only waste energy and leave one without the strength to do the daily practice. One must submit to the austerity of a sensible and regular life, concentrating all one's physical attention on building a body that comes as close to perfection as possible. To reach this ideal goal, one must strictly shun all excess and every vice, great or small; one must deny oneself the use of such slow poisons as tobacco, alcohol, etc., which men have a habit of developing into indispensable needs that gradually destroy the will and the memory.

The all-absorbing interest which nearly all human beings, even the most intellectual, have in food, its preparation and its consumption, should be replaced by an almost chemical knowledge of the needs of the body and a very scientific austerity in satisfying them. Another austerity must be added to that of food, the austerity of sleep. It does not consist in going without sleep but in knowing how to sleep. Sleep must not be a fall into unconsciousness which makes the body heavy instead of refreshing it. Eating with moderation and abstaining from all excess greatly reduces the need to spend many hours in sleep; however, the quality of sleep is much more important than its quantity. In order to have a truly effective rest and relaxation during sleep, it is good as a rule to drink something before going to bed, a cup of milk or soup or fruit-juice, for instance. Light food brings a quiet sleep. One should, however, abstain from all copious meals, for then the sleep becomes agitated and is disturbed by nightmares, or else is dense, heavy and dulling. But the most important thing of all is to make the mind clear, to quieten the emotions and calm the effervescence of desires and the preoccupations which accompany them.

If before retiring to bed one has talked a lot or had a lively discussion, if one has read an exciting or intensely interesting book, one should rest a little without sleeping in order to quieten the mental activity, so that the brain does not engage in disorderly movements while the other parts of the body alone are asleep. Those who practise meditation will do well to concentrate for a few minutes on a lofty and restful idea, in an aspiration towards a higher and vaster consciousness. Their sleep will benefit greatly from this and they will largely be spared the risk of falling into unconsciousness while they sleep.

After the austerity of a night spent wholly in resting in a calm and peaceful sleep comes the austerity of a day which is sensibly organised; its activities will be divided between the progressive and skilfully graded exercises required for the culture of the body, and work of some kind or other. For both can and ought to form part of the physical tapasya. With regard to exercises, each one will choose the ones best suited to his body and, if possible, take guidance from an expert on the subject, who knows how to combine and grade the exercises to obtain a maximum effect. Neither the choice nor the execution of these exercises should be governed by fancy. One must not do this or that because it seems easier or more amusing; there should be no change of training until the instructor considers it necessary. The self-perfection or even simply the self-improvement of each individual body is a problem to be solved, and its solution demands much patience, perseverance and regularity. In spite of what many people think, the athlete's life is not a life of amusement or distraction; on the contrary, it is a life of methodical efforts and austere habits, which leave no room for useless fancies that go against the result one wants to achieve.

In work too there is an austerity. It consists in not having any preferences and in doing everything one does with interest. For one who wants to grow in self-perfection, there are no great or small tasks, none that are important or unimportant; all are equally useful for one who aspires for progress and self-mastery. It is said that one only does well what one is interested in doing. This is true, but it is truer still that one can learn to find interest in everything one does, even in what appear to be the most insignificant chores. The secret of this attainment lies in the urge towards self-perfection. Whatever occupation or task falls to your lot, you must do it with a will to progress; whatever one does, one must not only do it as best one can but strive to do it better and better in a constant effort for perfection. In this way everything without exception becomes interesting, from the most material chore to the most artistic and intellectual work. The scope for progress is infinite and can be applied to the smallest thing.

This leads us quite naturally to liberation in action. For, in one's action, one must be free from all social conventions, all moral prejudices. However, this does not mean that one should lead a life of licence and dissoluteness. On the contrary, one imposes on oneself a rule that is far stricter than all social rules, for it tolerates no hypocrisy and demands a perfect sincerity. One's entire physical activity should be organised to help the body to grow in balance and strength and beauty. For this purpose, one must abstain from all pleasure-seeking, including sexual pleasure. For every sexual act is a step towards death. That is why from the most ancient times, in the most sacred and secret schools, this act was prohibited to every aspirant towards immortality.

The sexual act is always followed by a longer or shorter period of unconsciousness that opens the door to all kinds of influences and causes a fall in consciousness. But if one wants to prepare oneself for the supramental life, one must never allow one's consciousness to slip into laxity and inconscience under the pretext of pleasure or even of rest and relaxation.

One should find relaxation in force and light, not in darkness and weakness. Continence is therefore the rule for all those who aspire for progress. But especially for those who want to prepare themselves for the supramental manifestation, this continence must be replaced by a total abstinence, achieved not by coercion and suppression but by a kind of inner alchemy, as a result of which the energies that are normally used in the act of procreation are transmuted into energies for progress and integral transformation. It is obvious that for the result to be total and truly beneficial, all sexual impulses and desires must be eliminated from the mental and vital consciousness as well as from the physical will. All radical and durable transformation proceeds from within outwards, so that the external transformation is the normal, almost inevitable result of this process.

A decisive choice has to be made between lending the body to Nature's ends in obedience to her demand to perpetuate the race as it is, and preparing this same body to become a step towards the creation of the new race. For it is not possible to do both at the same time; at every moment one has to decide whether one wants to remain part of the humanity of yesterday or to belong to the superhumanity of tomorrow.

One must renounce being adapted to life as it is and succeeding in it if one wants to prepare for life as it will be and to become an active and efficient part of it.

One must refuse pleasure if one wants to open to the delight of existence, in a total beauty and harmony. This brings us quite naturally to vital austerity, the austerity of the sensations, the tapasya of power. For the vital being is the seat of power, of effective enthusiasm. It is in the vital that thought is transformed into will and becomes a dynamism for action. It is also true that the vital is the seat of desires and passions, of violent impulses and equally violent reactions, of revolt and depression. The normal remedy is to strangle and starve the vital by depriving it of all sensation; sensations are indeed its main sustenance and without them it falls asleep, grows sluggish and starves to death.

In fact, the vital has three sources of subsistence. The one most easily accessible to it comes from below, from the physical energies through the sensations.

The second is on its own plane, when it is sufficiently vast and receptive, by contact with the universal vital forces. The third, to which it usually opens only in a great aspiration for progress, comes to it from above by the infusion and absorption of spiritual forces and inspiration.

To these sources men always strive more or less to add another, which is for them at the same time the source of most of their torments and misfortunes. It is the interchange of vital forces with their fellows, usually in groups of two, which they most often mistake for love, but which is only the attraction between two forces that take pleasure in mutual interchange.

Thus, if we do not wish to starve our vital, sensations must not be rejected or diminished in number and intensity. Neither should we avoid them; rather we must make use of them with wisdom and discernment. Sensations are an excellent instrument of knowledge and education, but to make them serve these ends, they must not be used egoistically for the sake of enjoyment, in a blind and ignorant search for pleasure and self-satisfaction.

The senses should be capable of enduring everything without disgust or displeasure, but at the same time they must acquire and develop more and more the power of discerning the quality, origin and effect of the various vital vibrations in order to know whether they are favourable to harmony, beauty and good health or whether they are harmful to the balance and progress of the physical being and the vital. Moreover, the senses should be used as instruments to approach and study the physical and vital worlds in all their complexity; in this way they will take their true place in the great endeavour towards transformation.

It is by enlightening, strengthening and purifying the vital, and not by weakening it, that one can contribute to the true progress of the being. To deprive oneself of sensations is therefore as harmful as depriving oneself of food. But just as the choice of food must be made wisely and solely for the growth and proper functioning of the body, so too the choice of sensations and their control should be made with a very scientific austerity and solely for the growth and perfection of the vital, of this highly dynamic instrument, which is as essential for progress as all the other parts of the being.

It is by educating the vital, by making it more refined, more sensitive, more subtle and, one should almost say, more elegant, in the best sense of the word, that one can overcome its violence and brutality, which are in fact a form of crudity and ignorance, of lack of taste.

In truth, a cultivated and illumined vital can be as noble and heroic and disinterested as it is now spontaneously vulgar, egoistic and perverted when it is left to itself without education. It is enough for each one to know how to transform in himself the search for pleasure into an aspiration for the supramental plenitude. If the education of the vital is carried far enough, with perseverance and sincerity, there comes a time when, convinced of the greatness and beauty of the goal, the vital gives up petty and illusory sensorial satisfactions in order to win the divine delight.

The question of mental austerity immediately brings to mind long meditations leading to control of thought and culminating in inner silence. This aspect of yogic discipline is too well known to need dwelling upon. But there is another aspect of the subject which is usually given less attention, and that is control of speech. Apart from a very few exceptions, only absolute silence is set in opposition to loose talk. And yet it is a far greater and far more fruitful austerity to control one's speech than to abolish it altogether.

Man is the first animal on earth to be able to use articulate sounds. Indeed, he is very proud of this capacity and exercises it without moderation or discernment. The world is deafened with the sound of his words and sometimes one almost misses the harmonious silence of the plant kingdom.

Besides, it is a well-known fact that the weaker the mental power, the greater is the need to use speech. Thus there are primitive and uneducated people who cannot think at all unless they speak, and they can be heard muttering sounds more or less loudly to themselves, because this is the only way they can follow a train of thought, which would not be formulated in them but for the spoken word.

There are also a great many people, even among those who are educated but whose mental power is weak, who do not know what they want to say until they say it. This makes their speech interminable and tedious. For as they speak, their thought becomes clearer and more precise, and so they have to repeat the same thing several times in order to say it more and more exactly.

Some need to prepare beforehand what they have to say, and splutter when they are obliged to improvise, because they have not had time to elaborate step by step the exact terms of what they want to say.

Lastly, there are born orators who are masters of the spoken word; they spontaneously find all the words they need to say what they want to say and say it well. None of this, however, from the point of view of mental austerity, goes beyond the category of idle talk. For by idle talk I mean every word that is spoken without being absolutely indispensable. One may ask, how can one judge? For this, one must first make a general classification of the various categories of spoken words.

First, in the physical domain, we have all the words that are spoken for material reasons. They are by far the most numerous and most probably also the most useful in ordinary life.

A constant babble of words seems to be the indispensable accompaniment to daily work. And yet as soon as one makes an effort to reduce the noise to a minimum, one realises that many things are done better and faster in silence and that this helps to maintain one's inner peace and concentration.

If you are not alone and live with others, cultivate the habit of not externalising yourself constantly by speaking aloud, and you will notice that little by little an inner understanding is established between yourself and others; you will then be able to communicate among yourselves with a minimum of words or even without any words at all. This outer silence is most favourable to inner peace, and with goodwill and a steadfast aspiration, you will be able to create a harmonious atmosphere which is very conducive to progress.

In social life, in addition to the words that concern material life and occupations, there will be those that express sensations, feelings and emotions. Here the habit of outer silence proves of valuable help. For when one is assailed by a wave of sensations or feelings, this habitual silence gives you time to reflect and, if necessary, to regain possession of yourself before projecting the sensation or feeling in words. How many quarrels can be avoided in this way; how many times one will be saved from one of those psychological catastrophes which are only too often the result of uncontrolled speech.

Without going to this extreme, one should always control the words one speaks and never allow one's tongue to be prompted by a movement of anger, violence or temper. It is not only the quarrel that is bad in its results, but the fact of allowing one's tongue to be used to project bad vibrations into the atmosphere; for nothing is more contagious than the vibrations of sound, and by giving these movements a chance to express themselves, one perpetuates them in oneself and in others.

Among the most undesirable kinds of idle talk must also be included everything that is said about others. Unless you are responsible for certain people, as a guardian, a teacher or a departmental head, what others do or do not do is no concern of yours and you must refrain from talking about them, from giving your opinion about them and what they do, and from repeating what others may think or say about them.

It may happen that the very nature of your occupation makes it your duty to report what is taking place in a particular department, undertaking or communal work. But then the report should be confined to the work alone and not touch upon private matters. And as an absolute rule, it must be wholly objective. You should not allow any personal reaction, any preference, any like or dislike to creep in. And above all, never introduce your own petty personal grudges into the work that is assigned to you.

In all cases and as a general rule, the less one speaks of others, even to praise them, the better. It is already so difficult to know exactly what is happening in oneself—how can one know with certainty what is happening in others? So you must totally abstain from pronouncing upon anybody one of those final judgments which cannot but be foolish if not spiteful.

When a thought is expressed in speech, the vibration of the sound has a considerable power to bring the most material substance into contact with the thought, thus giving it a concrete and effective reality. That is why one must never speak ill of people or things or say things which go against the progress of the divine realisation in the world. This is an absolute general rule. And yet it has one exception. You should not criticise anything unless at the same time you have the conscious power and active will to dissolve or transform the movements or things you criticise. For this conscious power and active will have the capacity of infusing Matter with the possibility to react and refuse the bad vibration and ultimately to correct it so that it becomes impossible for it to go on expressing itself on the physical plane.

This can be done without risk or danger only by one who moves in the gnostic realms and possesses in his mental faculties the light of the spirit and the power of the truth. He, the divine worker, is free from all preference and all attachment; he has broken down the limits of his ego and is now only a perfectly pure and impersonal instrument of the supramental action upon earth.

There are also all the words that are uttered to express ideas, opinions, the results of reflection or study. Here we are in an intellectual domain and we might think that in this domain men are more reasonable, more self-controlled, and that the practice of rigorous austerity is less indispensable. It is nothing of the kind, however, for even here, into this abode of ideas and knowledge, man has brought the violence of his convictions, the intolerance of his sectarianism, the passion of his preferences. Thus, here too, one must resort to mental austerity and carefully avoid any exchange of ideas that leads to controversies which are all too often bitter and nearly always unnecessary, or any clash of opinion which ends in heated discussions and even quarrels, which are always the result of some mental narrowness that can easily be cured when one rises high enough in the mental domain.

For sectarianism becomes impossible when one knows that any formulated thought is only one way of saying something which eludes all expression. Every idea contains a little of the truth or one aspect of the truth. But no idea is absolutely true in itself.

This sense of the relativity of things is a powerful help in keeping one's balance and preserving a serene moderation in one's speech. I once heard an old occultist of some wisdom say, "Nothing is essentially bad; there are only things which are not in their place. Put each thing in its true place and you will have a harmonious world."

And yet, from the point of view of action, the value of an idea is in proportion to its pragmatic power. It is true that this power varies a great deal according to the individual on whom it acts. An idea that has great impelling force in one individual may have none whatsoever in another. But the power itself is contagious. Certain ideas are capable of transforming the world. They are the ones that ought to be expressed; they are the ruling stars in the firmament of the spirit that will guide the earth towards its supreme realisation.

Lastly, we have all the words that are spoken for the purpose of teaching. This category ranges from the kindergarten to the university course, not forgetting all the artistic and literary creations of mankind that seek to entertain or instruct. In this domain, everything depends on the worth of the creation, and the subject is too vast to be dealt with here. It is a fact that concern about education is very much in vogue at present and praiseworthy attempts are being made to make use of new scientific discoveries in the service of education. But even in this matter, austerity is demanded from the aspirant towards truth.

It is generally admitted that in the process of education a certain kind of lighter, more frivolous, more entertaining productions are necessary to reduce the strain of effort and give some relaxation to the children and even to adults. From a certain point of view, this is true; but unfortunately this concession has served as an excuse to justify a whole category of things which are nothing but the efflorescence of all that is vulgar, crude and base in human nature. Its coarsest instincts, its most depraved taste find in this concession a good excuse to display and impose themselves as an inevitable necessity. They are nothing of the kind, however; one can relax without being dissolute, take rest without being vulgar, enjoy oneself without allowing the grosser elements in the nature to rise to the surface. But from the point of view of austerity, these needs themselves change their nature; relaxation is transformed into inner silence, rest into contemplation and enjoyment into bliss.

This generally recognised need for entertainment, slackening of effort and more or less long and total forgetfulness of the aim of life and the purpose of existence should not be considered as something altogether natural and indispensable, but as a weakness to which one yields because of lack of intensity in the aspiration, because of instability in the will, because of ignorance, unconsciousness and sloth. Do not justify these movements and you will soon realise that they are unnecessary; there will even come a time when they become repugnant and unacceptable to you. Then the greater part of human creation, which is ostensibly entertaining but in reality debasing, will lose its support and cease to be encouraged.

However, one should not think that the value of spoken words depends on the nature of the subject of conversation. One can talk idly on spiritual matters just as much as on any other, and this kind of idle talk may well be one of the most dangerous. For example, the neophyte is always very eager to share with others the little he has learnt. But as he advances on the path, he becomes more and more aware that he does not know very much and that before trying to instruct others, he must be very sure of the value of what he knows, until he finally becomes wise and realises that many hours of silent concentration are needed to be able to speak usefully for a few minutes. Moreover, where inner life and spiritual effort are concerned, the use of speech should be subjected to a still more stringent rule and nothing should be said unless it is absolutely indispensable.

It is a well-known fact that one must never speak of one's spiritual experiences if one does not want to see vanishing in a flash the energy accumulated in the experience, which was meant to hasten one's progress. The only exception which can be made to the rule is with regard to one's guru, when one wants to receive some explanation or teaching from him concerning the content and meaning of one's experience. Indeed, one can speak about these things without danger only to one's guru, for only the guru is able by his knowledge to use the elements of the experience for your own good, as steps towards new ascents.

It is true that the guru himself is subject to the same rule of silence with regard to what concerns him personally. In Nature everything is in movement; thus, whatever does not move forward is bound to fall back. The guru must progress even as his disciples do, although his progress may not be on the same plane. And for him too, to speak about his experiences is not favourable: the greater part of the dynamic force for progress contained in the experience evaporates if it is put into words. But on the other hand, by explaining his experiences to his disciples he greatly helps their understanding and consequently their progress. It is for him in his wisdom to know to what extent he can and ought to sacrifice the one to the other. It goes without saying that no boasting or vainglory should enter into his account, for the slightest vanity would make him no longer a guru but an imposter.

As for the disciple, I would tell him: "In all cases, be faithful to your guru whoever he is; he will lead you as far as you can go. But if you have the good fortune to have the Divine as your guru, there will be no limit to your realisation."

Nevertheless, even the Divine, when incarnate on earth, is subject to the same law of progress. His instrument of manifestation, the physical being he has assumed, should be in a constant state of progress, and the law of his personal self-expression is in a way linked to the general law of earthly progress. Thus, even the embodied god cannot be perfect on earth until men are ready to understand and accept perfection. That day will come when everything that is now done out of a sense of duty towards the Divine will be done out of love for Him. Progress will be a joy instead of being an effort and often even a struggle. Or, more exactly, progress will be made in joy, with the full adherence of the whole being, instead of by coercing the resistance of the ego, which entails great effort and sometimes even great suffering.

In conclusion, I would say this: if you want your speech to express the truth and thus acquire the power of the Word, never think out beforehand what you want to say, do not decide what is a good or bad thing to say, do not calculate the effect of what you are going to say. Be silent in mind and remain unwavering in the true attitude of constant aspiration towards the All-Wisdom, the All-Knowledge, the All-Consciousness. Then, if your aspiration is sincere, if it is not a veil for your ambition to do well and to succeed, if it is pure, spontaneous and integral, you will then be able to speak very simply, to say the words that ought to be said, neither more nor less, and they will have a creative power.

Of all austerities the most difficult is the austerity of feelings and emotions, the tapasya of love. Indeed, in the domain of feelings, more perhaps than in any other, man has the sense of the inevitable, the irresistible, of a fatality that dominates him and which he cannot escape. Love (or at least what human beings call love) is particularly regarded as an imperious master whose caprice one cannot elude, who strikes you according to his fancy and forces you to obey him whether you will or not. In the name of love the worst crimes have been perpetrated, the greatest follies committed.

And yet men have invented all kinds of moral and social rules in the hope of controlling this force of love, of making it amenable and docile. But these rules seem to have been made only to be broken; and the restraint they impose on its free activity merely increases its explosive power. For it is not by rules that the movements of love can be disciplined. Only a greater, higher and truer power of love can subdue the uncontrollable impulses of love. Only love can rule over love by enlightening, transforming and exalting it. For here too, more than anywhere else, control does not consist of suppression and abolition but of transmutation—a sublime alchemy. This is because, of all the forces at work in the universe, love is the most powerful, the most irresistible. Without love the world would fall back into the chaos of inconscience.

Consciousness is indeed the creatrix of the universe, but love is its saviour. Conscious experience alone can give a glimpse of what love is, of its purpose and process. Any verbal transcription is necessarily a mental travesty of something which eludes all expression in every way. Philosophers, mystics, occultists, have all tried to define love, but in vain. I have no pretension of succeeding where they have failed. But I wish to state in the simplest possible terms what in their writings takes such an abstract and complicated form. My words will have no other aim than to lead towards the living experience, and I wish to be able to lead even a child to it.

Love is, in its essence, the joy of identity; it finds its ultimate expression in the bliss of union. Between the two lie all the phases of its universal manifestation. At the beginning of this manifestation, in the purity of its origin, love is composed of two movements, two complementary poles of the urge towards complete oneness. On one hand there is the supreme power of attraction and on the other the irresistible need for absolute self-giving. No other movement could have better bridged the abyss that was created when in the individual being consciousness was separated from its origin and became unconsciousness.

What had been projected into space had to be brought back to itself without, however, annihilating the universe which had thus been created. That is why love burst forth, the irresistible power of union.

It brooded over the darkness and the inconscience; it was scattered and fragmented in the bosom of unfathomable night. And then began the awakening and the ascent, the slow formation of Matter and its endless progression. It is indeed love, in a corrupted and darkened form, that is associated with all the impulses of physical and vital Nature, as the urge behind all movement and all grouping, which becomes quite perceptible in the plant kingdom.

In trees and plants, it is the need to grow in order to obtain more light, more air, more space; in flowers, it is the offering of their beauty and fragrance in a loving efflorescence. Then, in animals, it is love that lies behind hunger and thirst, the need for appropriation, expansion, procreation, in short, behind every desire, whether conscious or not. And among the higher species, it is in the self-sacrificing devotion of the female to her young. This brings us quite naturally to the human race in which, with the triumphant advent of mental activity, this association reaches its climax, for it has become conscious and deliberate.

Indeed, as soon as terrestrial development made it possible, Nature took up this sublime force of love and put it at the service of her creative work by linking and mixing it with her movement of procreation. This association has even become so close, so intimate, that very few human beings are illumined enough in their consciousness to be able to dissociate these movements from each other and experience them separately. In this way, love has suffered every degradation; it has been debased to the level of the beast.

From then on, too, there clearly appears in Nature's works the will to rebuild, by steps and stages and through ever more numerous and complex groupings, the primordial oneness. Having made use of the power of love to bring two human beings together to form the biune group, the origin of the family, after having broken the narrow limits of personal egoism, changing it into a dual egoism, Nature, with the appearance of children, brought forth a more complex unit, the family. And in course of time, with multifarious associations between families, individual interchanges and mingling of blood, larger groupings were formed: clans, tribes, castes, classes, leading to the creation of nations. This work of group formation proceeded simultaneously in the various parts of the world, crystallising in the different races. And little by little, Nature will fuse these races too in her endeavour to build a real and material foundation for human unity.

In the consciousness of most men, all this is the outcome of chance; they are not aware of the existence of a global plan and take circumstances as they come, for better or for worse according to their temperament: some are satisfied, others discontented.

Among the contented, there is a certain category of people who are perfectly adapted to Nature's ways: these are the optimists. For them the days are brighter because of the nights, colours are vivid because of the shadows, joy is more intense because of suffering, pain gives a greater charm to pleasure, illness gives health all its value; I have even heard some of them say that they are glad to have enemies because it made them appreciate their friends all the more. In any case, for all these people, sexual activity is one of the most enjoyable of occupations, satisfaction of the palate is a delight of life that they cannot go without; and it is quite normal to die since one is born: death puts an end to a journey which would become tedious if it were to last too long.

In short, they find life quite all right as it is and do not care to know whether it has a purpose or a goal; they do not worry about the miseries of others and do not see any need for progress.

Never try to "convert" these people; it would be a serious mistake. If they were unfortunate enough to listen to you, they would lose the balance they have without being able to find a new one. They are not ready to have an inner life, but they are Nature's favourites; they have a very close alliance with her, and this realisation should not be needlessly disturbed.

To a lesser degree, and above all, in a less durable way, there are other contented people in the world whose contentment is due to the magic effect of love. Each time an individual breaks the narrow limitations in which he is imprisoned by his ego and emerges into the open air, through self-giving, whether for the sake of another human being or his family, his country or his faith, he finds in this self-forgetfulness a foretaste of the marvellous delight of love, and this gives him the impression that he has come into contact with the Divine. But most often it is only a fleeting contact, for in the human being love is immediately mixed with lower egoistic movements which debase it and rob it of its power of purity. But even if it remained pure, this contact with the divine existence could not last for ever, for love is only one aspect of the Divine, an aspect which here on earth has suffered the same distortions as the others.

Besides, all these experiences are very good and useful for the ordinary man who follows the normal way of Nature in her stumbling march towards the future unity. But they cannot satisfy those who want to hasten the movement, or rather, who aspire to belong to another line of more direct and rapid movement, to an exceptional movement that will liberate them from ordinary mankind and its interminable march, so that they may take part in the spiritual advance which will lead them along the swiftest paths towards the creation of the new race, the race that will express the supramental truth upon earth. These rare souls must reject all forms of love between human beings, for however beautiful and pure they may be, they cause a kind of short-circuit and cut off the direct connection with the Divine.

For one who has known love for the Divine, all other forms of love are obscure and too mixed with pettiness and egoism and darkness; they are like a perpetual haggling or a struggle for supremacy and domination, and even among the best they are full of misunderstanding and irritability, of friction and incomprehension.

Moreover, it is a well-known fact that one grows into the likeness of what one loves. Therefore if you want to be like the Divine, love Him alone. Only one who has known the ecstasy of the exchange of love with the Divine can know how insipid and dull and feeble any other exchange is in comparison. And even if the most austere discipline is required to arrive at this exchange, nothing is too hard, too long or too severe in order to achieve it, for it surpasses all expression.

This is the marvellous state we want to realise on earth; it is this which will have the power to transform the world and make it a habitation worthy of the Divine Presence. Then will pure and true love be able to incarnate in a body that will no longer be a disguise and a veil for it. Many a time, in order to make the discipline easier and to create a closer and more easily perceptible intimacy, the Divine has sought, in his highest form of love, to assume a physical body similar in appearance to the human body; but each time, imprisoned within the gross forms of Matter, he was able to express only a caricature of himself. And in order to manifest in the fullness of his perfection he waits only for human beings to have made some indispensable progress in their consciousness and in their bodies; for the vulgarity of man's vanity and the stupidity of his conceit mistake the sublime divine love, when it expresses itself in a human form, for a sign of weakness and dependence and need.

And yet man already knows, at first obscurely, but more and more clearly as he draws nearer to perfection, that love alone can put an end to the suffering of the world; only the ineffable joy of love in its essence can sweep away from the universe the burning pain of separation. For only in the ecstasy of the supreme union will creation discover its purpose and its fulfilment.

That is why no effort is too arduous, no austerity too rigorous if it can illumine, purify, perfect and transform the physical substance so that it may no longer conceal the Divine when he takes on an outer form in Matter. For then this marvellous tenderness will be able to express itself freely in the world, the divine love which has the power of changing life into a paradise of sweet joy.

This, you will say, is the culmination, the crown of the effort, the final victory; but what must be done in order to achieve it? What is the path to be followed and what are the first steps on the way?

Since we have decided to reserve love in all its splendour for our personal relationship with the Divine, we shall replace it in our relations with others by a total, unvarying, constant and egoless kindness and goodwill that will not expect any reward or gratitude or even any recognition. However others may treat you, you will never allow yourself to be carried away by any resentment; and in your unmixed love for the Divine, you will leave him sole judge as to how he is to protect you and defend you against the misunderstanding and bad will of others.

You will await your joys and pleasures from the Divine alone. In him alone will you seek and find help and support. He will comfort you in all your sorrows, guide you on the path, lift you up if you stumble, and if there are moments of failure and exhaustion, he will take you up in his strong arms of love and enfold you in his soothing sweetness.

To avoid any misunderstanding, I must point out here that because of the exigencies of the language in which I am expressing myself, I am obliged to use the masculine gender whenever I mention the Divine. But in fact the reality of love I speak of is above and beyond all gender, masculine or feminine; and when it incarnates in a human body, it does so indifferently in the body of a man or a woman according to the needs of the work to be done.

In summary, austerity in feelings consists then of giving up all emotional attachment, of whatever nature, whether for a person, for the family, for the country or anything else, in order to concentrate on an exclusive attachment for the Divine Reality. This concentration will culminate in an integral identification and will be instrumental to the supramental realisation upon earth.

This leads us quite naturally to the four liberations which will be the concrete forms of this achievement. The liberation of the feelings will be at the same time the liberation from suffering, in a total realisation of the supramental oneness.

The mental liberation or liberation from ignorance will establish in the being the mind of light or gnostic consciousness, whose expression will have the creative power of the Word. The vital liberation or liberation from desire gives the individual will the power to identify itself perfectly and consciously with the divine will and brings constant peace and serenity as well as the power which results from them.

Finally, crowning all the others, comes the physical liberation or liberation from the law of material cause and effect. By a total self-mastery, one is no longer a slave of Nature's laws which make men act according to subconscious or semiconscious impulses and maintain them in the rut of ordinary life. With this liberation one can decide in full knowledge the path to be taken, choose the action to be accomplished and free oneself from all blind determinism, so that nothing is allowed to intervene in the course of one's life but the highest will, the truest knowledge, the supramental consciousness.

8

Aurobindo's Writings on Education

HUMAN MIND

The true basis of education is the study of the human mind—infant, adolescent and adult. Any system of education founded on theories of academic perfection, which ignores the instrument of study, is more likely to hamper and impair intellectual growth than to produce a perfect and perfectly equipped mind. For the educationist has to do, not with dead material like the artist or sculptor, but with an infinitely subtle and sensitive organism. He cannot shape an educational masterpiece out of human wood or stone; he has to work in the elusive substance of mind and respect the limits imposed by the fragile human body.

There can be no doubt that the current educational system of Europe is a great advance on many of the methods of antiquity, but its defects are also palpable. It is based on an insufficient knowledge of human psychology, and it is only safeguarded in Europe from disastrous results by the refusal of the ordinary student to subject himself to the processes it involves, his habit of studying only so much as he must to avoid punishment or to pass an immediate test, his resort to active habits and vigorous physical exercise. In India the disastrous effects of the system on body, mind and character are only too apparent. The first problem in a national system of education is to give an education as comprehensive as the European and more thorough, without the evils of strain and cramming. This can only be done by studying the instruments of knowledge and finding a system of teaching which shall be natural, easy and effective. It is only by strengthening and sharpening these instruments to their utmost capacity that they can be made effective for the increased work which modern conditions require. The muscles of the mind must be thoroughly trained by simple and easy means; then, and not till then, great feats of intellectual strength can be required of them.

The first principle of true teaching is that nothing can be taught. The teacher is not an instructor or task-master, he is a helper and a guide. His business is to suggest and not to impose. He does not actually train the pupil's mind, he only shows him how to perfect his instruments of knowledge and helps and encourages him in the process. He does not impart knowledge to him, he shows him how to acquire knowledge for himself. He does not call forth the knowledge that is within; he only shows him where it lies and how it can be habituated to rise to the surface.

The distinction that reserves this principle for the teaching of adolescent and adult minds and denies its application to the child, is a conservative and unintelligent doctrine. Child or man, boy or girl, there is only one sound principle of good teaching. Difference of age only serves to diminish or increase the amount of help and guidance necessary; it does not change its nature.

The second principle is that the mind has to be consulted in its own growth. The idea of hammering the child into the shape desired by the parent or teacher is a barbarous and ignorant superstition. It is he himself who must be induced to expand in accordance with his own nature. There can be no greater error than for the parent to arrange beforehand that his son shall develop particular qualities, capacities, ideas, virtues, or be prepared for a prearranged career. To force the nature to abandon its own *dharma* is to do it permanent harm, mutilate its growth and deface its perfection.

It is a selfish tyranny over a human soul and a wound to the nation, which loses the benefit of the best that a man could have given it and is forced to accept instead something imperfect and artificial, second-rate, perfunctory and common. Every one has in him something divine, something his own, a chance of perfection and strength in however small a sphere which God offers him to take or refuse. The task is to find it, develop it and use it. The chief aim of education should be to help the growing soul to draw out that in itself which is best and make it perfect for a noble use.

The third principle of education is to work from the near to the far, from that which is to that which shall be. The basis of a man's nature is almost always, in addition to his soul's past, his heredity, his surroundings, his nationality, his country, the soil from which he draws sustenance, the air which he breathes, the sights, sounds, habits to which he is accustomed. They mould him not the less powerfully because insensibly, and from that then we must begin. We must not take up the nature by the roots from the earth in which it must grow or surround the mind with images and ideas of a life which is alien to that in which it must physically move.

If anything has to be brought in from outside, it must be offered, not forced on the mind. A free and natural growth is the condition of genuine development. There are souls which naturally revolt from their surroundings and seems to belong to another age and clime. Let them be free to follow their bent; but the majority languish, become empty, become artificial, if artificially moulded into an alien form. It is God's arrangement that they should belong to a particular nation, age, society, that they should be children of the past, possessors of the present, creators of the future. The past is our foundation, the present our material, the future our aim and summit. Each must have its due and natural place in a national system of education.

Powers of the Mind

The instrument of the educationist is the mind or *anta]hkarana,* which consists of four layers. The reservoir of past mental impressions, the 'citta' or storehouse of memory, which must be distinguished from the specific act of memory, is the foundation on which all the other layers stand. All experience lies within us as passive or potential memory; active memory selects and takes what it requires from that storehouse. But the active memory is like a man searching among a great mass of locked-up material; sometimes he cannot find what he wants; often in his rapid search he stumbles across many things for which he has not immediate need; often too he blunders and thinks he has found the real thing when it is something else, irrelevant if not valueless, on which he has laid his hand.

The passive memory or *citta* needs no training, it is automatic and naturally sufficient to its task; there is not the slightest object of knowledge coming within its field which is not secured, placed and faultlessly preserved in that admirable receptacle. It is the active memory, a higher but less perfectly developed function, which is in need of improvement.

The second layer is the mind proper or *manas,* the sixth sense of our Indian psychology, in which all the others are gathered up. The function of the mind is to receive the images of things translated into sight, sound, smell, taste and touch, the five senses and translate these again into thought-sensations. It receives also images of its own direct grasping and forms them into mental impressions. These sensations and impressions are the material of thought, not thought itself; but it is exceedingly important that thought should work on sufficient and perfect material.

It is, therefore, the first business of the educationist to develop in the child the right use of the six senses; to see that they are not stunted or injured by disuse, but trained by the child himself under the teacher's direction to that perfect accuracy and keen subtle sensitiveness of which he is capable. In addition, whatever assistance can be gained by the organs of action, should be thoroughly employed. The hand, for instance, should be trained to reproduce what the eye sees and the mind senses. The speech should be trained to a perfect expression of the knowledge the whole *anta]hkarana* possesses.

The third layer is the intellect or 'buddhi', which is the real instrument of thought and that which orders and disposes of the knowledge acquired by the other parts of the machine. For the purpose of the educationist this is infinitely the most important of the three I have named. The intellect is an organ composed of several groups of functions, divisible into two important classes, the functions and faculties of the right-hand, the functions and faculties of the left-hand.

The faculties of the right-hand are comprehensive, creative and synthetic; the faculties of the left-hand critical and analytic. To the right-hand belong judgment, imagination, memory, observation; to the left-hand comparison and reasoning. The critical faculties distinguish, compare, classify, generalise, deduce, infer, conclude; they are the component parts of the logical reason. The right-hand faculties comprehend, command, judge in their own right, grasp, hold and manipulate. The right-hand mind is the master of the knowledge, the left-hand its servant. The left-hand touches only the body of knowledge, the right-hand penetrates its soul. The left-hand limits itself to ascertained truth, the right-hand grasps that which is still elusive or unascertained. Both are essential to the completeness of the human reason. These important functions of the machine have all to be raised to their highest and finest working-power, if the education of the child is not to be imperfect and one-sided.

There is a fourth layer of faculty which, not as yet entirely developed in man, is attaining gradually to a wider development and more perfect evolution. The powers peculiar to this highest stratum of knowledge are chiefly known to us from the phenomena of genius,—sovereign discernment, intuitive perception of truth, plenary inspiration of speech, direct vision of knowledge to an extent often amounting to revelation, making a man a prophet of truth. These powers are rare in their higher development, though many possess them imperfectly or by flashes. They are still greatly distrusted by the criticial reason of mankind because of the admixture of error, caprice and a biased imagination which obstructs and distorts their perfect workings.

Yet it is clear that humanity could not have advanced to its present stage if it had not been for the help of these faculties, and it is a question with which educationists have not yet grappled, what is to be done with this mighty and baffling element, the element of genius in the pupil. The mere instructor does his best to discourage and stifle genius, the more liberal teacher welcomes it. Faculties so important to humanity cannot be left out of our consideration. It is foolish to neglect them. Their imperfect development must be perfected, the admixture of error, caprice and biased fancifulness must be carefully and wisely removed. But the teacher cannot do it; he would eradicate the good corn as well as the tares if he interfered. Here, as in all educational operations, he can only put the growing soul into the way of its own perfection.

Moral Nature

In the economy of man the mental nature rests upon the moral, and the education of the intellect divorced from the perfection of the moral and emotional nature is injurious to human progress. Yet, while it is easy to arrange some kind of curriculum or syllabus which will do well enough for the training of the mind, it has not yet been found possible to provide under modern conditions a suitable moral training for the school and college.

The attempt to make boys moral and religious by the teaching of moral and religious text-books is a vanity and a delusion, precisely because the heart is not the mind and to instruct the mind does not necessarily improve the heart. It would be an error to say that it has no effect. It throws certain seeds of thoughts into the anta]hkara]na and, if these thoughts become habitual, they influence the conduct. But the danger of moral text-books is that they make the thinking of high things mechanical and artificial, and whatever is mechanical and artificial is inoperative for good.

There are three things which are of the utmost importance in dealing with a man's moral nature, the emotions, the *sa=msk"aras* or formed habits and associations, and the *svabh"ava* or nature. The only way for him to train himself morally is to habituate himself to the right emotions, the noblest associations, the best mental, emotional and physical habits and the following out in right action of the fundamental impulses of his essential nature. You can impose a certain discipline on children, dress them into a certain mould, lash them into a desired path, but unless you can get their hearts and natures on your side, the conformity to this imposed rule becomes a hypocritical and heartless, a conventional, often a cowardly compliance. This is what is done in Europe, and it leads to that remarkable phenomenon known as the sowing of wild oats as soon as the yoke of discipline at school and at home is removed, and to the social hypocrisy which is so large a feature of European life. Only what the man admires and accepts, becomes part of himself; the rest is a mask. He conforms to the discipline of society as he conformed to the moral routine of home and school, but considers himself at liberty to guide his real life, inner and private, according to his own likings and passions.

On the other hand, to neglect moral and religious education altogether is to corrupt the race. The notorious moral corruption in our young men previous to the saving touch of the Swadeshi movement was the direct result of the purely mental instruction given to them under the English system of education. The adoption of the English system under an Indian disguise in institutions like the Central Hindu College is likely to lead to the European result. That it is better than nothing, is all that can be said for it.

As in the education of the mind, so in the education of the heart, the best way is to put the child on the right road to his own perfection and encourage him to follow it, watching, suggesting, helping, but not interfering. The one excellent element in the English boarding school is that the master at his best stands there as a moral guide and example, leaving the boys largely to influence and help each other in following the path silently shown to them. But the method practised is crude and marred by the excess of outer discipline, for which the pupils have no respect except that of fear and the exiguity of the inner assistance. The little good that is done is outweighed by much evil. The old Indian system of the *guru* commanding by his knowledge and sanctity the implicit obedience, perfect admiration, reverent emulation of the student was a far superior method of moral discipline. It is impossible to restore that ancient system; but it is not impossible to substitute the wise friend, guide and helper for the hired instructor or the benevolent policeman which is all that the European system usually makes of the pedagogue.

The first rule of moral training is to suggest and invite, not command or impose. The best method of suggestion is by personal example, daily converse and the books read from day to day. These books should contain, for the younger student, the lofty examples of the past given, not as moral lessons, but as things of supreme human interest, and, for the elder student, the great thoughts of great souls, the passages of literature which set fire to the highest emotions and prompt the highest ideals and aspirations, the records of history and biography which exemplify the living of those great thoughts, noble emotions and aspiring ideals. This is a kind of good company, *satsa<nga,* which can seldom fail to have effect so long as sententious sermonising is avoided, and becomes of the highest effect if the personal life of the teacher is itself moulded by the great things he places before his pupils.

It cannot, however, have full force unless the young life is given an opportunity, within its limited sphere, of embodying in action the moral impulses which rise within it. The thirst of knowledge, the self-devotion, the purity, the renunciation of the Brahmin,—the courage, ardour, honour, nobility, chivalry, patriotism of the Kshatriya,—the beneficence, skill, industry, generous enterprise and large open-handedness of the Vaisya,—the self-effacement and loving service of the Sudra,—these are the qualities of the Aryan. They constitute the moral temper we desire in our young men, in the whole nation. But how can we get them if we do not give opportunities to the young to train themselves in the Aryan tradition, to form by the practice and familiarity of childhood and boyhood the stuff of which their adult lives must be made ?

Every boy should, therefore, be given practical opportunity as well as intellectual encouragement to develop all that is best in the nature. If he has bad qualities, bad babits, bad *sa=msk"aras*, whether of mind or body, he should not be treated harshly as a delinquent, but encouraged to get rid of them by the Rajayogic method of *sa=myama*, rejection and substitution. He should be encouraged to think of them, not as sins or offences, but as symptoms of a curable disease, alterable by a steady and sustained effort of the will,—falsehood being rejected whenever it rises into the mind and replaced by truth, fear by courage, selfishness by sacrifice and renunciation, malice by love. Great care will have to be taken that unformed virtues are not rejected as faults. The wildness and recklessness of many young natures are only the overflowings of an excessive strength, greatness and nobility. They should be purified, nor discouraged.

I have spoken of morality; it is necessary to speak a word of religious teaching. There is a strange idea prevalent that by merely teaching the dogmas of religion children can be made pious and moral. This is an European error, and its practice either leads to mechanical acceptance of a creed having no effect on the inner and little on the outer life, or it creates the fanatic, the pietist, the ritualist or the unctuous hypocrite. Religion has to be lived, not learned as a creed. The singular compromise made in the so-called National Education of Bengal making the teaching of religious beliefs compulsory, but forbidding the practice of *anu]s]th"ana* or religious exercise, is a sample of the ignorant confusion which distracts men's minds on this subject. The prohibition is a sop to secularism declared or concealed. No religious teaching is of any value unless it is lived, and the use of various kind of *s"adhan"a*, spiritual self-training and exercise is the only effective preparation for religious living. The ritual of prayer, homage, ceremony is craved for by many minds as an essential preparation and, if not made an end in itself, is a great help to spiritual progress; if it is withheld, some other form of meditation, devotion or religious duty must be put in its place. Otherwise, religious teaching is of little use and would almost be better ungiven.

But whether distinct teaching in any form of religion is imparted or not, the essence of religion, to live for God, for humanity, for country, for others and for oneself in these, must be made the ideal in every school which calls itself national. It is this spirit of Hinduism pervading our schools which—far more than the teaching of Indian subjects, the use of Indian methods or formal instruction in Hindu beliefs and Hindu scriptures—should be the essence of Nationalism in our schools distinguishing them from all others.

Successive Teaching

A very remarkable feature of modern training which has been subjected in India to a *reductio ad absurdum* is the practice of teaching by snippets. A subject is taught a little at a time, in conjunction with a host of others, with the result that what might be well learnt in a single year is badly learned in seven and the boy goes out ill-equipped, served with imperfect parcels of knowledge, master of none of the great departments of human knowledge. The system of education adopted by the National Council, an amphibious and twy-natured creation, attempts to heighten this practice of teaching by snippets at the bottom and the middle and suddenly change it to a grandiose specialism at the top. This is to base the triangle on its apex and hope that it will stand.

The old system was to teach one or two subjects well and thoroughly and then proceed to others, and certainly it was a more rational system than the modern. If it did not impart so much varied information, it built up a deeper, nobler and more real culture. Much of the shallowness, discursive lightness and fickle mutability of the average modern mind is due to the vicious principle of teaching by snippets.

The one defect that can be alleged against the old system was that the subject earliest learned might fade from the mind of the student while he was mastering his later studies. But the excellent training given to the memory by the ancients obviated the incidence of this defect. In the future education we need not bind ourselves either by the ancient or the modern system, but select only the most perfect and rapid means of mastering knowledge.

In defence of the modern system it is alleged that the attention of children is easily tired and cannot be subjected to the strain of long application to a single subject. The frequent change of subject gives rest to the mind. The question naturally arises : are the children of modern times then so different from the ancients, and, if so, have we not made them so by discouraging prolonged concentration? A very young child cannot, indeed, apply himself; but a very young child is unfit for school teaching of any kind.

A child of seven or eight, and that is the earliest permissible age for the commencement of any regular kind of study, is capable of a good deal of concentration if he is interested. Interest is, after all, the basis of concentration. We make his lessons supremely uninteresting and repellent to the child, a harsh compulsion the basis of teaching and then complain of his restless inattention! The substitution of a natural self-education by the child for the present unnatural system will remove this objection of inability. A child, like a man, if he is interested, much prefers to get to the end of his subject rather than leave it unfinished. To lead him on step by step, interesting and absorbing him in each as it comes, until he has mastered his subject is the true art of teaching.

The first attention of the teacher must be given to the medium and the instruments, and, until these are perfected, to multiply subjects of regular instruction is to waste time and energy. When the mental instruments are sufficiently developed to acquire a language easily and swiftly, that is the time to introduce him to many languages, not when he can only partially understand what he is taught and masters it laboriously and imperfectly. Moreover, one who has mastered his own language, has one very necessary facility for mastering another. With the linguistic faculty unsatisfactorily developed in one's own tongue, to master others is impossible. To study science with the faculties of observation, judgement, reasoning and comparison only slightly developed is to undertake a useless and thankless labour. So it is with all other subjects.

The mother-tongue is the proper medium of education and therefore the first energies of the child should be directed to the thorough mastering of the medium. Almost every child has an imagination, an instinct for words, a dramatic faculty, a wealth of idea and fancy. These should be interested in the literature and history of the nation. Instead of stupid and dry spelling and reading books, looked on as a dreary and ungrateful task, he should be introduced by rapidly progressive stages to the most interesting parts of his own literature and the life around him and behind him, and they should be put before him in such a way as to attract and appeal to the qualities of which I have spoken. All other study at this period should be devoted to the perfection of the mental functions and the moral character. A foundation should be laid at this time for the study of history, science, philosophy, art, but not in an obtrusive and formal manner.

Every child is a lover of interesting narrative, a hero-worshipper and a patriot. Appeal to these qualities in him and through them let him master without knowing it, the living and human parts of his nation's history. Every child is an inquirer, an investigator, analyser, a merciless anatomist. Appeal to those qualities in him and let him acquire without knowing it the right temper and the necessary fundamental knowledge of the scientist. Every child has an insatiable intellectual curiosity and turn for metaphysical enquiry. Use it to draw him on slowly to an understanding of the world and himself. Every child has the gift of imitation and a touch of imaginative power. Use it to give him the groundwork of the faculty of the artist.

It is by allowing Nature to work that we get the benefit of the gifts she has bestowed on us. Humanity in its education of children has chosen to thwart and hamper her processes and, by so doing, has done much to thwart and hamper the rapidity of its onward march. Happily, saner ideas are now beginning to prevail. But the way has not yet been found. The past hangs about our necks with all its prejudices and errors and will not leave us; it enters into our most radical attempts to return to the guidance of the all-wise Mother. We must have the courage to take up clearer knowledge and apply it fearlessly in the interests of posterity. Teaching by snippets must be relegated to the lumber-room of dead sorrows. The first work is to interest the child in life, work and knowledge, to develop his instruments of knowledge with the utmost thoroughness, to give him mastery of the medium he must use. Afterwards, the rapidity with which he will learn will make up for any delay in taking up regular studies, and it will be found that, where now he learns a few things badly, then he will learn many things thoroughly well.

Training of the Senses

There are six senses which minister to knowledge, sight, hearing, smell, touch and taste, mind, and all of these except the last look outward and gather the material of thought from outside through the physical nerves and their end organs, eye, ear, nose, skin, palate. The perfection of the senses as ministers to thought must be one of the first cares of the teacher. The two things that are needed of the senses are accuracy and sensitiveness. We must first understand what are the obstacles to the accuracy and sensitiveness of the senses, in order that we may take the best steps to remove them. The cause of imperfection must be understood by those who desire to bring about perfection.

The senses depend for their accuracy and sensitiveness on the unobstructed activity of the nerves which are the channels of their information and the passive acceptance of the mind which is the recipient. In themselves the organs do their work perfectly, the eye gives the right form, the ear the correct sound, the palate the right taste, the skin the right touch, the nose the right smell. This can easily be understood if we study the action of the eye as a crucial example, a correct image is reproduced automatically on the retina, if there is any error in appreciating it, it is not the fault of the organ, but of something else.

The fault may be with the nerve currents. The nerves are nothing but channels, they have no power in themselves to alter the information given by the organs.

But a channel may be obstructed and the obstruction may interfere either with the fullness or the accuracy of the information, not as it reaches the organ where it is necessarily and automatically perfect, but as it reaches the mind. The only exception is in case of a physical defect in the organ as an instrument. That is not a matter for the educationist, but for the physician.

If the obstruction is such as to stop the information reaching the mind at all, the result is an insufficient sensitiveness of the senses. The defects of sight, hearing, smell, touch, taste, anesthesia in its various degrees, are curable when not the effect of physical injury or defect in the organ itself. The obstructions can be removed and the sensitiveness remedied by the purification of the nerve system. The remedy is a simple one which is now becoming more and more popular in Europe for different reasons and objects, the regulation of the breathing. This process inevitably restores the perfect and unobstructed activity of the channels and, if well and thoroughly done, leads to a high activity of the senses. The process is called in Yogic discipline, *n"ad$û-«suddhi* or nerve-purification.

The obstruction in the channel may be such as not absolutely to stop in however small a degree, but to distort the information. A familiar instance of this is the effect of fear or alarm on the sense action. The startled horse takes the sack on the road for a dangerous living thing, the startled man takes a rope for a snake, a waving curtain for a ghostly form. All distortions due to actions in the nervous system can be traced to some kind of emotional disturbance acting in the nerve channels. The only remedy for them is the habit of calm, the habitual steadiness of the nerves. This also can be brought about by *n"ad$û-«suddhi* or nerve-purification, which quiets the system, gives a deliberate calmness to all the internal processes and prepares the purification of the mind.

If the nerve channels are quiet and clear, the only possible disturbance of the information is from or through the mind. Now the *manas* or sixth sense is in itself a channel like the nerves, a channel for communication with the *buddhi* or brain-force. Disturbance may happen either from above or from below.

The information outside is first photographed on the end organ, then reproduced at the other end of the nerve system in the *citta* or passive memory. All the images of sight, sound, smell, touch and taste are deposited there and the *manas* reports them to the *buddhi*. The *manas* is both a sense organ and a channel. As a sense organ it is as automatically perfect as the others, as a channel it is subject to disturbance resulting either in obstruction or distortion.

As a sense organ the mind receives direct thought impressions from outside and from within. These impressions are in themselves perfectly correct, but in their report to the intellect they may either not reach the intellect at all or may reach it so distorted as to make a false or partially false impression. The disturbance may affect the impression which attends the information of eye, ear, nose, skin or palate, but it is very slightly powerful here. In its effect on the direct impressions of the mind, it is extremely powerful and the chief source of error.

The mind takes direct impressions primarily of thought, but also of form, sound, indeed of all the things for which it usually prefers to depend on the sense organs. The full development of this sensitiveness of the mind is called in our Yogic discipline *'s"uk]smad]r]s]ti'* or subtle reception of images. Telepathy, clairvoyance, clairaudience, presentiment, thought-reading, character-reading and many other modern discoveries are very ancient powers of the mind which have been left undeveloped, and they all belong to the *manas*. The development of the sixth sense has never formed part of human training. In a future age it will undoubtedly take a place in the necessary preliminary training of the human instrument. Meanwhile there is no reason why the mind should not be trained to give a correct report to the intellect so that our thought may start with absolutely correct if not with full impressions.

The first obstacle, the nervous emotional, we may suppose to be removed by the purification of the nervous system. The second obstacle is that of the emotions themselves warping the impression as it comes. Love may do this, hatred may do this, any emotion or desire according to its power and intensity may distort the impression as it travels. This difficulty can only be removed by the discipline of the emotions, the purifying of the moral habits. This is a part of moral training and its consideration may be postponed for the moment.

The next difficulty is the interference of previous associations formed or ingrained in the *citta* or passive memory. We have a habitual way of looking at things and the conservative inertia in our nature disposes us to give every new experience the shape and semblance of those to which we are accustomed. It is only more developed minds which can receive first impressions without an unconscious bias against the novelty experience. For instance, if we get a true impression of what is happening—and we habitually act on such impressions true or false—if it differs from what we are accustomed to expect, the old association meets it in the *citta* and sends a changed report to the intellect in which either the new impression is overlaid and concealed by the old or mingled with it.

To go farther into this subject would be to involve ourselves too deeply into the details of psychology. This typical instance will suffice. To get rid of this obstacle is impossible without *citta«suddhi* or purification of the mental and moral habits formed in the *citta*. This is a preliminary process of Yoga and was effected in our ancient system by various means, but would be considered out of place in a modern system of education.

It is clear, therefore, that unless we revert to our old Indian system in some of its principles, we must be content to allow this source of disturbance to remain. A really national system of education would not allow itself to be controlled by European ideas in this all-important matter. And there is a process so simple and momentous that it can easily be made a part of our system.

It consists in bringing about passivity of the restless flood of thought sensations rising of its own momentum from the passive memory independent of our will and control. This passivity liberates the intellect from the siege of old associations and false impressions. It gives it power to select only what is wanted from the storehouse of the passive memory, automatically brings about the habit of getting right impressions and enables the intellect to dictate to the *citta* what *sa=msk"aras* or associations shall be formed or rejected. This is the real office of the intellect,—to discriminate, choose, select, arrange. But so long as there is no *citta«suddhi*, instead of doing this office perfectly, it itself remains imperfect and corrupt and adds to the confusion in the mind channel by false judgment, false imagination, false memory, false observation, false comparison, contrast and analogy, false deduction, induction and inference. The purification of the *citta* is essential for the liberation, purification and perfect action of the intellect.

Sense-Improvement by Practice

Another cause of the inefficiency of the senses as gatherers of knowledge, is insufficient use. We do not observe sufficiently or with sufficient attention and closeness and a sight, sound, smell, even touch or taste knocks in vain at the door for admission This 'tamasic' inertia of the receiving instruments is no doubt due to the inattention of the *buddhi,* and therefore its consideration may seem to come properly under the training of the functions of the intellect, but it is more convenient, though less psychologically correct, to notice it here. The student ought to be accustomed to catch the sights, sounds, etc., around him, distinguish them, mark their nature, properties and sources and fix them in the *citta* so that they may be always ready to respond when called for by the memory.

It is a fact which has been proved by minute experiments that the faculty of observation is very imperfectly developed in men, merely from want of care in the use of the sense and the memory. Give twelve men the task of recording from memory something they all saw two hours ago and the accounts will all vary from each other and from the actual occurrence. To get rid of this imperfection will go a long way towards the removal of error. It can be done by training the senses to do their work perfectly, which they will do readily enough if they know the *buddhi* requires it of them, and giving sufficient attention to put the facts in their right place and order in the memory.

Attention is a factor in knowledge, the importance of which has been always recognised. Attention is the first condition of right memory and of accuracy. To attend to what he is doing is the first element of discipline required of the student, and, as I have suggested, this can easily be secured if the object of attention is made interesting. This attention to a single thing is called concentration. One truth is, however, sometimes overlooked; that concentration on several things at a time is often indispensable. When people talk of concentration, they imply centring the mind on one thing at a time; but it is quite possible to develop the power of double concentration, triple concentration, multiple concentration. When a given incident is happening, it may be made up of several simultaneous happenings or a set of simultaneous circumstances, a sight, a sound, a touch or several sights, sounds, touches occurring at the same moment or in the same short space of time. The tendency of the mind is to fasten on one and mark others vaguely, may not at all or, if compelled to attend to all, to be distracted and mark none perfectly. Yet this can be remedied and the attention equally distributed over a set of circumstances in such a way as to observe and remember each perfectly. It is merely a matter of *abhyasa* or steady natural practice.

It is also very desirable that the hand should be capable of coming to the help of the eye in dealing with the multitudinous objects of its activity so as to ensure accuracy. This is of a use so obvious and imperatively needed, that it need not be dwelt on at length. The practice of imitation by the hand of the thing seen is of use both in detecting the lapses and inaccuracies of the mind, in noticing the objects of sense and in registering accurately what has been seen. Imitation by the hand ensures accuracy of observation. This is one of the first uses of drawing and it is sufficient in itself to make the teaching of this subject a necessary part of the training of the organs.

Training of the Mental Faculties

The first qualities of the mind that have to be developed are those which can be grouped under observation. We notice some things, ignore others. Even of what we notice, we observe very little. A general perception of an object is what we all usually carry away from a cursory half-attentive glance. A closer attention fixes its place, form, nature as distinct from its surroundings. Full concentration of the faculty of observation gives us all the knowledge that the three chief senses can gather about the object, or if we touch or taste, we may gather all that the five senses can tell of its nature and properties. Those who make use of the sixth sense, the poet, the painter, the Yogin, can also gather much that is hidden from the ordinary observer.

The scientist by investigation ascertains other facts open to a minuter observation. These are the components of the faculty of observation and it is obvious that its basis is attention, which may be only close or close and minute. We may gather much even from a passing glance at an object, if we have the habit of concentrating the attention and the habit of *sattwic* receptivity. The first thing the teacher has to do is to accustom the pupil to concentrate attention.

We may take the instance of a flower. Instead of looking casually at it and getting a casual impression of scent, form and colour, he should be encouraged to know the flower—to fix in his mind the exact shade, the peculiar glow, the precise intensity of the scent, the beauty of curve and design in the form. His touch should assure itself of the texture and its peculiarities. Next, the flower should be taken to pieces and its structure examined with the same carefulness of observation. All this should be done not as a task, but as an object of interest by skilfully arranged questions suited to the learner which will draw him on to observe and investigate one thing after the other until he has almost unconsciously mastered the whole.

Memory and judgement are the next qualities that will be called upon, and they should be encouraged in the same unconscious way. The student should not be made to repeat the same lesson over again in order to remember it. That is a mechanical, burdensome and unintelligent way of training the memory. A similar but different flower should be put in the hands and he should be encouraged to note it with the same care, but with the avowed object of noting the similarities and differences. By this practice daily repeated the memory will naturally be trained. Not only so, but the mental centres of comparison and contrast will be developed. The learner will begin to observe as a habit the similarities of things and their differences.

The teacher should take every care to encourage the perfect growth of this faculty and habit. At the same time, the laws of species and genus will begin to dawn on the mind and, by a skilful following and leading of the young developing mind, the scientific habit, the scientific attitude and the fundamental facts of scientific knowledge may in a very short time be made part of its permanent equipment. The observation and comparison of flowers, leaves, plants, trees will lay the foundations of botanical knowledge without loading the mind with names and that dry set acquisition of informations which is the beginning of cramming and detested by the healthy human mind when it is fresh from nature and unspoiled by unnatural habits.

In the same way by the observation of the stars, astronomy, by the observation of earth, stones, etc., geology, by the observation of insects and animals, entomology and zoology may be founded. A little later chemistry may be started by interesting observation of experiments without any formal teaching or heaping on the mind of formulas and book knowledge. There is no scientific subject the perfect and natural mastery of which cannot be prepared in early childhood by this training of the faculties to observe, compare, remember and judge various classes of objects. It can be done easily and attended with a supreme and absorbing interest in the mind of the student. Once the taste is created, the boy can be trusted to follow it up with all the enthusiasm of youth in his leisure hours. This will prevent the necessity at a later age of teaching him everything in class.

The judgement will naturally be trained along with the other faculties. At every step the boy will have to decide what is the right idea, measurement, appreciation of colour, sound, scent, etc., and what is the wrong. Often the judgements and distinctions made will have to be exceedingly subtle and delicate. At first many errors will be made, but the learner should be taught to trust his judgment without being attached to its results. It will be found that the judgement will soon begin to respond to the calls made on it, clear itself of all errors and begin to judge correctly and minutely. The best way is to accustom the boy to compare his judgements with those of others. When he is wrong, it should at first be pointed out to him how far he was right and why he went wrong; afterwards he should be encouraged to note these things for himself. Every time he is right, his attention should be prominently and encouragingly called to it so that he may get confidence.

While engaged in comparing and constrasting, another centre is certain to develop, the centre of analogy. The learner will inevitably draw analogies and argue from like to like. He should be encouraged to use this faculty while noticing its limitations and errors. In this way he will be trained to form the habit of correct analogy which is an indispensable aid in the acquisition of knowledge.

The one faculty we have omitted, apart from the faculty of direct reasoning, is Imagination. This is a most important and indispensable instrument. It may be divided into three functions, the forming of mental images, the power of creating thoughts, images and imitations or new combinations of existing thoughts and images, the appreciation of the soul in things, beauty, charm, greatness, hidden suggestiveness, the emotion and spiritual life that pervades the world. This is in every way as important as the training of the faculties which observe and compare outward things. But that demands a separate and fuller treatment.

The mental faculties should first be exercised on things, afterwards on words and ideas. Our dealings with language are much too perfunctory and the absence of a fine sense for words impoverishes the intellect and limits the fineness and truth of its operation. The mind should be accustomed first to notice the word thoroughly, its form, sound and sense; then to compare the form with other similar forms in the points of similarity and difference, thus forming the foundation of the grammatical sense; then to distinguish between the fine shades of sense of similar words and the formation and rhythm of different sentences, thus forming the formation of the literary and the syntactical faculties. All this should be done informally, drawing on the curiosity and interest, avoiding set teaching and memorising of rules. The true knowledge takes its base on things, *arthas,* and only when it has mastered the thing, proceeds to formalise its information.

Training of the Logical Faculty

The training of the logical reason must necessarily follow the training of the faculties which collect the material on which the logical reason must work. Not only so but the mind must have some development of the faculty of dealing with words before it can deal successfully with ideas. The question is, once this preliminary work is done, what is the best way of teaching the boy to think correctly from premises. For the logical reason cannot proceed without premises. It either infers from facts to a conclusion, or from previously formed conclusions to a fresh one, or from one fact to another. It either induces, deduces or simply infers. I see the sunrise day after day,

I conclude or induce that it rises as a law daily after a varying interval of darkness. I have already ascertained that wherever there is smoke, there is fire. I have induced that general rule from an observation of facts. I deduce that in a particular case of smoke there is a fire behind. I infer that a man must have lit it from the improbability of any other cause under the particular circumstances. I cannot deduce it because fire is not always created by human kindling; it may be volcanic or caused by a stroke of lightning or the sparks from some kind of friction in the neighbourhood.

There are three elements necessary to correct reasoning : first, the correctness of the facts or conclusions I start from, secondly, the completeness as well as the accuracy of the data I start from, thirdly, the elimination of other possible or impossible conclusions from the same facts. The fallibility of the logical reason is due partly to avoidable negligence and looseness in securing these conditions, partly to the difficulty of getting all the facts complete, most of all, to the extreme difficulty of eliminating all possible conclusions except the one which happens to be right. No fact is supposed to be more perfectly established than the universality of the Law of Gravitation as an imperative rule, yet a single new fact inconsistent with it would upset this supposed universality. And such facts exist. Nevertheless by care and keenness the fallibility may be reduced to its minimum.

The usual practice is to train the logical reason by teaching the science of Logic. This is an instance of the prevalent error by which book knowledge of a thing is made the object of the study instead of the thing itself. The experience of reasoning and its errors should be given to the mind and it should be taught to observe how this works for itself; it should proceed from the example to the rule and from the accumulating harmony of rules to the formal science of the subject, not from the formal science to the rule, and from the rule to the example.

The first step is to make the young mind interest itself in drawing inferences from the facts, tracing cause and effect. It should then be led on to notice its successes and its failures and the reason of the success and of the failure; the incorrectness of the fact started from, the haste in drawing conclusions from insufficient facts, the carelessness in accepting a conclusion which is improbable, little supported by the data or open to doubt, the indolence or prejudice which does not wish to consider other possible explanations or conclusions. In this way the mind can be trained to reason as correctly as the fallibility of human logic will allow, minimising the chances of error. The study of formal logic should be postponed to a later time when it can easily be mastered in a very brief period, since it will be only the systematising of an art perfectly well-known to the student.

9

The Mother's Writings on Education

Education

The education of a human being should begin at birth and continue throughout his life. Indeed, if we want this education to have its maximum result, it should begin even before birth; in this case it is the mother herself who proceeds with this education by means of a twofold action: first, upon herself for her own improvement, and secondly, upon the child whom she is forming physically. For it is certain that the nature of the child to be born depends very much upon the mother who forms it, upon her aspiration and will as well as upon the material surroundings in which she lives.

To see that her thoughts are always beautiful and pure, her feelings always noble and fine, her material surroundings as harmonious as possible and full of a great simplicity—this is the part of education which should apply to the mother herself. And if she has in addition a conscious and definite will to form the child according to the highest ideal she can conceive, then the very best conditions will be realised so that the child can come into the world with his utmost potentialities. How many difficult efforts and useless complications would be avoided in this way?

Education to be complete must have five principal aspects corresponding to the five principal activities of the human being; the physical, the vital, the mental, the psychic and the spiritual. Usually, these phases of education follow chronologically the growth of the individual; this, however, does not mean that one of them should replace another, but that all must continue, completing one another until the end of his life.

We propose to study these five aspects of education one by one and also their interrelationships. But before we enter into the details of the subject, I wish to make a recommendation to parents. Most parents, for various reasons, give very little thought to the true education which should be imparted to children. When they have brought a child into the world, provided him with food, satisfied his various material needs and looked after his health more or less carefully, they think they have fully discharged their duty. Later on, they will send him to school and hand over to the teachers the responsibility for his education.

There are other parents who know their children must be educated and who try to do what they can. But very few, even among those who are most serious and sincere, know that the first thing to do, in order to be able to educate a child, is to educate oneself, to become conscious and master of oneself so that one never sets a bad example to one's child. For it is above all through example that education becomes effective. To speak good words and to give wise advice to a child has very little effect if one does not oneself give him an example of what one teaches. Sincerity, honesty, straightforwardness, courage, disinterestedness, unselfishness, patience, endurance, perseverance, peace, calm, self-control are all things that are taught infinitely better by example than by beautiful speeches. Parents, have a high ideal and always act in accordance with it and you will see that little by little your child will reflect this ideal in himself and spontaneously manifest the qualities you would like to see expressed in his nature. Quite naturally a child has respect and admiration for his parents; unless they are quite unworthy, they will always appear to their child as demi-gods whom he will try to imitate as best he can.

With very few exceptions, parents are not aware of the disastrous influence that their own defects, impulses, weaknesses and lack of self-control have on their children. If you wish to be respected by a child, have respect for yourself and be worthy of respect at every moment. Never be authoritarian, despotic, impatient or ill-tempered. When your child asks you a question, do not give him a stupid or silly answer under the pretext that he cannot understand you. You can always make yourself understood if you take enough trouble; and in spite of the popular saying that it is not always good to tell the truth, I affirm that it is always good to tell the truth, but that the art consists in telling it in such a way as to make it accessible to the mind of the hearer.

In early life, until he is twelve or fourteen, the child's mind is hardly open to abstract notions and general ideas. And yet you can train it to understand these things by using concrete images, symbols or parables. Up to quite an advanced age and for some who mentally always remain children, a narrative, a story, a tale well told teaches much more than any number of theoretical explanations.

Another pitfall to avoid: do not scold your child without good reason and only when it is quite indispensable. A child who is too often scolded gets hardened to rebuke and no longer attaches much importance to words or severity of tone. And above all, take good care never to scold him for a fault which you yourself commit. Children are very keen and clear-sighted observers; they soon find out your weaknesses and note them without pity.

When a child has done something wrong, see that he confesses it to you spontaneously and frankly; and when he has confessed, with kindness and affection make him understand what was wrong in his movement so that he will not repeat it, but never scold him; a fault confessed must always be forgiven. You should not allow any fear to come between you and your child; fear is a pernicious means of education : it invariably gives birth to deceit and lying. Only a discerning affection that is firm yet gentle and an adequate practical knowledge will create the bonds of trust that are indispensable for you to be able to educate your child effectively. And do not forget that you have to control yourself constantly in order to be equal to your task and truly fulfil the duty which you owe your child by the mere fact of having brought him into the world.

Physical Education

Of all the domains of human consciousness, the physical is the one most completely governed by method, order, discipline, process. The lack of plasticity and receptivity in matter has to be replaced by a detailed organisation that is both precise and comprehensive. In this organisation, one must not forget the interdependence and interpenetration of all the domains of the being. However, even a mental or vital impulse, to express itself physically, must submit to an exact process. That is why all education of the body, if it is to be effective, must be rigorous and detailed, far-sighted and methodical. This will be translated into habits; the body is a being of habits. But these habits should be controlled and disciplined, while remaining flexible enough to adapt themselves to circumstances and to the needs of the growth and development of the being.

All education of the body should begin at birth and continue throughout life. It is never too soon to begin nor too late to continue.

Physical education had three principal aspects:

— control and discipline of the functioning of the body;

— an integral, methodical and harmonious development of all the parts and movements of the body; and

— correction of any defects and deformities.

It may be said that from the very first days, even the first hours of his life, the child should undergo the first part of this programme as far as food, sleep, evacuation, etc. are concerned. If the child, from the very beginning of his existence, learns good habits, it will save him a good deal of trouble and inconvenience for the rest of the life; and besides, those who have the responsibility of caring for him during his first years will find their task very much easier.

Naturally, this education, if it is to be rational, enlightened and effective, must be based upon a minimum knowledge of the human body, of its structure and its functioning. As the child develops, he must gradually be taught to observe the functioning of his internal organs so that he may control them more and more, and see that this functioning remains normal and harmonious. As for positions, postures and movements, bad habits are formed very early and very rapidly, and these may have disastrous consequences for his whole life. Those who take the question of physical education seriously and wish to give their children the best conditions for normal development will easily find the necessary indications and instructions. The subject is being more and more thoroughly studied, and many books have appeared and are still appearing which give all the information and guidance needed.

It is not possible for me here to go into the details of the application, for each problem is different from every other and the solution should suit the individual case. The question of food has been studied at length and in detail; the diet that helps children in their growth is generally known and it may be very useful to follow it. But it is very important to remember that the instinct of the body, so long as it remains intact, is more reliable than any theory. Accordingly, those who want their child to develop normally should not force him to eat food which he finds distasteful, for most often the body possesses a sure instinct as to what is harmful to it, unless the child is particularly capricious.

The body in its normal state, that is to say, when there is no intervention of mental notions or vital impulses, also knows very well what is good and necessary for it; but for this to be effective in practice, one must educate the child with care and teach him to distinguish his desires from his needs. He should be helped to develop a taste for food that is simple and healthy, substantial and appetising, but free from any useless complications. In his daily food, all that merely stuffs and causes heaviness should be avoided; and above all, he must be taught to eat according to his hunger, neither more nor less, and not to make his meals an occasion to satisfy his greed or gluttony. From one's very childhood, one should know that one eats in order to give strength and health to the body and not to enjoy the pleasures of the palate.

Children should be given food that suits their temperament, prepared in a way that ensures hygiene and cleanliness, that is pleasant to the taste and yet very simple. This food should be chosen and apportioned according to the age of the child and his regular activities. It should contain all the chemical and dynamic elements that are necessary for his development and the balanced growth of every part of his body.

Since the child will be given only the food that helps to keep him healthy and provide him with the energy he needs, one must be very careful not to use food as a means of coercion and punishment. The practice of telling a child, "You have not been a good boy, you won't get any dessert", etc., is most harmful. In this way you create in his little consciousness the impression that food is given to him chiefly to satisfy his greed and not because it is indispensable for the proper functioning of his body.

Another thing should be taught to a child from his early years: to enjoy cleanliness and observe hygienic habits. But, in obtaining this cleanliness and respect for the rules of hygiene from the child, one must take great care not to instill into him the fear of illness. Fear is the worst instrument of education and the surest way of attracting what is feared. Yet, while there should be no fear of illness, there should be no inclination for it either. There is a prevalent belief that brilliant minds are found in weak bodies. This is a delusion and has no basis. There was perhaps a time when a romantic and morbid taste for physical unbalance prevailed; but, fortunately, that tendency has disappeared.

Nowadays a well-built, robust, muscular, strong and well-balanced body is appreciated at its true value. In any case, children should be taught to respect health and admire the healthy man whose vigorous body knows how to repel attacks of illness. Often a child feigns illness to avoid some troublesome obligation, a work that does not interest him, or simply to soften his parent's hearts and get them to satisfy some caprice. The child must be taught as early as possible that this does not work and that he does not become more interesting by being ill, but rather the contrary. The weak have a tendency to believe that their weakness makes them particularly interesting and to use this weakness and if necessary even illness as a means of attracting the attention and sympathy of the people around them. On no account should this pernicious tendency be encouraged. Children should therefore be taught that to be ill is a sign of weakness and inferiority, not of some virtue or sacrifice.

That is why, as soon as the child is able to make use of his limbs, some time should be devoted every day to the methodical and regular development of all the parts of his body. Every day some twenty or thirty minutes, preferably on waking, if possible, will be enough to ensure the proper functioning and balanced growth of his muscles while preventing any stiffening of the joints and of the spine, which occurs much sooner than one thinks. In the general porgramme of the child's education, sports and outdoor games should be given a prominent place; that, more than all the medicines in the world, will assure the child good health.

An hour's moving about in the sun does more to cure weakness or even anaemia than a whole arsenal of tonics. My advice is that medicines should not be used unless it is absolutely impossible to avoid them; and this "absolutely impossible" should be very strict. In this programme of physical culture, although there are well-known general lines to be followed for the best development of the human body, still, if the method is to be fully effective in each case, it should be considered individually, if possible with the help of a competent person, or if not, by consulting the numerous manuals that have already been and are still being published on the subject.

But in any case a child, whatever his activities, should have a sufficient number of hours of sleep. The number will vary according to his age. In the cradle, the baby should sleep longer than he remains awake. The number of hours of sleep will diminish as the child grows. But until maturity it should not be less than eight hours, in a quiet, well-ventilated place. The child should never be made to stay up late for no reason. The hours before midnight are the best for resting the nerves. Even during the waking hours, relaxation is indispensable for all who want to maintain their nervous balance. To know how to relax the muscles and the nerves is an art which should be taught to children when they are very young. There are many parents who, on the contrary, push their child to constant activity.

When the child remains quiet, they imagine that he is ill. There are even parents who have the bad habit of making their child do household work at the expense of his rest and relaxation. Nothing is worse for a developing nervous system, which cannot stand the strain of too continuous an effort or of an activity that is imposed upon it and not freely chosen. At the risk of going against many current ideas and ruffling many prejudices, I hold that it is not fair to demand service from a child, as if it were his duty to serve his parents.

The contrary would be more true, and certainly it is natural that parents should serve their child or at least take great care of him. It is only if a child chooses freely to work for his family and does this work as play that the thing is admissible. And even then, one must be careful that it in no way diminishes the hours of rest that are absolutely indispensable for his body to function properly.

I have said that from a young age children should be taught to respect good health, physical strength and balance. The great importance of beauty must also be emphasised. A young child should aspire for beauty, not for the sake of pleasing others or winning their admiration, but for the love of beauty itself; for beauty is the ideal which all physical life must realise. Every human being has the possibility of establishing harmony among the different parts of his body and in the various movements of the body in action. Every human body that undergoes a rational method of culture from the beginning of its existence can realise its own harmony and thus become fit to manifest beauty. When we speak of the other aspect of an integral education, we shall see what inner conditions are to be fulfilled so that this beauty can one day be manifested.

So far I have referred only to the education to be given to children; for a good many bodily defects can be rectified and many malformations avoided by an enlightened physical education given at the proper time. But if for any reason this physical education has not been given during childhood or even in youth, it can begin at any age and be pursued throughout life. But the later one begins, the more one must be prepared to meet bad habits that have to be corrected, rigidities to be made supple, malformations to be rectified. And this preparatory work will require much patience and perseverance before one can start on a constructive programme for the harmonisation of the form and its movements. But if you keep alive within you the ideal of beauty that is to be realised, sooner or later you are sure to reach the goal you have set yourself.

Vital Education

Of all education, vital education is perhaps the most important, the most indispensable. Yet it is rarely taken up and pursued with discernment and method. There are several reasons for this: first, the human mind is in a state of great confusion about this particular subject; secondly, the undertaking is very difficult and to be successful in it one must have endless endurance and persistence and a will that no failure can weaken.

Indeed, the vital in man's nature is a despotic and exacting tyrant. Moreover, since it is the vital which holds power, energy, enthusiasm, effective dynamism, many have a feeling of timorous respect for it and always try to please it. But it is a matter that nothing can satisfy and its demands are without limit. Two ideas which are very widespread, especially in the West, contribute towards making its domination more sovereign. One is that the chief aim of life is to be happy; the other that one is born with a certain character and that it is impossible to change it.

The first idea is a childish deformation of a very profound truth: that all existence is based upon delight of being and without delight of being there would be no life. But this delight of being, which is a quality of the Divine and therefore unconditioned, must not be confused with the pursuit of pleasure in life, which depends largely upon circumstances. The conviction that he has the right to be happy leads, as a matter of course, to the will to "live one's own life" at any cost. This attitude, by its obscure and aggressive egoism, leads to every kind of conflict and misery, disappointment and discouragement, and very often ends in catastrophe.

In the world as it is now the goal of life is not to secure personal happiness, but to awaken the individual progressively to the Truth-consciousness.

The second idea arises from the fact that a fundamental change of character demands an almost complete mastery over the subconscient and a very rigorous disciplining of whatever comes upon from the inconscient, which, in ordinary natures, expresses itself as the effects of atavism and of the environment in which one was born. Only an almost abnormal growth of consciousness and the constant help of Grace can achieve this Herculean task. That is why this task has rarely been attempted and many famous teachers have declared it to be unrealisable and chimerical. Yet it is not unrealisable. The transformation of character has in fact been realised by means of a clear-sighted discipline and a perseverance so obstinate that nothing, not even the most persistent failures, can discourage it.

The indispensable starting-point is a detailed and discerning observation of the character to be transformed. In most cases, that itself is a difficult and often a very baffling task. But there is one fact which the old traditions knew and which can serve as the clue in the labyrinth of inner discovery. It is that everyone possesses in a large measure, and the exceptional individual in an increasing degree of precision, two opposite tendencies of character, in almost equal proportions, which are like the light and the shadow of the same thing. Thus someone who has the capacity of being exceptionally generous will suddenly find an obstinate avarice rising up in his nature, the courageous man will be a coward in some part of his being and the good man will suddenly have wicked impulses. In this way life seems to endow everyone not only with the possibility of expressing an ideal, but also with contrary elements representing in a concrete manner the battle he has to wage and the victory he has to win for the realisation to become possible. Consequently, all life is an education pursued more or less consciously, more or less willingly.

In certain cases this education will encourage the movements that express the light, in others, on the contrary, those that express the shadow. If the circumstances and the environment are favourable, the light will grow at the expense of the shadow; otherwise the opposite will happen. And in this way the individual's character will crystallise according to the whims of Nature and the determinisms of material and vital life, unless a higher element comes in in time, a conscious will which, refusing to allow Nature to follow her whimsical ways, will replace them by a logical and clear-sighted discipline. This conscious will is what we mean by a rational method of education.

That is why it is of prime importance that the vital education of the child should begin as early as possible, indeed, as soon as he is able to use his senses. In this way many bad habits will be avoided and many harmful influences eliminated.

This vital education has two principal aspects, very different in their aims and methods, but both equally important. The first concerns the development and use of the sense organs. The second progressing awareness and control of the character, culminating in its transformation.

The education of the senses, again, has several aspects, which are added to one another as the being grows; indeed it should never cease. The sense organs, if properly cultivated, can attain a precision and power of functioning far exceeding what is normally expected of them.

In some ancient initiations it was stated that the number of senses that man can develop is not five but seven and in certain special cases even twelve. Certain races at certain times have, out of necessity, developed more or less perfectly one or the other of these supplementary senses. With a proper discipline persistently followed, they are within the reach of all who are sincerely interested in this development and its results. Among the faculties that are often mentioned, there is, for example, the ability to widen the physical consciousness, project it out of oneself so as to concentrate it on a given point and thus obtain sight, hearing, smell, taste and even touch at a distance.

To this general education of the senses and their functioning there will be added, as early as possible, the cultivation of discrimination and of the aesthetic sense, the capacity to choose and adopt what is beautiful and harmonious, simple, healthy and pure. For there is a psychological health just as there is a physical health, a beauty and harmony of the sensations as of the body and its movements. As the capacity of understanding grows in the child, he should be taught, in the course of his education, to add artistic taste and refinement to power and precision. He should be shown, led to appreciate, taught to love beautiful, lofty, healthy and noble things, whether in Nature or in human creation. This should be a true aesthetic culture, which will protect him from degrading influences. For, in the wake of the last wars and the terrible nervous tension which they provoked, as a sign, perhaps, of the decline of civilisation and social decay, a growing vulgarity seems to have taken possession of human life, individual as well as collective, particularly in what concerns aesthetic life and the life of the senses.

A methodical and enlightened cultivation of the senses can, little by little, eliminate from the child whatever is by contagion vulgar, commonplace and crude. This education will have very happy effects even on his character. For one who has developed a truly refined taste will, because of this very refinement, feel incapable of acting in a crude, brutal or vulgar manner. This refinement, if it is sincere, brings to the being a nobility and generosity which will spontaneously find expression in his behaviour and will protect him from many base and perverse movements.

And this brings us quite naturally to the second aspect of vital education which concerns the character and its transformation.

Generally, all disciplines dealing with the vital being, its purification and its control, proceed by coercion, suppression, abstinence and asceticism. This procedure is certainly easier and quicker, although less deeply enduring and effective, than a rigorous and detailed education. Besides, it eliminates all possibility of the intervention, help and collaboration of the vital. And yet this help is of the utmost importance if one wants the individual's growth and action to be complete.

To become conscious of the various movements in oneself and be aware of what one does and why one does it, is the indispensable starting-point. The child must be taught to observe, to note his reactions and impulses and their causes, to become a discerning witness of his desires, his movements of violence and passion, his instincts of possession and appropriation and domination and the background of vanity which supports them, together with their counterparts of weakness, discouragement, depression and despair.

Evidently, for this process to be useful, along with the growth of the power of observation the will for progress and perfection must also grow. This will should be instilled into the child as soon as he is capable of having a will, that is to say, at a much earlier age than is usually believed.

In order to awaken this will to surmount and conquer, different methods are appropriate in different cases; with certain individuals rational arguments are effective, for others their feelings and goodwill should be brought into play, with yet others the sense of dignity and self-respect. For all, the most powerful method is example constantly and sincerely shown.

Once the resolution has been firmly established, one has only to proceed rigorously and persistently and never to accept any defeat as final. To avoid all weakening and backsliding, there is one important point you must know and never forget: the will can be cultivated and developed just as the muscles can by methodical and progressive exercise. You must not shrink from demanding the maximum effort of your will even for a thing that seems of no importance, for it is through effort that its capacity grows, gradually acquiring the power to apply itself even to the most difficult things. What you have decided to do, you must do, whatever the cost, even if you have to renew your effort over and over again any number of times in order to do it. Your will will be strengthened by the effort and you will have only to choose with discernment the goal to which you will apply it.

To sum up: one must gain full knowledge of one's character and then acquire control over one's movements in order to achieve perfect mastery and the transformation of all the elements that have to be transformed.

Now all will depend upon the ideal which the effort for mastery and transformation seeks to achieve. The value of the effort and its result will depend upon the value of the ideal. This is the subject we shall deal with next, in connection with mental education.

Mental Education

Of all lines of education, mental education is the most widely known and practised, yet except in a few rare cases there are gaps which make it something very incomplete and in the end quite insufficient.

Generally speaking, schooling is considered to be all the mental education that is necessary. And when a child has been made to undergo, for a number of years, a methodical training which is more like cramming than true schooling, it is considered that whatever is necessary for his mental development has been done. Nothing of the kind. Even conceding that the training is given with due measure and discrimination and does not permanently damage the brain, it cannot impart to the human mind the faculties it needs to become a good and useful instrument. The schooling that is usually given can, at the most, serve as a system of gymnastics to increase the suppleness of the brain. From this standpoint, each branch of human learning represents a special kind of mental gymnastics, and the verbal formulations given to these various branches each constitute a special and well-defined language.

A true mental education, which will prepare man for a higher life, has five principal phases. Normally these phases follow one after another, but in exceptional individuals they may alternate or even proceed simultaneously. These five phases, in brief, are:

— Development of the power of concentration, the capacity of attention.

— Development of the capacities of expansion, widening, complexity and richness.

— Organisation of one's ideas around a central idea, a higher ideal or a supremely luminous idea that will serve as a guide in life.

— Thought-control, rejection of undesirable thoughts, to become able to think only what one wants and when one wants.

— Development of mental silence, perfect calm and a more and more total receptivity to inspirations coming from the higher regions of the being.

It is not possible to give here all the details concerning the methods to be employed in the application of these five phases of education to different individuals. Still, a few explanations on points of detail can be given.

Undeniably, what most impedes mental progress in children is the constant dispersion of their thoughts. Their thoughts flutter hither and thither like butterflies and they have to make a great effort to fix them. Yet this capacity is latent in them, for when you succeed in arousing their interest, they are capable of a good deal of attention. By his ingenuity, therefore, the educator will gradually help the child to become capable of a sustained effort of attention and a faculty of more and more complete absorption in the work in hand.

All methods that can develop this faculty of attention from games to rewards are good and can all be utilised according to the need and the circumstances. But it is the psychological action that is most important and the sovereign method is to arouse in the child an interest in what you want to teach him, a liking for work, a will to progress. To love to learn is the most precious gift that one can give to a child: to love to learn always and everywhere, so that all circumstances, all happenings in life may be constantly renewed opportunities for learning more and always more.

For that, to attention and concentration should be added observation, precise recording and faithfulness of memory. This faculty of observation can be developed by varied and spontaneous exercises, making use of every opportunity that presents itself to keep the child's thought wakeful, alert and prompt.

The growth of the understanding should be stressed much more than that of memory. One knows well only what one has understood. Things learnt by heart, mechanically, fade away little by little and finally disappear; what is understood is never forgotten. Moreover, you must never refuse to explain to a child the how and the why of things. If you cannot do it yourself, you must direct the child to those who are qualified to answer or point out to him some books that deal with the question. In this way you will progressively awaken in the child the taste for true study and the habit of making a persistent effort to know.

This will bring us quite naturally to the second phase of development in which the mind should be widened and enriched.

You will gradually show the child that everything can become an interesting subject for study if it is approached in the right way. The life of every day, of every moment, is the best school of all, varied, complex, full of unexpected experiences, problems to be solved, clear and striking examples and obvious consequences. It is so easy to arouse healthy curiosity in children, if you answer with intelligence and clarity the numerous questions they ask. An interesting reply to one readily brings others in its train and so the attentive child learns without effort much more than he usually does in the classroom. By a choice made with care and insight, you should also teach him to enjoy good reading-matter which is both instructive and attractive. Do not be afraid of anything that awakens and pleases his imagination; imagination develops the creative mental faculty and through it study becomes living and the mind develops in joy.

In order to increase the suppleness and comprehensiveness of his mind, one should see not only that he studies many varied topics, but above all that a single subject is approached in various ways, so that the child understands in a practical manner that there are many ways of facing the same intellectual problem, of considering it and solving it. This will remove all rigidity from his brain and at the same time it will make his thinking richer and more supple and prepare it for a more complex and comprehensive synthesis. In this way also the child will be imbued with the sense of the extreme relativity of mental learning and, little by little, an aspiration for a truer source of knowledge will awaken in him.

Indeed, as the child grows older and progresses in his studies, his mind too ripens and becomes more and more capable of forming general ideas, and with them almost always comes a need for certitude, for a knowledge that is stable enough to form the basis of a mental construction which will permit all the diverse and scattered and often contradictory ideas accumulated in his brain to be organised and put in order. This ordering is indeed very necessary if one is to avoid chaos in one's thoughts.

All contradictions can be transformed into complements, but for that one must discover the higher idea that will have the power to bring them harmoniously together. It is always good to consider every problem from all possible standpoints so as to avoid partiality and exclusiveness; but if the thought is to be active and creative, it must, in every case, be the natural and logical synthesis of all the points of view adopted. And if you want to make the totality of your thoughts into a dynamic and constructive force, you must also take great care as to the choice of the central idea of your mental synthesis; for upon that will depend the value of this synthesis. The higher and larger the central idea and the more universal it is, rising above time and space, the more numerous and the more complex will be the ideas, notions and thoughts which it will be able to organise and harmonise.

It goes without saying that this work of organisation cannot be done once and for all. The mind, if it is to keep its vigour and youth, must progress constantly, revise its notions in the light of new knowledge, enlarge its framework to include fresh notions and constantly reclassify and reorganise its thoughts, so that each of them may find its true place in relation to the others and the whole remains harmonious and orderly.

All that has just been said concerns the speculative mind, the mind that learns. But learning is only one aspect of mental activity; the other, which is at least equally important, is the constructive faculty, the capacity to form and thus prepare action. This very important part of mental activity has rarely been subject of any special study or discipline. Only those who want, for some reason, to exercise a strict control over their mental activities think of observing and disciplining this faculty of formation; and as soon as they try it, they have to face difficulties so great that they appear almost insurmountable.

And yet control over this formative activity of the mind is one of the most important aspects of self-education; one can say that without it no mental mastery is possible. As far as study is concerned, all ideas are acceptable and should be included in the synthesis, whose very function is to become more and more rich and complex; but where action is concerned, it is just the opposite. The ideas that are accepted for translation into action should be strictly controlled and only those that agree with the general trend of the central idea forming the basis of the mental synthesis should be permitted to express themselves in action. This means that every thought entering the mental consciousness should be set before the central idea; if it finds a logical place among the thoughts already grouped, it will be admitted into the synthesis; if not, it will be rejected so that it can have no influence on the action. This work of mental purification should be done very regularly in order to secure a complete control over one's actions.

For this purpose, it is good to set apart time every day when one can quietly go over one's thoughts and put one's synthesis in order. Once the habit is acquired, you can maintain control over your thoughts even during work and action, allowing only those which are useful for what you are doing to come to the surface. Particularly, if you have continued to cultivate the power of concentration and attention, only the thoughts that are needed will be allowed to enter the active external consciousness and they then become all the more dynamic and effective. And if, in the intensity of concentration, it becomes necessary not to think at all, all mental vibration can be stilled and an almost total silence secured. In this silence one can gradually open to the higher regions of the mind and learn to record the inspirations that come from there.

But even before reaching this point, silence in itself is supremely useful, because in most people who have a somewhat developed and active mind, the mind is never at rest. During the day, its activity is kept under a certain control, but at night, during the sleep of the body, the control of the waking state is almost completely removed and the mind indulges in activities which are sometimes excessive and often incoherent. This creates a great stress which leads to fatigue and the diminution of the intellectual faculties.

The fact is that like all the other parts of the human being, the mind too needs rest and it will not have this rest unless we know how to provide it. The art of resting one's mind is something to be acquired. Changing one's mental activity is certainly the way of resting; but the greatest possible rest is silence. And as far as the mental faculties are concerned a few minutes passed in the calm of silence are a more effective rest than hours of sleep.

When one has learned to silence the mind at will and to concentrate it in receptive silence, then there will be no problem that cannot be solved, no mental difficulty whose soultion cannot be found. When it is agitated, thought becomes confused and impotent; in an attentive tranquillity, the light can manifest itself and open up new horizons to man's capacity.

Psychic Education and Spiritual Education

So far we have dealt only with the education that can be given to all children born upon earth and which is concerned with purely human faculties. But one need not inevitably stop there. Every human being carries hidden within him the possibility of a greater consciousness which goes beyond the bounds of his present life and enables him to share in a higher and a vaster life. Indeed, in all exceptional beings it is always this consciousness that governs their lives and organises both the circumstances of their existence and their individual reaction to these circumstances. What the human mental consciousness does not know and cannot do, this consciousness knows and does. It is like a light that shines at the centre of the being, radiating through the thick coverings of the external consciousness.

Some have a vague intimation of its presence; a good many children are under its influence, which shows itself very distinctly at times in their spontaneous actions and even in their words. Unfortunately, since parents most often do not know what it is and do not understand what is happening in their child, their reaction to these phenomena is not a good one and all their education consists in making the child as unconscious as possible in this domain and concentrating all his attention on external things, thus accustoming him to think that they are the only ones that matter. It is true that this concentration on external things is very useful, provided that it is done in the proper way.

The three lines of education—physcial, vital and mental—deal with that and could be defined as the means of building up the personality, raising the individual out of the amorphous subconscious mass and making him a well-defined self-conscious entity. With psychic education we come to the problem of the true motive of existence, the purpose of life on earth, the discovery to which this life must lead and the result of that discovery: the consecration of the individual to his eternal principle. Normally this discovery is associated with a mystic feeling, a religious life, because it is mainly the religions that have concerned themselves with this aspect of life. But it need not necessarily be so: the mystic notion of God may be replaced by the more philosophical notion of truth and still the discovery will remain essentially the same, but the road leading to it may be taken even by the most intransigent positivist. For mental notions and ideas have only a very secondary importance in preparing one for the psychic life.

The important thing is to live the experience; that carries with it its own reality and force apart from any theory that may precede or accompany or follow it, for most often theories are no more than explanations that one gives to oneself in order to have, more or less, the illusion of knowledge. Man clothes the ideal or the absolute he seeks to attain with different names according to the environment in which he is born and the education he has received. The experience is essentially the same, if it is sincere; it is only the words and phrases in which it is formulated that differ according to the belief and the mental education of the one who has the experience.

All formulation is thus only an approximation that should be progressive and grow in precision as the experience itself becomes more and more precise and co-ordinated. Still, to sketch a general outline of psychic education, we must give some idea, however relative it may be, of what we mean by the psychic being. One could say, for example, that the creation of an individual being is the result of the projection, in time and space, of one of the countless possibilities latent in the supreme origin of all manifestation which, through the medium of the one and universal consciousness, takes concrete form in the law or the truth of an individual and so, by a progressive development, becomes his soul or psychic being.

I must emphasise that what is stated briefly here does not claim to be a complete exposition of the reality and does not exhaust the subject—far from it. It is only a very summary explanation for a practical purpose, to serve as a basis for the education which we intend to consider now.

It is through this psychic presence that the truth of an individual being comes into contact with him and the circumstances of his life. In most cases the presence acts, so to say, far behind the veil, unrecognised and unknown; but in some, it is perceptible and its action recognisable and even, in a very few, the presence becomes tangible and its action fully effective. These go forward in life with an assurance and a certitude all their own; they are masters of their destiny. It is for the purpose of obtaining this mastery and becoming conscious of the psychic presence that psychic education should be practised. But for that there is need of a special factor, the personal will. For till now, the discovery of the psychic being and identification with it have not been among the recognised subjects of education, and although one can find in special treatises useful and practical hints on the subject, and although in exceptional cases one may have the good fortune of meeting someone who is capable of showing the way and giving the help that is needed to follow it, most often the attempt is left to one's own personal initiative.

The discovery is a personal matter and a great determination, a strong will and an untiring perseverance are indispensable to reach the goal. Each one must, so to say, trace out his own path through his own difficulties. The goal is known to some extent, for most of those who have reached it have described it more or less clearly. But the supreme value of the discovery lies in its spontaneity, its ingenuousness, and that escapes all ordinary mental laws. And that is why anyone wanting to take up the adventure usually first seeks out some person who has successfully undertaken it and is able to sustain him and enlighten him on his way. Yet there are some solitary travellers and for them a few general indications may be useful.

The starting-point is to seek in yourself that which is independent of the body and the circumstances of life, which is not born of the mental formation that you have been given, the language you speak, the habits and customs of the environment in which you live, the country where you are born or the age to which you belong. You must find, in the depths of your being, that which carries in it a sense of universality, limitless expansion, unbroken continuity. Then you decentralise, extend and widen yourself; you begin to live in all things and in all beings; the barriers separating individuals from each other break down. You think in their thoughts, vibrate in their sensations, feel in their feelings, live in the life of all. What seemed inert suddenly becomes full of life, stones quicken, plants feel and will and suffer, animals speak in a language more or less inarticulate, but clear and expressive; everything is animated by a marvellous consciousness without time or limit.

And this is only one aspect of the psychic realisation; there are others, many others. All help you to go beyond the barriers of your egoism, the walls of your external personality, the impotence of your reactions and the incapacity of your will.

But, as I have already said, the path to that realisation is long and difficult, strewn with snares and problems to be solved, which demand an unfailing determination. It is like the explorer's trek through virgin forest in quest of an unknown land, of some great discovery. The psychic being is also a great discovery which requires at least as much fortitude and endurance as the discovery of new continents. A few simple words of advice may be useful to one who has resolved to undertake it.

The first and perhaps the most important point is that the mind is incapable of judging spiritual things. All those who have written on this subject have said so; but very few are those who have put it into practice. And yet, in order to proceed on the path, it is absolutely indispensable to abstain from all mental opinion and reaction.

Give up all personal seeking for comfort, satisfaction, enjoyment or happiness. Be only a burning fire for progress, take whatever comes to you as an aid to your progress and immediately make whatever progress is required.

Try to take pleasure in all you do, but never do anything for the sake of pleasure.

Never get excited, nervous or agitated. Remain perfectly calm in the face of all circumstances. And yet be always alert to discover what progress you still have to make and lose no time in making it.

Never take physical happenings at their face value. They are always a clumsy attempt to express something else, the true thing which escapes our superficial understanding.

Never complain of the behaviour of anyone, unless you have the power to change in his nature what makes him act in this way; and if you have the power, change him instead of complaining.

Whatever you do, never forget the goal which you have set before you. There is nothing great or small once you have set out on this great discovery; all things are equally important and can either hasten or delay its success. Thus before you eat, concentrate a few seconds in the aspiration that the food you are about to eat may bring your body the substance it needs to serve as a solid basis for your effort towards the great discovery, and give it the energy for persistence and perseverance in the effort.

Before you go to sleep, concentrate a few seconds in the aspiration that the sleep may restore your fatigued nerves, bring calm and quietness to your brain so that on waking you may, with renewed vigour, begin again your journey on the path of the great discovery.

Before you act, concentrate in the will that your action may help or at least in no way hinder your march forward towards the great discovery.

When you speak, before the words come out of your mouth, concentrate just long enough to check your words and allow only those that are absolutely necessary to pass, only those that are not in any way harmful to your progress on the path of the great discovery.

To sum up, never forget the purpose and goal of your life. The will for the great discovery should be always there above you, above what you do and what you are, like a huge bird of light dominating all the movements of your being.

Before the untiring persistence of your effort, an inner door will suddenly open and you will emerge into a dazzling splendour that will bring you the certitude of immortality, the concrete experience that you have always lived and always shall live, that external forms alone perish and that these forms are, in relation to what you are in reality, like clothes that are thrown away when worn out. Then you will stand erect, freed from all chains, and instead of advancing laboriously under the weight of circumstances imposed upon you by Nature, which you had to endure and bear if you did not want to be crushed by them, you will be able to walk on, straight and firm, conscious of your destiny, master of your life.

And yet this release from all slavery to the flesh, this liberation from all personal attachment is not the supreme fulfilment. There are other steps to climb before you reach the summit. And even these steps can and should be followed by others which will open the doors to the future. These following steps will form the object of what I call spiritual education.

But before we enter on this new stage and deal with the question in detail, an explanation is necessary. Why is a distinction made between the psychic education of which we have just spoken and the spiritual education of which we are about to speak now ? Because the two are usually confused under the general term of "yogic discipline", although the goals they aim at are very different: for one it is a higher realisation upon earth, for the other an escape from all earthly manifestation, even from the whole universe, a return to the unmanifest.

So one can say that the psychic life is immortal life, endless time, limitless space, ever-progressive change, unbroken continuity in the universe of forms. The spiritual consciousness, on the other hand, means to live the infinite and the eternal, to be projected beyond all creation, beyond time and space. To become conscious of your psychic being and to live a psychic life you must abolish all egoism; but to live a spiritual life you must no longer have an ego.

Here also, in spiritual education, the goal you set before you will assume, in the mind's formulation of it, different names according to the environment in which you have been brought up, the path you have followed and the affinities of your temperament. Those who have a religious tendency will call it God and their spiritual effort will be towards identification with the transcendent

God beyond all forms, as opposed to the immanent God dwelling in each form. Others will call it the Absolute, the Supreme Origin, others Nirvana; yet others, who view the world as an unreal illusion, will name it the Only Reality and to those who regard all manifestation as falsehood it will be the Sole Truth. And every one of these expressions contains an element of truth, but all are incomplete, expressing only one aspect of that which is. Here too, however, the mental formulation has no great importance and once you have passed through the intermediate stages, the experience is identical.

In any case, the most effective starting-point, the swiftest method is total self-giving. Besides, no joy is more perfect than the joy of a total self-giving to whatever is the summit of your conception: for some it is the notion of God, for others that of Perfection. If this self-giving is made with persistence and ardour, a moment comes when you pass beyond the concept and arrive at an experience that escapes all description, but which is almost always identical in its effects. And as your self-giving becomes more and more perfect and integral, it will be accompanied by the aspiration for identification, a total fusion with That to which you have given yourself, and little by little this aspiration will overcome all differences and all resistances, especially if with the aspiration there is an intense and spontaneous love, for then nothing can stand in the way of its victorious drive.

There is an essential difference between this identification and the identification with the psychic being. The latter can be made more and more lasting and, in certain cases, it becomes permanent and never leaves the person who has realised it, whatever his outer activities may be. In other words, the identification is no longer realised only in meditation and concentration, but its effects are felt at every moment of one's life, in sleep as well as in waking.

On the other hand, liberation from all form and the identification with that which is beyond form cannot last in an absolute manner; for it would automatically bring about the dissolution of the material form. Certain traditions say that this dissolution happens inevitably within twenty days of the total identification. Yet it is not necessarily so; and even if the experience is only momentary, it produces in the consciousness results that are never obliterated and have repercussions on all states of the being, both internal and external. Moreover, once the identification has been realised, it can be renewed at will, provided that you know how to put yourself in the same conditions.

This merging into the formless is the supreme liberation sought by those who want to escape from an existence which no longer holds any attraction for them. It is not surprising that they are dissatisfied with the world in its present form. But a liberation that leaves the world as it is and in no way affects the conditions of life from which others suffer, cannot satisfy those who refuse to enjoy a boon which they are the only ones, or almost the only ones, to possess, those who dream of a world more worthy of the splendours that lie hidden behind its apparent disorder and widespread misery. They dream of sharing with others the wonders they have discovered in their inner exploration. And the means to do so is within their reach, now that they have arrived at the summit of their ascent.

From beyond the frontiers of form a new force can be evoked, a power of consciousness which is as yet unexpressed and which, by its emergence, will be able to change the course of things and give birth to a new world. For the true solution to the problem of suffering, ignorance and death is not an individual escape from earthly miseries by self-annihilation into the unmanifest, nor a problematical collective flight from universal suffering by an integral and final return of the creation to its Creator, thus curing the universe not by abolishing it, but a transformation, a total transfiguration of matter brought about by the logical continuation of Nature's ascending march in her progress towards perfection, by the creation of a new species that will be to man what man is to the animal and that will manifest upon earth a new force, a new consciousness and a new power. And so will begin a new education which can be called the supramental education; it will, by its all-powerful action, work not only upon the consciousness of individual beings, but upon the very substance of which they are built and upon the environment in which they live.

In contrast with the types of education we have mentioned previously, which progress from below upwards by an ascending movement of the various parts of the being, the supramental education will progress from above downwards, its influence spreading from one state of being to another until at last the physical is reached. This last transformation will only occur visibly when the inner states of being have already been considerably transformed. It is therefore quite unreasonable to try to recognise the presence of the supramental by physical appearances. For these will be the last to change and the supramental force can be at work in an individual long before anything of it becomes perceptible in his bodily life.

10

Framework for Integral Education

For each major stage of studies (lower primary, higher primary, etc.) there could normally be sections or groups of about 100 students. The differences of levels of capacities should not very much count in the formation of these large groupings. These groupings would be valid and useful for those areas of studies which yield easily to cooperative work, mass media or to the means of environmental influence. These would include works of productive labour, large portions of language-learning, as also introductory or panoramic portions of a number of subjects where demonstrations, exhibitions or stimulating and interesting lectures and suitable means of communication. These would also be relevant to what may be regarded as peripheral areas of studies, where the imparting of general information is intended. Areas of general explanations, general knowledge, general instructions are also appropriate to these large groupings.

In the general working of the organisations, it is better not to have any fixed time-table for the work of these large groupings. Or, if it is found necessary for some reason to have a regular fixed timing, it is better to have it not for the main work but to confine it to what may be termed 'time for supplementary work'.

In any case, the fixed timings of various programmes of education should be so arranged that the hours of fresh study and labour which can be done by individual self-learning are not affected in any way.

For purposes of the individual self-learning, there will be, in a sense, no groupings since each individual will be free to choose his own area of work and pursue it at his own pace.

(a) But each teacher will have a number of students who will come to him more or less regularly for consultation on the subject of his competence. These students would, in a sense, constitute for the teacher in question a kind of a natural group. For, although these students will mostly come individually for consultations, they might also come in the form of a group from time to time.

(b) There will be, however, another kind of grouping or break-up of the large group, depending upon the mode of learning that a given topic imposes or upon the mode of learning chosen by the student There are topics or areas which need to be pursued regularly, systematically, step by step, with rigour, measure and regulated or accelerated speed. Those who choose such topics or such a mode of learning will form a kind of a group-even though each of them may do his work mostly by himself. There are other areas or topics, which may permit a leisurely and free pursuit. Those who choose such topics or such a mode of learning will from another group. These groupings will, however, be not tight and inflexible. The same student may belong to one group for a few topics and to another group for other topics; or, with regard to the same topic, he may offer to do both these kinds of work appropriate to both these groups. Thus, he will belong to both the groups.

It may be noted that the grouping mentioned above under (a) and (b) will be, more or less, temporary, meant for some specific purpose or project and therefore dissoluble with the purpose in view. These groups will normally tend to be homogeneous from the point of view of capacities, or interests, but these will often need to have group classes, and sometimes, even a fixed time-table for short or long periods. Normally, time-tables should be fixed for a month or two, renewable for a longer period, if necessary.

Individual consultations with the teachers will also tend in the direction of regular prior fixation of timings in regard to each student. There are some obvious advantages and conveniences in such fixed appointments. But care should be taken to see that the teachers keep always one or two hours daily unfixed so that students may have the opportunity to come to them from time to time without any prior engagement.

One final point about grouping. If we are watchful, we shall find that, from time to time, there emerge spontaneously extremely small groups of students who have common inclinations of high aspirations, some common character or common trait of personality, even though they may differ in respect of capacities. Their homogeneity is by virtue of character or personality rather than capacities. Such groups are very valuable. They should be recognised, and they should be given all the help needed individually or collectively. Such groups become, if properly encouraged, transmitters of enthusiasm, dedication and devotion to studies, work and ideas.

In regard to the above system of grouping, three obvious advantages can be mentioned:

(1) There has recently been a strong plea for multi-point entry system, particularly, in relation to the solutions

which have been suggested for the implementation of the programme for the universalisation of elementary education. It will be noted that this idea of multi-point entry system is extremely valuable, and this system will find a natural setting in the structure that is suggested here. Similarly, this structure will provide a favourable setting for 'unit' studies. And a new system of tests can easily operate in the proposed structure so that tests become a part of the natural rhythm of the process of learning.

(2) It would be possible in this flexible organisation to ensure facilities for individual attention which is indispensable, particularly, in the field of moral and spiritual education.

(3) Works of productive labour can flourish in this setting with naturalness that is so essential to the joy of work. These works needs not be given as tasks. But students can be stimulated and encouraged by means of nourishment of interests, environmental needs and influences, as also through the medium of hobbies. In this setting, even specialisation of vocational training can be initiated at early stages. General education, diversification of courses and vocationalisation - all can blend harmoniously together.

Teachers

(a) The role of teachers in this new organisation is crucial. The teachers should have not only competence with regard to their subjects but also the necessary spirit and zeal.

(b) In the initial stages, students will need to learn how to organise their freedom; teachers should, therefore, help students in this regard.

(c) For every unit of 100 students, there should be a Coordinator or a 'First Teacher' whose functions will be as follows:

(i) He will be available to students for guidance so as to help them in organising their work and in learning the art of self-learning as also other ways of learning;

(ii) He may, by personal contact, provide motivation to the students for various works, topics or subjects, accordings to the needs and circumstances;

(iii) he will ensure that all the material needs of studies and work are provided for;

(iv) He will keep an overall record of the work of every student in the unit, and will see that the students get the necessary guidance from himself or from the other teachers, or else from the environment;

(v) He will also ensure that the entire organisation runs smoothly and harmoniously;

(vi) He will work as a brother among brothers and will consult all concerned before arriving at decisions; and

(vii) He will also give the necessary help in framing time-table, particularly, in view of the fact that, since there will be no time-tables fixed in advance for the whole year, there will be the need to frame *ad hoc* time-tables for short or long durations in consultation with students and teachers for various subjects and for various purposes.

(d) In addition to the First Teachers, it seems practicable that, for each major subject, a full-time competent teacher could take charge of about 30-40 students (this number may vary according to the special needs of a given subject and also the age and capacity of the students). These teachers may form themselves into a small committee to help the Coordinator, and maintain a personal contact with the students in the Unit.

(e) Problems of irregularity, indiscipline and misuse of facilities will primarily be dealt with by the Coordinator and his Committee. To this Committee may be nominated some of the best students of the Unit.

(f) All administrative problems should be handled carefully so that all points of view are given their due weight, and decisions emerge out of consultations.

(g) All work should be carried out by utmost goodwill and cooperative action, rather than by any arbitrary authority.

(h) There should be no place for gossips, politics, canvassing, maneuvering, ugliness and untidiness. There should be an atmosphere of self-control and utmost inner discipline.

(i) A full-fledged working of this model will presuppose new educational material in the form of booklets, work-sheets, charts, maps, pictures, albums, tapes, slides, film-strips, magazines, journals, exhibits, tools, and equipment and apparatus. And new curricula and syllabi have to be worked out, particularly, in regard to interdisciplinary studies and interweaving of work and knowledge. In these tasks, teachers will have to make their own contribution.

ORGANISATION

In the proposed organisation, a special emphasis will fall

upon 'individual work'. 'Individual Work' may be pursued in several different ways that have already been enumerated elsewhere.

At the end of every two or three months, each student will submit to the Coordinator a report on his work in regard to each topic, subject or work under study. This report will give details of the progress he has made in regard to what he has read or written or the reflections and conclusions he has arrived at.

Tests will be given to the students where necessary, and their aim will be to provide to the students occasions for exercise, revision, comprehension, encouragement and self-evaluation.

Tests for placement in the employment market should be conducted by a National Testing Service, and they should be open to anyone who wants to take them. These tests should be related to specific jobs or employment opportunities or certain pursuits of studies and disciplines of knowledge and skill.. They will also test physical fitness, and other talent, practical skills and value orientation.

To learn the secret of self-education and to work hard so as to remain steadily on the road to self-perfection - this will be the student's constant endeavour.

To study and work widely and intensely, to study and work with joy and application, to study and work to grow and to remain perpetually youthful-this will be the content of his main work.

But to become a fearless hero-warrior in the quest of Truth, Harmony, and Liberty, and to surpass the limitations of his nature by an inner change and transformation - this will be regarded as the very heart of his work.

EDUCATION CONTENTS

Aims of education determine the contents and methods of education. If our aim is that of life-long integral education, the contents of education have to be conceived quite differently from what are normally pursued in our present system of education.

In India, almost all schools follow a curriculum which was originally designed to arrive at the end of the educational process within a limited period and to fashion clerical abilities among students. Gradually, it has been expanded to suit the needs of producing lawyers, engineers, medical doctors, businessmen and teachers. Vocational courses have only been recently introduced, even through they have not flourished to any expected degree. Moreover, curricula are so designed that they do not cater to the needs of those who want to or are required to drop out of school system at early stages. Even the curriculum of class X, which is the first terminal point in our Indian system, is geared to the needs of higher levels of education. Upto class X, all prescribed studies are compulsory for everybody. Hence, no child can have an experience of free choice and free joy of learning until the completion of class X.

If a student wants to become a mason or a carpenter, our schools have nothing to offer to him. Similarly, if he wants to be a poet, there is hardly anything which would be directly related in our curriculum which would nourish his abilities to become even a budding poet. If one wants to be musician, the student will hardly find anything in his curriculum excepting a few classes in music meant as a part of general education. Examples of this kind can be multiplied.

Let us take the example of physical education, which has somehow secured some place in recent decades in our system of education. There are periods allotted to physical training or to Yoga classes. But what exactly is physical education, what is the importance of the human body, how miraculously human body works, what are different forms of physical education, - these and allied questions receive hardly any place in the curriculum. Something about the human body is, of course, taught in courses relating to physiology and hygiene, but the orientation is not related to physical education.

Moreover, we find that there are a number of interesting questions and studies which come up if we allow freedom of enquiry and freedom of pursuit of subjects of interest. Students often ask questions like this: "What is below the waters of the ocean?" "What kinds of animals live in the ocean?" "What has been the history of costumes?" "What has been the history of weapons?" "How to learn?" "How to widen interest?" " How to concentrate?" These and allied questions are hardly answered because they do not form part of curriculum or syllabus.

A very important question is being debated in regard to value education. Should there be a special curriculum for this subject? Or else, should the study of values be integrated in different studies? The debate has been inconclusive, and in the meantime, no serious effort has been made to spell out the curriculum in respect of value education.

In regard to the study of languages, curricula do not manifest any concern for developing adequate competence to express oneself faultlessly, perfectly, and beautifully. Where more than one languages are taught, there is no concern to correlate these languages and to advance the capacity of translating from one language to the other. In fact, there are no courses on translations in our schools or in colleges.

In one of his essays of national system of education, Sri Aurobindo had underlined the importance of language in the development of mental faculties. He had said that mental faculty should first be exercised on things, afterwards on words and ideas. But he had added, "Our dealings with language are much too perfunctory and absence of fine sense for words impoverishes the intellect and limits the fineness and truth of its operation. The mind should be accustomed first to notice the word thoroughly, its form, sound and sense; then to compare the form with other similar forms in the points of similarity and difference, thus forming the foundation of the grammatical sense; then to distinguish between the fine shades of sense of similar words and the formation and rhythm of different sentences, thus forming the formation of the literary and the syntactical faculties. All this should be done informally, drawing on the curiosity and interest, avoiding set teaching and memorising of rules. The true knowledge takes its base on things, arthas, and only when it has mastered the things, proceeds to formalise its information".

If these ideas of dealings with language have to be fulfilled, we have to think both of new contents and new methods of teaching languages.

The field of history needs a very special attention. It is not sufficiently realised that Indian history, with its uninterrupted continuity of more than five thousand years, has a rich account to be conveyed to students Excepting China, no other country has had such a long historical account, and even in regard to China, the continuity is not so great as in the case of India. As compared to the students in other countries, the Indian students have, therefore, to be obliged to receive and assimilate a much greater burden not only of the quantity of information but also of the complexity of numerous currents of civilisation and culture which had again landmarks of various kinds, the interpretations of which are varied and numerous.

The history books which are now used in our educational system were written during the British period, and they have only been slightly modified during the last fifty years. The question as to how we must present Indian history to Indian students poses many problems, and they have not received the attention that they deserve. Very often, the history of northern India over-shadows the history of southern India; the accounts of various dynasties that ruled parts of India at different times overshadow the accounts of civilisation and culture that developed in various forms in various parts in the country, retaining yet some kind of essential unity; much of the cultural ethos is treated marginally by proclaiming that the concerned literature is legendary or mythological in character; even the basic facts of the most important texts of the ancient Indian history - and for that matter of world history, - namely, of the Vedas, are not known even to the most educated Indians of today; the sheer poetic excellence of the Vedas should have merited the full attention of the whole nation; even the three great national poets of Indian history, Valmiki, Vyasa and Kalidasa, and their works are hardly known and only very briefly mentioned in our history books; the great achievements which were registered by ancient Indians in the fields of astronomy, mathematics, natural sciences, metallurgy, as also in the fields of grammar, ethics, philosophy, religion, psychic and spiritual sciences, yoga, art, music, dance, and architecture, hardly figure in our history books. Even the political account of Indian history suffers from great short-comings and Indian students remain ignorant of how Indian polity developed through the ages and what great dreams and deeds were nurtured by the leading personalities of the country in different epochs.

Again, Indian history is taught in such a way that while a student becomes conversant with, say, Maratha period, he remains quite unacquainted with the Mughal period or earlier periods or subsequent periods. Inter-connections of history are hardly presented or grasped.

It is true that many important facts about India's development are besieged by controversies in regard to their historical accuracies; it is also true that much is not known about many great men and women who flourished in different epochs of history; it is also true that the meanings of some of the greatest products of Indian literature have been interpreted differently by different scholars. But the answer to these questions is to undertake a programme of thorough-going research instead of subjecting them to neglect or even oblivion. Our students deserve to be given a rich account of the heritage to which they have a natural right.

The question of the study of history is further complicated by the fact that, in order to keep abreast with the increasing drift towards human unity, which is spreading all over the world, we have to teach our students the entire history of the world in a meaningful manner. This subject is very vast, but at this stage, we need not enter into any further details. We may only make a remark that there is a need to present world history and its relationships with Indian history at least in three forms: in synoptic form, in the form of an outline, and in the form of detailed exposition, so that they can suit the needs of atleast three categories of students, namely, those who want to have a general and rapid view, those who want to be acquainted, and those who want to study at a deeper or scholarly level.

Before we leave the subject of history, we may make a few important remarks which are associated with this subject. The first is in connection with the study of legends and mythologies. At one time, there was a great prejudice against ancient beliefs, their symbolism, and their literature which lacked scientific or philosophic rigour. This prejudice is gradually being corrected, and there is today a salutary movement to understand ancient legends and mythologies with fresh eyes. It seems, therefore, desirable that a study of legends and mythologies in so far as they constitute a part of the cultural ethos, should be brought to the notice of our young generations. In any case, our students should not have wrong facts about legends and mythologies.

Accuracy of information on this subject is very important. Secondly, we have deplorable dearth of good biographies of great men and women of our country; a similar deficiency is not there in regard to world history, but our own knowledge of books concerning the same is very limited, and even that limited knowledge does not find any route of transmission to our teachers and students. This is a very important subject, and we must give considerable place to biographies, and accounts of important events should from a part of the contents of education.

Thirdly, we have to take a great care to ensure that the study of the past and the present does not become a prison preventing the visions of the future. There are golden reaches of our consciousness, and from them and from the reaches between them and our ordinary mental consciousness there have descended forces and forms which have become embodied in literature, philosophy, science, in music, drama, art, architecture, sculpture, in great and heroic deeds and in all that is wonderful and precious in the different organised or as yet unorganised aspects of life. To put students in contact with these, Eastern and Western, ancient and present, would be to provide them with the air and atmosphere in which they can breathe an inspiration to reach again to those peaks of consciousness and to create still newer forms and forces which would bring the golden day nearer - this should be the aim of the study of history.

A very important area that is developing today is that of inter-disciplinary studies. At present, this is pursued only at the higher level of education or at the level of research. But there is an urgent need to develop this subject even at lower levels of education. Basically, all subjects are complementary to each other; and there is no subject which is not interesting, provided we can show the interrelationship, of a subject with those subjects which are supposed to be interesting. Many may not know how much mathematics is connected with music, and how Pythagoras saw the relationship between these two subjects; and many do not know or appreciate the relationship between music and poetry.

Again, mathematics is closely connected with logic, - there is even a view that mathematics and logic are one and the same and logic is often considered to be the key of metaphysics; there is an obvious connection between metaphysics and physics; and physics, chemistry and biology are closely interconnected ; again, the main theme of biology is that of evolution, and evolution is closely related to the theme of man. Now, the study of man leads us to the study of history and geography; study of geography leads to the study of the earth, and the study of earth is connected with the study of planets and stars and galaxies and of the entire universe.

In fact, it must be said that the pursuit of man to know himself and the universe and to relate himself with the universe as effectively and harmoniously as possible is the underlying idea of all education. This interrelationship of man and the universe is central to the aim of integral education. If integral education is concerned with the development of the physical, vital, mental, psychic and spiritual parts of the human being, it is also connected with the knowledge that links universal

Matter with universal Spirit. And this covers the entire gamut of knowledge and the means by which all knowledge can be united in one unity.

Closely connected with the problem of unity of knowledge is the contemporary problem of explosion of knowledge. Considering this unprecedented explosion, one is obliged to ask as to how one can relate oneself to this explosion in such a way that one is not crushed under the increasing flow of information On the one hand, there is a pressure towards specialisation; on the other hand, there is a pressure for inter-disciplinary and holistic knowledge. Knowing more and more about less and less bestows upon the individual a specialised capacity and proficiency but it also creates disabling inefficiencies in respect of larger questions where multi-sided knowledge is indispensable.

There is more to perplex us. Specialised knowledge and efficiency that the individual possesses today tend to become obsolete at a rapid rate. There is, consequently, increasing pressure to continue to learn all the time. But this leaves very little time to expand horizons in fields other than those of specialisation. With the passage of time, our inefficiency to deal with general questions of life goes on increasing.

At a certain state, this situation, if not corrected, can really become alarming. Crises of various kinds are bound to multiply and this is what we witness today all over the world.

Against this background, an important question that can be raised is whether there is something like "essential knowledge" which every human being, as a human being, ought to possess and which ought to be communicated to every student during the educational career.

Reflecting on this question, it seems that there are at least three global subjects which can be considered to be essential and at the same time inherently interdisciplinary; if they could be taken up as the basic umbrella of curriculum, we can more easily combine the needs of general and specialised education. The first subject is that of man and the environment, the second subject, which is closely related to the first, is that of man and evolution; and the third subject is that of the aim of life.

As these areas are quite neglected, they acquire special consideration of educationists. Two final remarks need to be made. We find that most of the books which are prescribed in schools and colleges are so written that they are extremely uninteresting. Students read them because they want to pass examinations, and often they take to short-cuts and resort to guide books which are even more boring and less instructive. There is a need to prepare learning materials in such a way that every subject is made interesting, vivid and even charming. It may be said that this is a tall order, but when we are thinking not of narrow or immediate goals, and when we are thinking of education for tomorrow, we need not hesitate to make tall orders.

Secondary, if integral education is to be freed from the evils of subject-oriented, book-oriented and examination-oriented system of education, if liberty and self-discipline are to be the hallmark of the methods of integral education, and if the emphasis is to be laid on self-education, we shall need to write books in different forms that will be required for different kinds of students, different kinds of backgrounds and different modes of learning. We have to think of preparing worksheets, workbooks, monographs, reference books, documentation books, and books which can be read along with TV or audio-tapes.

11

Education and Personality Development

The modern educationist has come to realise that the child is not a plastic material to be moulded and pressed into a shape as desired and decided upon by the parents and educators. There is an insistence on free choice for the student to choose his own subjects of study, his pace of progress, and even (within limits) his teachers. There is a recognition of individual differences, necessitating variation in psychological treatment, presentation of materials of study, and criteria for judgement of performance. There is a demand for new syllabi and for flexible syllabi which would correspond to the psychological needs of the growth of the personality abolition of the examination system, and need, therefore, to discover a more rational and psychological system that can replace the system of tests, checks and counter-checks. All these demands and needs point to the idea of education for the all-round development of personality.

But what is personality? And how to prepare ourselves for the education for personality development? Personality is sometimes identified with character, but very often a distinction is made between the two. According to this distinction, character means the fixed structure of certain recognisable qualities while personality means the flux of self-expressive or sensitive and responsive being. But when we examine the distinction between the fixed structure and the flux, we find that the fixity and the flux are only relative terms, and in the movement of Nature, nothing is fixed. Personality may then be regarded as a plastic expression of certain forces and ends of Nature combined for the time being. Deeper psychological research affirms, as in the system of Yoga, that this combination of forces can be disturbed, it can be modified, it can be totally changed. Personalities can be multiplied within the same individual; the conflicting personalities in the individual can be harmonised; one can become capable of putting forth the needed personality according to the circumstances or the demands of the work or situation, even while the other personalities would remain behind, contributing to the efficacy of the personality put in the front. One can even go beyond all personality and know the real person that assumes so many personalities.

One can make a distinction between the real Person and the instruments of the person, viz. the body, life and mind. And between the person and the instruments there is what one might call the force of the person that expresses itself and gives a special turn, a special power of configuration, a certain stamp to the instruments. It is this special stamp or power of configuration that gives rise to the specific formation of a pattern of qualities and drives to our body, life and mind. It is that which we should call properly 'personality'. In the language of the Samkhya psychology, we might say that body, life and mind are the expressions of Prakriti marked by the three gunas: *sattva, rajas and tamas.*

The normal human being is simply an instrument of *Prakriti,* dominated largely by *tamas* or *rajas,* expressing indeed some pattern of these qualities, but as yet unable to become aware of the inner person, *Purusha.* In the

Samkhya, the *Purusha* is a mere Witness which is inactive, and it is not proper to speak of the Force of the *Purusha.* But in the Vedanta, especially in the original Vedanta of the Upanishads, and in some of its best developed forms, the inner person has its own force, often called the soul-force, which when awakened, pours itself into the instruments of *Prakriti,* and it is this meeting of the Soul-Force and *Prakriti* of Nature that causes the real formation of Personality.

The greater the opening of Nature to receive the flow of the Soul-Force, the greater is the resultant personality, and the fullness of Personality would be achieved initially by full development of mind, life and body under the sovereign guidance, rule and will of the Soul-Force, and a complete coursing of the energies of the Soul-Force, into the stuff, vibrations, activities, modes of mind, life and body, into the movements of *sattva, rajas* and *tamas,* with the power of their complete refinement, change and transformation.

The Soul-Force vibrates with the power and presence of the inner person, the true individual, which is quite different from the ego, a product of Nature or *Prakriti.* The true individual is called, in Sanskrit, the *Chaitya Purusha,* the one which is described in the Upanishads as *'no bigger than the thumb'*. It is, indeed, no bigger than the thumb when there is as yet no awakening in us of its presence and its force, but it is that which grows in us in answer to the needs of our internal and external growth, and the secret of all development of personality lies in that presence and in its force. It has, therefore, been affirmed that if one wants to develop the needed personality or wants to have mastery over one's own personal development, and even of the circumstances of our development, then the right method is to discover and seek a living contract with that inner person. In the absence of this contract, one will always remain subject to the formations of qualities in oneself, and will have no power to control, guide and perfect these formations. It is, therefore, concluded that the fullness of personality can come about only by the complete emergence of the inner person and the full expression of its force.

This force has, if we study closely, four basic expressions. It expresses itself through four Powers: a Power for knowledge, a Power for strength, a Power for mutuality and active and productive relation and interchange, a Power for works and labour and service. Accordingly, we have four basic personalities: the personality of knowledge, the personality of strength, the personality of harmony and the personality of skill.

"The psychological fact is", says Sri Aurobindo, "that there are these four active powers and tendencies of the Spirit and its executive Shakti within us and the predominance of one or the other in the more well-formed part of our personality gives us our main tendencies, dominant qualities and capacities, effective turn in action and life. But they are more or less present in all men, here manifest, there latent, here developed, there subdued and depressed or subordinate, and in the perfect man will be raised up to a fullness and harmony which in the spiritual freedom will burst out into the free play of the infinite quality of the spirit in the inner and the outer life and in the self-enjoying creative play of the Purusha with his and the world's Nature-Power."

The full richness of personality is the splendid, opulent and marvellous integration of the four-fold personality. The full heart of Love is tranquilised by knowledge into a calm ecstasy and vibrates with strength; the strong hands of Power labour for the world in a radiant fullness of joy and light; the luminous brain of Knowledge accepts and transforms the heart's obscure inspirations and lends itself to the workings of the high-seated Will. All these powers are founded together on a soul of sacrifice that lives in unity with all the world and accepts all things to transmute them. This, we may say, is the condition of man's integrality.

Such then is the basic idea of the integral personality and the process of its formation. In this idea we find the completion of several other ideas of personality of the remedy of dangers presented in several processes of exaggerated formations of egoism and individuality. According to one conception, personality is identified with egoistic individuality having a certain sense of ends or values. And fullness of personality in this sense would mean an enlarged development of egoistic individuality by means of an increased power of mind, an increased power of vital force, by a refined or dense and massive exaggerations of the forces of what Yoga calls 'Ignorance'.

This would manifest even a violent and turbulent, exaggerated, vital ego, satisfying itself with a supreme tyrannous or anarchic strength of self-fulfilment. Or, it would manifest a mighty exhibition of an overpowering force, self-possessed, self-held, even an ascetically self-restrained mind-capacity and life-power, strong, calm or cold or formidable in collected vehemence, subtle, dominating, a sublimation at once of the mental and vital ego. These are indeed superhuman manifestations, but even on a lower key, these manifestations are appalling, and one shudders at the idea of personality development if such is to be the result of education for personality development.

There is, of course, an idea of a harmonious development of personality in which body, life and mind are developed integrally and with a kind of balance that would avoid exaggerations of the vital or mental ego. Something of this kind was attempted as an ideal in the early Greek culture, and this is often proposed all over the world as a salutary aim for education. At its highest, it attempts a harmony of the triangular disposition of the individual, a harmony of the aesthetic, ethical and rational tendencies. The highest ideal that is formulated is that of the pursuit of the Truth, Goodness and Beauty.

But modern psychological studies have revealed the tendencies of intrinsic conflict of these three ideals as understood and practised by the human mind. There have also been revealed the tendencies of the unconscious which constantly bombard the shifting harmonies of personality, and the researches made in the fields of parapsychology reveal deeper complexes and compactions whose harmony is extremely difficult to achieve. What we call harmony is most often a compromise of tendencies, an apparently working order concealing under a brittle cover a mass of uncontrolled and unregenerate or unregulated impulses, tendencies, dreams, imaginations, systems of ideas and motives. There is, in fact, a sort of controlled disequilibrium, but not a happy mastery of a rich harmony.

The inner soul, the inner person of the Indian psychology, has an inherent power of purification and harmonisation. It detects the error and falsehood spontaneously; it turns effortlessly to all that is noble and mysterious and wonderful. The development of personality that is accompanied with or initiated by an awakening to this inmost soul, this psychic entity, prevents egoism and exaggerated formation of egoism; it harmonises effectively the aesthetic, the ethical and the rational. It has even a power to transmute the passions and impulses; it can even set right the subconscious and open it to the supreme light by which it can finally be transformed.

> "It is", in the words of Sri Aurobindo, "this secret psychic entity which is the original Conscience in us deeper than the constructed and conventional conscience of the moralist, for it is this which points always towards Truth and Right and Beauty, towards Love and Harmony and all

> that is a divine possibility in us, and persists till these things become the major need of our nature. It is the psychic personality in us that flowers as the saint, the sage, the seer; when it reaches its full strength, it turns the being towards the Knowledge of Self and the Divne, towards the supreme Truth, the supreme Good, the supreme Beauty, Love and Bliss, the divine heights and largenesses, and opens us to the touch of spiritual sympathy, universality, oneness."

The coming forward of the psychic person marks a momentous stage in the development of personality. It then begins to govern overtly and entirely our outer nature of mind, life and body, and then this can be cast into soul-image of what is true, right and beautiful, and in the end, the whole nature can be turned towards the real aim of life, the supreme victory. A transformation of the mind, life and body by the presence and the power of the psychic being is effected. This process may be rapid or tardy accordingly to the resistance in our developed nature.

But ultimately, by the greater and greater infusion of the psychic light, every part of the being is psychicised. As Sri Aurobindo describes it :

> "Every region of the being, every nook and corner of it, every movement, formation, direction, inclination of thought, will, emotion, sensation, action, reaction, motive, disposition, propensity, desire, habit of the conscious or subconscious physical, even the most concealed, camouflaged, mute recondite, is lighted up with the unerring psychic light, their confusions dissipated, their tangles disentangled, their obscurities, deceptions, self-deceptions precisely indicated and removed; all is purified set right, the whole nature harmonised, modulated in the psychic key, put in spiritual order."

There are, still, according to Sri Aurobindo, higher levels of consciousness, ranges of the powers of the fourfold personality in the superconscious. These ranges are those of what Sri Aurobindo has termed the Higher Mind, the Illumined Mind, Intuitive Mind, Overmind and

Supermind. An account of all this would form a subject by itself, and in an introductory paper as this we cannot dare enter into this field.

What we need to stress now is that the secret of personality development is an awakening to the psychic person and the development of body, life and mind in such a manner that they might aid in this awakening and might become well-trained instruments of the fourfold personality of knowledge, strength, harmony and skill.

It should be evident that the personality development as conceived here is a life-long education. And yet, it is a process that must begin right from the earliest stage, and must determine the drift, the content, and method of all our stages of education. And it seems inevitable that an education motivated by the development of personality demands a radical change in our approach, attitudes, methods, structure, system of evaluation, of syllabus and of contact with the students.

And, first, we may ask if we could find some principles which would guide us in our work of organising some practical organisation of education for personality development. In a series of articles that Sri Aurobindo wrote in 1909-10, as a leader of Indian nationalism, in order to expound what he conceived to be the lines on which a system of National Education could be evolved, he enunciated three fundamental principles to which reference is made earlier.

There are several other guidelines that we find in Sri Aurobindo. While explaining the instruments of the work of the teacher, he writes in his Synthesis of Yoga,

> "Teaching, example, influence, - these are the three instruments of the Guru. But the wise Teacher will not seek to impose himself or his opinions on the passive acceptance of the receptive mind; he will throw in only what is productive and sure as a seed which will grow under the divine fostering within. He will seek to awaken

> much more than to instruct; he will aim at the growth of the faculties and the experiences by a natural process and free expansion. He will give a method as an aid, as a utilisable device, not as an imperative formula or a fixed routine. And he will be on his guard against any turning of the means into a limitation, against the mechanising of process."

"What is his method and his system?" asks Sri Aurobindo and answers,

> "He has no method and every method. His system is a natural organisation of the highest processes and movements of which the nature is capable. Applying themselves even to the pettiest details and to the actions the most insignificant in their appearance with as much care and thoroughness as to the greatest, they in the end lift all into the Light and transform all."

"This imperfect nature of ours", explains Sri Aurobindo, "contains the materials of our perfection, but inchoate, distorted, misplaced, thrown together in disorder to a poor imperfect order. All this material has to be patiently perfected, purified, reorganised, new-moulded and transformed, not hacked and hewn and slain or mutilated, not obliterated by simple coercion and denial."

These principles, it will be observed, are subtle and complex, and no rigid formula of practice can be derived from them. They impose a great responsibility on the teacher and demand from him extraordinary qualities of a profound psychologist.

It would also seem that the education governed by these principles stands in need of a very flexible structure or organisation, in which the paramount place is automatically assigned to the varied needs of student's growth. In such a system, it is not merely the 'subjects' of study that should count. A much greater importance will have to be assigned to the inner aspiration, experience of freedom, possibility of educating oneself, self-experimentation, discovery of the inner needs and their relation with the programme of studies, and the discovery of the aim of life and the art of life.

A great stress will fall upon each student's individual work, and there has to be subtlety in forming flexible groupings of the students.

Our present structure of education is imprisoned within the walls of a triple system, and if we wish to make education for personality development a practical proposition, we must examine this triple system in some depth and suggest some practicable solutions. This imprisoning system is the lecture system, syllabus system, and the examination system.

We may begin with a few remarks regarding the Lecture System. A lecture or a speech as a creative expression of the inner spirit is a living vibration and it has an indispensable place in any ideal system of education.

Again, a lecture which is an informal talk has also an important place in education.

Also, lectures have a great utility in (a) introducing a subject, (b) stimulating an interest for a subject, (c) presenting a panoramic view of a subject, (d) explaining general difficulties or hurdles which are commonly met by a large number of students in their studies, (e) creating a collective atmosphere with regard to certain pervasive ideas, and (f) initiating rapid and massive programmes of training.

Finally, lectures as reports of research work have their undeniable place and value. But where the above aims or conditions are absent, lectures become dry, boring, ineffective, irrelevant to the interests of the students, and therefore useless.

Also, instead of being given a legitimate and rightful place, lectures in the present system are given almost a central place. It has been regarded as the central task of teachers to lecture and to cover the syllabus through their lectures. As a result, teachers are most often uncreative in their lectures; they are in a hurry to pour out their knowledge without much regard for the interest and attention of the students. Students tend to remain mostly passive, often inattentive and become in due course restless, and even violent. The present lecture system is thus quite unpsychological and devoid of much educational value. This must be changed radically.

Next, we may examine the syllabus system with which our lecture system is so closely connected.

A syllabus as an over-all view of an idea of a subject has necessary place in any ideal system of education.

A curriculum as an instrument of certain goals to be achieved has also an important place.

Also, a syllabus has a great utility in presenting to the student the various elements involved in what he is going to learn, in stimulating his interest in those elements, and in creating in him a 'prospective' attitude towards his studies.

Also, a syllabus as an instrument of a graded system of learning has its value and usefulness (at least in some areas of studies).

But a syllabus cut out rigidly and fixed uniformly for all the students alike is a heavy chain that smothers the innate tendencies of curiosity, variation, digression, play and spontaneity. It also cuts across a genuine development towards the synthesis and globality of a wide sweep of integral comprehension.

A wrong notion also grows that only what is given in the syllabus is that which is to be learnt; what falls outside the syllabus is often ignored and remains ignored indefinitely.

Instead of giving a legitimate place to the syllabus, it has come to be regarded as a backbone of the entire structure of the educational system.This situation must radically change.

A syllabus as a general panoramic view in the vision of the teacher and as a guideline for the student has a legitimate function, and this function has to be preserved. But in the actual operation of the educational process, there have to be what may be called 'evolutionary' syllabi. A syllabus should grow according to the needs of the inner growth of the student, and the student should be free to develop and weave the various elements of his studies into a complex harmonious whole on the lines of his deeper quest and according to the rhythm of the inner flowering of his personality.

We should aid at progress, but at free progress. We should aid at perfection, but a perfection that is a spontaneous and happy flowering.

The progress of the student has to be related to the motivation of the student. Curiosity as a motive has to be fostered and nourished. It has to be deepened and enlarged. But a time must come when mere curiosity is transformed into a serious search after the Truth. It is this transformation that marks a real progress.

A time comes in the process of learning when the student is awakened to the necessity of mastery or perfection. When this motivation begins to operate, more and more thorough programmes of training can be proposed, for it is with this motivation that training becomes a rigorous but joyous exercise.

Many of the difficulties of the teachers in dealing with the students arise because most programmes of study are programmes of training, and these are presented to the students whether they are psychologically ready or not.

There has to be a long period of general culture during which attention is to be paid to the cultivation of deep interest and love for studies and a large and wide grasp of the world and its mysteries. Stress on specialisation and mastery and perfection has also to be there, but a serious attention to this aspect should be given, it seems, only when the motivation for it begins to arise in the consciousness of the student.

All this implies a new handling of the students and their interests. It also implies the paramount importance of the observation of students and a deep psychological understanding of their motivation and their needs of growth.

A sound principle of teaching is, as we have noted elsewhere, that the child should be consulted in his own growth, and so, instead of imposing a programme of studies, the teacher has to work with the student pointing out to him the various paths of progress and asking him to choose what he would like to pursue. The teacher can certainly guide, counsel, help in choosing, but he should not impose.

It is true that finding a vocation and the necessary training for the chosen vocation are indeed important motivation of study, and they have to be given an important part in our total scheme. But we have at first to note that the chief vocation of man is to be Man and to transcend the limitations of manhood. And the key to the making of a Man is to develop the faculties of original, subtle, and complex thinking capable of seizing the heart of things and men and events, and the will-power to control and harmonise the various impulses, instincts and desires by means of the perception of a noble ideal and an unfailing resolution to realise that ideal. There has also to be a full growth of the body and its powers of strength, agility, plasticity, health and grace. And all this development of the body, life and mind is to be under the guidance of a secret knowledge and was the privilege of India to have once possessed in a great measure, and she can now recover and develop it even in a greater measure. This is the knowledge of the psychic and the spiritual.

Whatever else may be the vocation of the individual, to possess this knowledge of the inner spiritual being and to guide his mind, life and body in the light of this knowledge – this has to be chief programme of the vocation of every student. A wide, special and flexible syllabus for the discovery of and training for this vocation has to be the major concern of New Education.

But this chief programme has also to be related to each student for the specific role that he has to play in the world- activities.

A psychological handling of the student reveals the fact that every child has in him the materials for his perfection but these materials are in an undeveloped state or they are ill- organised. The specific role and vocation of each is intrinsically related to the harmonisation and perfection of these materials and to the natural and right rhythm of this process of perfection.

It will also be found that each man's natural vocation is intrinsically related to a natural tendency towards the mastery of a specific Technology, if we use that term in its widest sense in which not only scientific technologies but also language and law are included in its connotation. It is this natural tendency towards technology that should be encouraged right from the early stages of education. And for this purpose, there should always be available ample facilities for the cultivation of interests in various technologies and for their mastery in due course.

But care has to be taken to see that the study of technology does not become mechanical. And to prevent this we must realise that technology is a tool of expression. This would mean that the over-all emphasis should fall upon the inner springs of self-development which would necessitate expression, and which ; in turn, would necessitate the use of tools of expression.

It is also to be noted that while technology is oriented towards utility, and therefore all technological training has to be for serving certain utilities of life, the ultimate aim of technological training should not be 'utilitarian' in its vulgar sense. The aim of technology is and must be to be the vehicle of the expression of an ideal, an aspiration, an inspiration and a perfection.

A new organisation and syllabus for Technology would result from the above considerations.

And now we come to the Examination System. Tests as means of judging achievement are necessary and often indispensable. As such, they have an important place in any ideal system of education.

Tests are also useful for stimulation, for providing opportunities to the students to think clearly and formulate ideas adequately, for achieving precision, exactness, for arriving at a global view of the subjects of study, for self-evaluation, and for gaining self-confidence.

Tests can also be a matter of fun and play. But tests as a threat and as a means of securing the students' motivation for studies are a barbaric misuse of a useful instrument.

Tests coming as they do only once in a year in a decisive way, the uniformity of tests in disregard of the individual differentiation, an almost exclusive reliance on written tests which encourage cramming or unreflective reproduction of the material read or studied – these are among the elements that hurt the sensitivity of psychologists and educationists whose hearts yearn to foster the minds and hearts of the students with deep understanding, tenderness and affection in relation to the psychological needs of their growth of personality.

The fact that even a silly, mechanical mind can pass the tests, and that too with honours, is sufficient to pass a verdict against the present system of tests.

The fact that the most important aspects of culture that we wish our children to cultivate lie entirely beyond the scope of our tests is sufficient to show what a marginal place tests should occupy in our total system of education. The great values of truthfulness; sincerity, cheerfulness, benevolence, right judgement, sacrifice, friendship – these are some of the things which we wish our children to possess. As these do not come under the sweep of the examination system, they tend to be neglected or ignored or given a very inferior place in the educational process. But it is these rather than many other superficial things that should have a sovereign place. Means must be found by which sovereign things achieve their sovereignty.

The examination system must be radically changed. The motivation for studies has to come from a natural curiosity, a sense of inner need of a profound quest, and an inevitable necessity for the search after the Truth and Perfection. The teacher's genius will be judged by the way in which he can give the right and timely contact to his students and provide the necessary nourishment to their curiosity and need for a quest or stimulate them by striking ideas, projects, stories, and daily conversations, and much more by example and influence.

Let not tests be a substitute for these profound and deep things which constitute the very heart of education. There are what may be called 'romantic' periods of study and they come to different students at different stages of development, These are the periods of general expansion or a passion for a given preoccupation or falling in love with education. These are the periods entirely unsuitable for tests.

There are others when students need to clarify their vague ideas and sentiments ; they need precision and system. These are the periods when oral or written tests appropriate to these needs can be given.

There are again periods of assimilation at the end of which there is need to review in a connected manner the different elements of study. Here tests for comprehension or an extensive exposition would be relevant.

There are also periods when there is a will to undergo a rigorous programme of training. During such periods, even a series of difficult and strenuous tests would be perfectly justified.

Tests would be particularly needed where the courses of Technology (understood in its largest sense) are concerned.

Tests have thus to be a varied nature, and for each students, tests must come to such a way that they are helpful to his growth.

Tests must not be the means of passing or failing, of promotion or detention, but means of a self-evaluation, stimulation, and for correction and perfection. Moreover, tests may be oral or written or practical, according to the need and circumstance. It is also to be realised that impromptu tests can be more effective both in their power of stimulation and in arriving at a right judgement of the actual capacity of performance of the student.

It will be seen that in this view of tests, there will be no need to prefix any time-table for tests; they should be given to the students as and when necessary.

In any case, it has to be realised that the right way of judging a student and his progress is by an inner contact, an inner feeling for the student, an inner tact and discrimination. These qualities have to be developed by the teachers. And it is when these qualities are developed that they will vibrate in the atmosphere a power that encourages and nourishes the great virtues of the inner soul of the student.

These considerations suggest some lines on which a new organisation for New Education suitable for personality development could be evolved. But before we come to further precisions, it may seem necessary to state some over-all propositions regarding the spirit in which the new organisation should function, and the general role of the teachers in this New Education.

There will be, it may be said, four features of New Education :

> A sincere pursuit of the Truth, persistent seeking of an organisation of progressive Harmony, and a spontaneous Freedom fulfilling itself through growing order and perfection.

Informality in instruction, joy in learning, utter dedication, strictness in training, and the widest comprehension in the student-teacher relationship – these will govern the new methods of education.

An ever-fresh youthfulness, a constant prospective thrust towards New Future, and a happy thirst for continuous progress – these will govern the atmosphere on New Education.

A search for the highest aim of life, a stress on the integral development of personality, and a living expression of the unity of mankind – these will be the universal preoccupations of the teachers and students.

In New Education, students will not go to schools and colleges in order to listen to lectures, but for a quest, for finding out the answers to their questions, for consulting the teachers, when needed.

The very disposition of the classes will be radically changed, so that students have facilities to consult the teachers for a short or long time according to the needs. Instead of their being at the head of the class, the teachers will be found at convenient places so that they are readily available to those who need them for help, guidance, consultation.

The teacher's main occupation will be to observe his students, their inclinations and capacities, so as to be able to help them with deep sympathy and understanding. One of his important activities will be to write out something special for each of his students which will be useful for his general and specific growth. This involves a great deal of research work, but that is the privilege of his station in life.

The teacher will not be a mere lecturer; rather he will be an animator. He will inspire much more than instruct; he will guide by example and by the influence of his inner soul and its noble aspirations.

To aid the student in awakening the inner will to grow and to progress – that will be the constant endeavour of the teacher.

To evolve a programme of education for each student in accordance with the felt needs of the student's growth, to watch the students with deep sympathy, understanding and patience, ready to intervene and guide when necessary, to stimulate the students with striking words, ideas, questions, stories, projects and programmes – this will be the main work of the teachers.

But to radiate an inner calm and a cheerful dynamism so as to create an atmosphere conducive to the development of the higher faculties of inner knowledge and intuition – that will be regarded as the very heart of the work of the teacher.

As hinted earlier, there are, it seems, two important stages or aspects in the process of learning, the aspect of what may be called 'culture' and that of what may be called 'training'. The two are indeed interlocked, and in such a complex process as that of education, it is impossible to make clear-cut distinctions and compartments. An yet, it seems important to make some pragmatic distinctions, and some definite provisions for these two aspects.

Both these words 'culture' and 'training' have certain associations, and they need to be clarified after a detailed discussion. For our present purpose, however, we shall attribute to the word 'culture' that process of learning which is a result of a spontaneous and natural growth of faculties, capacities and personality by virtue of an easy stimulation of the environment, or a happy and attractive influence, something that may in a way be described as a leisurely growth of genius. And by 'training', we shall mean the process of learning which involves regular, persistent, methodical, rigorous and meticulous exercises. This occurs where the natural growth has reached a high point of maturity which demands a further development of precision, clarity, efficiency, and over-all perfection. It is also needed sometimes or often where the inherent urge is either absent or not so prominent, or else where there is an obstacle or a blockade in the growth. Or, again, there may be a need to stimulate an interest or capacity which is not active, either because it is only latent or it is absent. Or, finally, it may be needed where there is a mere laxity due to inertia and indifference.

If we examine them carefully, we shall find that most of our educational methods aim at providing some adequate-inadequate aids which are pertinent only to the aspect of training. But since they do not apply to the stage or aspect of culture, there is an artificiality in the atmosphere, and there is an undercurrent of a psychological revolt on the part of the students.

In the New Education, this defect must be eliminated. For this elimination, it seems, two things are needed.

Firstly, there must be on the part of the teacher a recognition that:

— Education must be a happy process, and happiness is a fruit of the inherent urge to grow, unhampered by external pressures.

— All educational processes must aim at achieving this happiness among the students. And all help, guidance and facilities should be provided towards this end.

— The right method of education has therefore to be that of 'culture', and all processes of training should gradually or rapidly be transformed into those of culture.

However, where this transformation has still not taken place, the right time for the programme of 'training' is when the student feels inwardly the need for clarity, precision or perfection, and when he is willing to impose upon himself an outer discipline for a short or long period) (according to the needs of the situation) of vigorous and persistent (or even repetitive) exercises.

In the absence of this inner will, there may be a need to impose outer discipline; but this imposition should be only a temporary device, and the aim should be to eliminate it gradually and totally. In any case, the imposition from outside must not be arbitrary and should not be offensive to the sensitiveness and sensibility of the students.

Secondly, for purposes of organisation, it may be convenient to have different organisations for 'culture' and for 'training', with a kind of flexibility so that students can use these organisations easily according to the psychological needs of their growth.

All programmes of 'training' should be conducted in what may be called 'Laboratories'. Normally, we have laboratories only for natural and applied sciences; and the normal work there is called 'practicals'. Recently, with the advent of language laboratories, the conception has gained in connotation, and we can, for our present purposes, enlarge it still further. Thus, we might propose that there should be laboratories for each branch of knowledge, and these laboratories might be organised in about the following way : Information will be available here about:

— what the subject in question means, and why it should be studied;

— a few alternative syllabi for the subject;

— an analysis of the various steps involved in the learning of the subject systematically and thoroughly;

— an idea of the different ways of preparing for these various steps.

There will also be available here :

— selected standard and reference books related to the subject;

— interesting and stimulating booklets or story books and other relevant documentation pertaining to the various topics of the subject;

— programmed books pertaining to the subject; these books often need to be supplemented by what may be called 'Work Sheets', i.e. educational material so prepared that it can be studied only by student's intelligent reflection and application. These work sheets should be of various types to permit alternative approaches;

— a series of graded exercises which the students can handle on their own with the least help from he teacher; (there should be a facility for self-correction);

— various kinds of test papers, including what may be called 'final test papers'; (these final test papers are those which the students under training may be required to answer in order to judge for themselves if they have achieved the necessary mastery).

The following activities will be encouraged :

— determination to work hard, work regularly, and to develop the habits of punctuality and discipline;

— to fix up a short or long programme of work, and to stick to it rigorously (laxity in this may disqualify a student from the joining of the given programme of the laboratory work);

— to arrange, from time to time, a short programme of lectures and seminars where a number of difficult problems will be discussed and dealt with rapidly and effectively;

— to give written reports of the work done;

— to pass certain tests (written, oral or practical);

— any other activities to achieve clarity, precision, efficiency, mastery.

We may now suggest a few ideas for the organisation of the stage or aspect of culture or of spontaneous and natural growth. Every student is normally in this stage with regard to most of his activities and returns to it after every short or long period of growth by training. He is often in this stage in regard to most of his activities simultaneously with his being in the other stage with regard to one or more of the other activities.

This is the interlocking of the two stages, and therefore, many of the features envisaged for laboratory work should more or less be available for what we have called 'cultural work'. But in cultural work, there will be a stress on freedom, a sense of leisurebness, a natural rhythm of work, daily conversation, and easy passage from one activity to another, fostering of interests and 'romance' of learning, warmth of friendliness and free collaboration in work, joy of discovery and invention, deep and profound reflection, spontaneous meditation, creative expression, fun and frolic of exercise, free consultation and discussion, development of consciousness, growth of spherical thought and action. These elements should also be present in the 'laboratory work', but there the stress will be on rigour, measure and mastery.

An adequate organisation of the 'cultural work' will need the following rooms :

— A Room or Rooms of Silence to which students who would like to do uninterrupted work or to reflect or meditate in silence can go when they like;

— Rooms of Consultation, where students can meet their teachers and consult with them on various points of their seeking;

— Rooms of Collaboration, where students can work in collaboration with each other on projects, etc.;

— Rooms of Exhibition, where students can organise various exhibitions of their work, — charts, paintings, etc.;

— Hobby Rooms, where students can work freely on various hobbies, such as aeromodelling, carpentry, fret-work, etc.;

— Rooms for Dancing, Music, Paining, Dramatics, etc.;

— Lecture Rooms where teachers can hold discussions with their students and where they can deliver lectures - short or long, according to the need;

— Store Rooms where materials for exhibitions, hobbies, etc., can be stored carefully and systematically.

We may call these Rooms 'Halls of Culture' and it may be suggested that all these Halls as well as Laboratories should be quite contiguous in location so that there is not much movement from one place to another.

And now, a few ideas may be suggested which will describe the actual working of New Education. It is necessary to point out that while the New Education will be proposed for general acceptance, it will not be imposed upon any one. Having ensured this basic assumption, the following points may be suggested for the actual operation of the work :

— There will be no compulsion with regard to any subject of study;

— The choice of a subject for study will be freely made with each student, and this choice should reflect a real and serious quest of the student;

— At the beginning of the session, students will be invited to indicate what lines of study or what particular topics they would like to explore;

— In order to facilitate the choice of topics, teachers may present to the students a suggestive but detailed list of suitable topics; teachers who may so wish, may also give a few talks to the students to explain the main outline of their subjects in order to stimulate their interest; students may also be advised to consult the material available in respect of laboratories to have a detailed idea of the various subjects;

— Each topic thus selected will constitute a short or a long project according to the nature of the topic;

— In exploring each project, students will take the help of the teacher or teachers whom they might choose from among those competent to deal with it;

— Teachers, on their part, will endeavour to relate the exploration of the projects to the inner needs of the students and the methods of exploration will be so organised as to permit the cultivation of intuition and higher faculties of knowledge and action;

— In guiding students, teachers will be expected to endeavour to widen and intensify the area of exploration so as to avoid narrow specialisation or mere idle superficiality;

— Normally, students will work in the Halls of Culture but, according to the needs, students will be permitted or recommended to join laboratories for a given topic or subject;

— Each student's programme of studies will be flexible, supple and evolutionary;

— In the selection of topics of study, students will not be restricted to any single faculty;

— There will be no lecture classes fixed in advance for the whole year. But teachers may arrange, by agreement with their students, lecture classes when necessary particularly in relation to the 'laboratory' work;

— Lectures will be confined to their legitimate and justifiable purposes indicated earlier;

— The over-all duration of various courses operating at present in the ordinary system need not be changed;

— Tests will be given to the students, when necessary, particularly in relation to the 'laboratory work'; tests will be confined to their legitimate and justifiable purposes as indicated earlier;

— At the end of every two or three months, each student will submit to the 'Coordinator' a report of his work in regard to each topic or subject. This report will give details of the progress he made in regard to what he has read or written or the reflections and the conclusions which might have been reached. It will also give an account of various activities in which he may be engaged whether under the supervision of the teachers or not. No activity will be regarded as extra-curricular, since all activities will be a part of education and of his programme of self-development;

— These reports will be transmitted to the Coordinator through the respective teachers (or directly where in regard to certain activities work is done without the supervision of any teacher). In doing so, they will mention the students' regularity of sustained effort, development of capacities, understanding of their subjects and the power of answering questions orally, practically or in writing with sufficient clarity and precision;

— Teachers will also give help by suggesting if a given student needs to do laboratory work in regard to a given topic or subject;

— The quality of the work will be considered more important than the quantity of the work, although the latter should not be meagre, but commensurate with high standards.

It will be seen that in this working, a special emphasis falls upon individual attention and upon providing necessary facilities for the maximum development of each student. There will thus be a great stress on 'individual work'. The individual work may be pursued in several different ways:

— by quiet reflection or meditation;

— by referring to books or relevant portions of books suggested by the teacher;

— by working on 'work-sheets';

— by consultations or interviews with the teachers;

— by carrying out experiments;

— by solving problems;

— by writing compositions;

— by drawing, designing, painting, etc.;

— by any other work, such as decoration, cooking, carpentry, stitching, embroidery, etc.

At the same time, there can be several situations in which a 'group work' is desirable and necessary. There are a number of projects in which there can be a division of labour and the need for the coordination of the work done by the participants; there can be educational games of team work, and there are often needs for joint exploration and experimentation, joint pursuit of a subject, useful lectures. In all these cases, collective work is very useful, and it should be encouraged.

But care should be taken to see that the needs for individual excellence are not sacrificed for the sake of the demands resulting from the consideration of the economy of the collective work. Often the collective work tends to be mechanical, and this tendency should be discouraged. It is preferable that the collective works are of a short duration of one or two months at a time. Longer periods may be needed in relation to 'laboratory' work, but in the determination of the general working of the individual and group work, there should be no rigidity. Grouping is best done when it is encouraged to be formed spontaneously on the basis of natural affinities of character of personality. The organisation should constantly grow so as to make the working supple and plastic.

It will also be seen that in this working there is no compulsion with regard to any subject of study, and the student will be free to choose any combination of subjects and to progress at his own pace. At the same time, this imposes upon the student a good deal of discrimination and an intimate understanding of the process of education itself. The aim of education, the value of different subjects of study, the need for mastery and perfection, and the psychological process by which one can develop one's own personality are some of the most important and difficult things on which students have to reflect deeply in order to take intelligent decisions with regard to their progress.

It should be the function of the teacher to provide to the students all the necessary elements of information and material relevant to these important questions and to present them in their full perspective.

In doing so, the following recommendations may be useful :

— *Learning by practising:* One of the great defects of learning through reading and through books and lectures is the gulf that has been created between theoretical knowledge and realisation by experience. Much of our knowledge is theoretical, and we do not know how much of it is really true in experience; much of our knowledge is abstract, and we do not enjoy it as a matter of deep and intimate possession of our very being. Much of our knowledge is ineffective, impotent, and we do not know in experience that knowledge is Power; much of our knowledge is a burden, and under the weight of the 'explosion' in knowledge, we do not know how to master knowledge, how to look 'steadily and whole'.

This situation is due to the fact that we have lost the real art of learning; for the secret of learning is, as was known to the ancient seers, the experience which comes by an inner and sincere practice.

To know what is the Truth, one must practice the Truth in words, thoughts and actions. To be able to posses the Truth, one must practice day and night self-control and self-mastery.

There are, as the ancients declared, states of consciousness in which the necessary knowledge occurs intuitively; and it is the knowledge occurring in the right consciousness that is effective and fruit-bearing. Not that knowledge as information is not important; for all operations of action, precise and detailed information is indispensable; but information received by mere listening or reading is most often a dead burden or a source of our imprisonment within narrow grooves and partial beliefs and opinions.

Information must grow from consciousness, and paramount importance must be given to the growth of profound and sincere states of consciousness rather than to the feeding of information.

And these states of consciousness come by an intense aspiration to know, by a great calm and silence, by stopping of the chattering noise of words and turmoil and riots in the mind. And this means a constant, persistent and steady practice of concentration and purification.

This process can greatly be aided by inner and outer action, by a process of creativity, by a process of experimentation and productivity. If we examine life closely, we find that every circumstance of life has a message in it. Life is the great teacher of life. Every incident of life can be a field of experimentation of inner or outer action. Our attempt should be to cultivate the right attitude towards life-situations and derive from them the educational experience proper to the need of our growth. We are here on the earth not merely to be deep and wide in our consciousness, but also to deal with outer situations, to control and master them, and also to create situations appropriate to the needs of our inner growth and our internal and external perfection.

A good teacher will always utilise daily situations of the student's life and turn them into occasions for the inner art of learning.

In recent times, there is a great awakening to the value of learning by doing. A number of programmes and projects are being suggested to use as stimulation which would evoke active responses. A great stress is being laid on learning through craft and manual work, works of production and experimental exercises, handling of material and technological occupation. There is also a powerful and salutary movement to utilise creative activities such as art, music, dance, composition of poetry, prose, drama. All education is, it is contended, ecstasy that comes from creativity.

All these ideas are undoubtedly excellent, but often each one of them is made into an exclusive gospel of right education, and in stressing this activity or that, the inner heart of learning is missed, namely, the growth of inner consciousness, inner concentration, and inner life of sincerity. Outer action may and often does help the inner; the outer perfection has undoubtedly to be a part of the total; but the foundation has to be inward, and if this is not centrally understood and practiced, there is in the end bound to be a failure.

Search for meaning and unity of knowledge: There is fundamentally no subject which is not interesting, and there is no subject which is not immediately or remotely related to any other subject.

A subject is uninteresting only so long as it is not sufficiently understood, and nothing is understood unless everything is understood.

And yet, when we pursue everything we are led into an endless movement and we seem to be drifting away somewhere towards a greater vagueness and incomprehension.

We are baffled by multiplicity, variety, endlessness. There are details and details, and there is a constant explosion of knowledge. We are in a stage of constant disequilibrium. We seem to have no standing ground.

Is there a secret knowledge knowing which everything can be known? The ancient Upanishads affirm such a Secret Something. But it is neither this subject nor that subject, nor it is all subjects put together. And yet it is in every subject, and in all subjects. In a sense, to learn this subject or that subject is not so important, nor is it important to learn the interrelation of subjects. The important thing is to learn and understand that Secret. That Something is the Meaning of Meaning, the Meaning of this, or that, of all.

The method of learning That is an entirely inner process. It cannot really be taught. One can only awaken to it and realise it. No learning is that awakening, and yet all learning can be made an occasion for that awakening.

Three things may be suggested as an aid to this process of learning:

(a) Whatever be the subject of topic on hand, there should be a constant endeavour at 'understanding', 'comprehension' To get at the heart, at the meaning to grasp, to hold it in the centre of consciousness, — this should be the primary indispensable operation of learning.

(b) Not to limit or narrow down to a limited number of subjects, but to encourage the development of interests for larger and larger fields of knowledge and activity, constant enlargement of interests, faculties and frontiers of knowledge, — this should be a necessary general operation of learning. It is this enlargement that brings the perception of the inner meaning of all. We begin to perceive that there is in every field and all fields taken together an essentiality, universal generality or commonness, and an endless variety of particulars, details and uniqueness. All superficiality is a waste of time and energy; to do something and not to do it well betrays an insincerity which is the enemy of all progress. Therefore, while enlarging interests there should be a measure, so that the multiplicity of activities does not necessitate superficiality or inadequate attention. To do a thing as quickly as possible and as perfectly as possible gives us the right measure and balance. A great help in this process is the growth of panoramic view of the world, a synoptic vision of the whole, the spherical thought, spherical consciousness.

(c) The third aid is the development of skill of perfection, efficiency, speed of performance, mastery. This should be a consequential operation of all learning. There may be here a selection of a limited number of fields and, in certain circumstances, where there is a need to invention and some pioneering work, even narrow specialisation. But even here, the stress will be on the discovery of That, the secret Something. Given this motivation, this stress, the defects of specialisation will intrinsically be corrected. In recent times, a greater and greater need for specialisation is felt, but also a greater sense and value for enlargement and for general education. To arrive at some satisfactory solution, two things have been suggested.

(1) Man, it is said, is the best subject of study for Man. And in the study of man, it has been argued, we have all the wideness and generality that we need and hope for.

There has thus grown the idea of 'core' or 'common' subjects of which the study of Man or some humanistic study form an indispensable part. This study is proposed as an obligatory study in the syllabi of various humanistic and technological courses.

(2) The second powerful and salutary idea is that of an inter-disciplinary approach to studies. A stress is laid upon the perception of connections, relations, the underlying unity of knowledge.

These are, indeed, excellent ideas, but they are often thought of and presented as a real remedy for our complex and difficult problems of curricula and syllabi. But the psychology of education is subtle and does easily make itself subservient to rigid formulas. Such an attempt is therefore not likely to be the final solution.

A good teacher will no doubt regard man and his future, his circumstances and the events that shape his destiny as extremely important, and will undoubtedly underline the necessity and importance of the study of Man, but he will not impose it. A good teacher will no doubt encourage the study of multiplicity of subjects and interdisciplinary approach, and he will take care to see that it does turn into an artificiality and superficiality. He will see that globality of thought and sphericity of thought are encouraged; but he will permit them to grow naturally and spontaneously. He will not impose them in the form of a logical web. He will remember constantly that he is not a teacher of a subject or subjects, but a helper in the search after the Meaning of Meaning of Meaning, the secret of the Unity of all knowledge.

12

Importance of Value-oriented Education

Education is intrinsically and by definition value-oriented. To speak, therefore, of value-oriented education is, in a sense, tautologous. In fact, education is a subset of a larger setting of culture, and culture consists of cultivation of faculties and powers pertaining to reason, ethics and aesthetics in the light of the pursuit of values of Truth, Beauty and Goodness *(satyam, sivam, sundaram)*. Culture also consists of infusing the influences of this pursuit into physical and vital impulses, so as to refine them and sublimate them to the highest possible degrees, and to transmit the resultant fund of experience through various modes of expression, including those of poetry, music, dance, drama, art, architecture, and craft. The height of a culture is to be judged by the depth and height that are reached in terms of an ascending process of harmonisation and, in that process, development of quest of spiritual inspiration and revelation and their manifestation in various domains of physical life.

Every developed culture, therefore, inspires methodologies of transmission of accumulated normative lessons of culture to succeeding generations, and this process of transmission is greatly secured by a process of education which, in turn, discovers and implements a more and more ripened system of acceleration of progress. Thus, the basic thrust of culture and education is inevitably value-oriented.

The question that arises as to why we are then obliged to think of value-oriented education. The answer is that there have intervened, during the last 200 years and more, certain factors that have retarded the right upward impulses of culture and education. This has happened all over the world, and everywhere there is a new awakening today to infuse value-oriented both in culture and in education.

In India, we can see that since the eighteenth century, and even before that, there came about the decline of intellectual activity and freedom, the waning of great ideals, the loss of the gust of life, and, even in the moral and spiritual life, the rise of excessive ritualism. Public life began to become more and more irreligious, egoistic, and self-seeking. This entire process became accentuated by three factors, which can be summed up in terms of influences emerging from Macaulay, Materialism and Mercantile barbarism.

As is very well-known, Macaulay had explicitly stated the purpose of the education system that was introduced under his initiative by the British in India, namely, to create a "class Indian in blood and colour but English in taste, in opinion, in morals and intellect" who would be interpreters between the British and the teeming millions that they ruled. Unfortunately, the scheme of education that was introduced has even now continued to persist with peripheral modifications. If we examine that scheme objectively, and in the light of the basic foundations of Indian culture, we shall find that it knocked off four main elements with perilous consequences. First of all, it eliminated the study of poetry, music and art, which constitutes perfect education of the soul; secondly, it eliminated the study of philosophy, dharma and spiritual knowledge ¾ three elements which are the supreme components of the Indian heritage; thirdly, while it introduced some elements of world history and world geography and modern science, it presented the dominant British view of history and disturbed the Indian view of science, which always looked upon scientific inquiry as a part of the holistic quest in which Science, Philosophy and Yoga had a sound system of interrelationship; and fourthly, it omitted altogether physical education and skills of art and craft and others related to science of living, which were kept alive in India throughout the ages. What has been lost in terms of pedagogy and richness of contents of knowledge and skills has still not been remedied, and urgent steps are necessary to review the entire scheme so that we can provide to our students a genuine national system of education, which is at the same time open to the benefits of modern knowledge and modern ideals of progress towards Liberty, Equality and Fraternity.

The advent of the British rule in India coincided with the high tide of modern science in the West, and along with it the extensive spread of materialism ¾ a phenomenon of mixed blessings. While science and scientific spirit are deep rooted in the genius of India, materialism does not fit very well with the Indian ethos, although material poverty was never a national ideal, and abundance of wealth was a high achievement of Indian culture, until our economy was greatly shattered by the British policy.

It is mistakenly supposed that science and materialism are logically interrelated with each other, even though the triumph of physical sciences has tended to emphasise materialistic approach to knowledge and reality. In any case, the Macaulayan scheme of education does not provide the kind of scientific rigour, which is manifested in the Indian history of scientific knowledge; nor does it promote that avenue of inquiry by which the limitations of materialism can be understood and overcome.

Materialism has promoted what can be called mercantile barbarism, and that too, even in the setting of a science-based civilisation. It is barbarism because its gospel is to support and aggrandise the needs of physical life, and it seeks triumph of consumerism, which can be sustained only by supporting an unjust economic and social order, environmental disasters and by inducing people to remain confined to a perpetual bondage to increasing physical wants. We have today for the entire human race a possibility to be uplifted to a higher and nobler way of life and to an order of unity and harmony, but mercantilism compels competition and strife, and we see today the horror of terrorism spreading on a global scale. We speak of globalisation today, but the dominant quest today is the quest of global markets and not the quest of global brotherhood.

The issues that confront us relate not only to promote education widely and universally, but also *what kind of education,* so that India can recover her true spirit and it is empowered to stand out in the world as a leader of the future, in spirituality and science, in philosophy and art and in all fields of professions and occupations so as to be opulent and prosperous capable of fostering universal culture of peace, harmony and world-unity. For this aim to be fulfilled we need to liberate our educational system from the Macaulayan mould, we need to deal with materialism both scientifically and philosophically, as also morally and spiritually, and we need to combat forces of barbarism, ignorance and division so as to inspire among the youth a burning quest for wisdom and courage, for excellence in works and skills, and for universality and all that contributes to individual and collective perfection.

One of the best means of achieving these goals is the task that we have begun earnestly during the last few years the task of Value-Oriented education.

The task is difficult and enormous, but there are several favourable circumstances which can aid us and encourage us to undertake this task and accomplish it.

We must first take into account the fact that during the freedom struggle, five greatest leaders of modern India, who were also educationists, challenged the British system of education and developed powerful philosophies of education so as to provide to the students not only the lessons of the Indian heritage but also to prepare them for the future greatness of India. The first leonine call came from Maharshi Dayananda Saraswati who went back to the Vedic foundations and put forth a system of education that would reform India and make it progressive. He inspired the Gurukula system of education and underlined the great role of the teacher in uplifting the talent and character of the pupil. The second great effort was that of Swami Vivekananda who spoke of man-making education and, accepting Vedantic knowledge as the base, and acknowledging the truth of every religion and a synthesis of yoga, he opened the gates of the future before the youths, filling them with a new spirit of inspiration, heroism and dynamic action. Another line of educational experiment was initiated by Mahatma Gandhi, who emphasised the training of the Hand, Heart and Head, overarched by the values of Truth, Non-Violence, Self-Control, Non-Covetousness and Renunciation, as also equal respect towards all religions and life of simplicity that aims at reconstruction and reform of rural, social, and political organisations based on equality, empowerment of the weak and the oppressed, decentralisation and brotherhood. Gurudev Rabindranath Tagore, the great poet of modern India, established at Shantiniketan an experimental Institution for a new aim and mode of education where the beauty and sublimity of Nature can serve as a living partner of teaching and learning and where the values of poetry, music and art can vibrate in the rhythms of life of the development of personality and mingling of cultures of Asia and of the world that would promote internationalism and world- -citizenship, and universal fraternity that transcends all divisions of race and religion in the Religion of Man. And there arose also the Nationalist call of 'Bande Mataram' that gave birth to the movement of the National System of Education with the aim of recreating the ancient Indian Spirit that was at once spiritual, intellectual, scientific, artistic and productive, and empowered now with new vigour to assimilate all that is new and progressive and to create new forms of expression and synthesis of powers of personality and knowledge and harmony of the East and the West. Sri Aurobindo formulated the philosophy of this system in 1909 and developed it further in subsequent decades so as to embody the light and power of the Synthesis of Yoga and a programme of integral transformation of human life on the earth that would lead the evolution of Nature into the birth of a new humanity and superhumanity.

All these initiatives and experiments have been bold and great and inspiring, and all of them are still in various stages of growth and development; great lessons have to be learnt from these experiments, and we have here a great fund of educational research that can guide us in the tasks of value-oriented education and of the entire transformation of our educational system.

We have also a favourable climate being created by some of the progressive experiments in the West, such as those promoted by Pestalozzi, Montessori, Bertrand Russell and others; the trend is towards child-centred education, and the basic idea is that the individual is not merely a social unit, but a soul, a being, who has to fulfil his own individual truth and law as well as his natural or his assigned part in the truth and law of the collective existence. Happily, this Western idea agrees at its root with the profoundest and highest spiritual conceptions of Asia and it can easily play a great role in harmonising our national effort at reconstruction of education with similar efforts in the West.

In this task, UNESCO's initiatives are also helpful. The two great reports: *Learning to Be* brought out in 1971 and *Learning: Treasure Within* brought out in 1996 have underlined education for values of international understanding, peace and integral development of personality. Emphasis on Complete Education for the Complete Human Being and on four pillars of learning, viz., Learning to Know, Learning to Do, Learning to Live With Others, and Learning to Be, points to the need for a radical paradigm shift impelling all-round reforms in aims, contents and methods of education, as also of the system of examination, evaluation and certification.

In the wide sweep of values which are incontrovertibly admitted universally are those contained in the Declaration of Human Rights as also those in the Declaration of Human Responsibilities. Nearer home, we have also a remarkable and unique declaration in our own Constitution under Article 51 A of Fundamental Duties, which I believe, if implemented in full ¾ as we have resolved to do ¾ we shall have secure guidance as to what values we have to promote in our educational system, so that all citizens can be empowered to fulfil their duties.

Contemporary explosion of information and increasing spread of sophisticated information technology have brought forth deeper issues of education and educational methodology, in the context of which value-oriented education assumes wider dimensions. Not only open system of education can now become very effective, but it will also open new channels of communication of the message of value-oriented education, since they can be at once adapted to the needs of the individual and of groups and masses. At a higher dimension, one question that will have to be answered is of the ways and means to ensure that knowledge does not get lost in information, and wisdom does not get lost in knowledge. I believe that more and more we shall have to address ourselves to the question that the Upanishad had raised, viz., what is that knowing which everything can be known? *(yasmin vijnate sarvam vijnatam bhavati).* For advancement of knowledge demands methods by which knowledge can be summed up and possessed in a state of self-possession. In this context, it may also be suggested that value-oriented education should ultimately issue from and result in the knowledge of what can be described as all-embracing Self and universal Reality.

Philosophy, which is today highly dominated by Science is also likely to undergo a major change and enlarge itself in its scope so as to admit the phenomena of Consciousness, which are now being studied more and more at the level of microcosm as also at the level of macrocosm. In this light, it will not be difficult for philosophy to detect the logical error of Materialism involved in its attempt to derive from the premise that Matter is real, the conclusion that Matter alone is real. The circularity of the argument becomes obvious and is rendered invalid. As Sri Aurobindo points out:

> "This vulgar or rustic error of our corporeal organs does not gain in validity by being promoted into the domain of philosophical reasoning. Obviously, their pretension is unfounded. Even in the world of Matter there are existences of which the physical senses are incapable of taking cognisance. Yet the denial of the suprasensible as necessarily an illusion or a hallucination depends on this

> constant sensuous association of the real with the materially perceptible, which is itself a hallucination. Assuming throughout what it seeks to establish, it has the vice of the argument in a circle and can have no validity for an impartial reasoning."

At the stage at which we stand today, the recent advances in the field of knowledge provide us sounder foundations for the philosophy of value and philosophy of value-oriented education. Already great scientists and philosophers of science have begun to acknowledge the need to bridge the gulf between science and value, just as there is a need to bridge the gulf between art and value. It is recognised that the development of science should be supplemented by enormous development of the value of human kindness.

What emerges from the foregoing is that the programme of value-oriented education should emphasise the relationship between Science and Value. In our presentation of values, we do not need to be prescriptive; we should encourage methods of explorations. As we explore deeper and deeper, we shall find that there are values which are relative and subjective; but we shall also find that there is in us a dimension of Value and that this is an undeniable objective fact. There is also the fact that the more one advances in the theory and practice of Value, the more is one obliged to overcome selfishness, egoism and subjectivity, and the more is one led to the discovery of the Categorical Imperative, the criterion of which is translatable in some kind of objectivity and universality, as Kant showed, although not entirely satisfactorily, and as shown by the Bhagavad-Gita in its concept of *lokasangraha*. What we call good actions can be relative, and our judgement about them can be subjective; but there can be no denial that, objectively speaking, the highest goodwill for the highest good of all is the highest conceivable Value. To my mind, the first and the last message of value-oriented education should be to develop among all the highest Goodwill, *siva sankalpam.*

Social Problems in India

India is today sinking under the weight of problems, some of which, like those of violence, division, corruption and plutocracy are proving to be most obstinate and most difficult to resolve. We are trying to find solutions but there seem to be certain tendencies and factors which require remedies at a level that is far deeper than the level at which we are now thinking and acting.

At present, we are engrossed within narrow boundaries, and what we lack most is perception of perspectives. We want democracy, but narrowed down in our adoption of the Western form of parliamentary democracy, we do not go to the root of the truth of democracy, namely, the development of the individual to grow into his/her highest possibilities, physical, vital, mental, aesthetic, ethical and spiritual.

True democracy demands self-determination by the individual and the collection at the highest levels of consciousness. This demand is consistently and systematically ignored or obstructed, and therefore, democracy is being increasingly collapsing in plutocracy, -the rule of money, the rule of crime and rule of muscle power. Our Constitution speaks of socialism, but we are not adequately cognisant of the way in which socialism tends to grow into deification of the State. As a result, we are not working consciously for the development of collective consciousness that takes care of the liberties of the individual nor are we developing the ethos in which the individual and the collectivity are prepared to sacrifice their egoisms for their harmonious and inter-dependent relationships. The only way by which we are reducing the impact of socialism is by reviving the grip of capitalism in the name of liberalisation and globalisation. We are not inquiring as to how we can devise means and methods by which, consistent with individual liberty, we can also bring about welfare not merely of a few but of all. Our Constitution also speaks of secularism, but while we easily yield to the tendency to equate secularism with materialism, we do not strain ourselves to transcend the limitations of consciousness where exclusivism of religions is over passed so as to create a dynamic Dharma and dynamic spirituality, which does not shun material life but transforms it for the highest possible synthesis of Spirit and Matter.

We want rapid social transformation, but we are still nourishing those institutions that foster casteism and narrow loyalties. We want rapid economic growth, but confine ourselves to the stifling attitudes, and thus we are unable to inspire adequate individual and collective initiative or required generosity and nobility in our institutions of commerce and industry. While we need sustained effort for development, we are riddled with fluctuations in regard to our priorities. We do think sometimes of education as of highest importance but we remain restricted merely to multiplying the number of educational institutions which continuously increase the impact of Macaulayan ideology of education instead of making bold efforts to transform the objectives, contents and methods of education that will educate all and educate them for development of wisdom and character. In this situation, it has become imperative to underline that the most important theme of India today is that of education for character development.

This theme is also reinforced when we consider not only the Indian situation but the global situation which is constantly influencing and shaping our Indian situation. A huge structure is being built up with an increasing insistence on mechanisation, standardisation and dehumanisation, leaving practically no room for the growth of profounder, ethical and spiritual consciousness which alone can rightly and wisely guide human volition in taking decisions in the critical times that seem to lie ahead of us. While under the pressure of the technological development, the world is shrinking and we are dreaming of the possibility of a planetary civilisation, we have not yet the required corresponding psychological development which can enable the human consciousness and character to sustain such a planetary civilisation.

On the contrary, there is growing preponderance of those impulses which can thrive only through ignorance, fragmentation, discord and violence. As we study the situation, we feel convinced that it is a vain chimera to believe that the world of today and tomorrow can be safe without a radical change in human consciousness and character. It is true that the wisest leaders of today have declared unambiguously that the future of the human race is dependent exclusively upon a radical transformation of human consciousness, and that one of the most important means of effecting this transformation is an integral and value-oriented education. Unfortunately, this counsel is heard dimly and ignored greatly when we frame our plans of action for education.

It is, therefore, necessary that a voluntary effort is initiated and conferences, seminars and workshops are organised where the theme of integral and value-oriented education and the theme of education for character development are studied in depth. It is only through this method that a wide awakening among people can be generated. Without this awakening, such a difficult thing as education for character development cannot be conceived and implemented.

In the first place, we need to clarify ourselves as to what we mean by education for character development.

In simplest terms, character implies well-trained will to be straightforward, fearless and honest coupled with sincerity to act and even to fight nobly and courageously in order to embody in one's own life and in the life of the society all that is true and all that can foster solidarity and unity.

Character may be considered to have four dimensions, dimension of wisdom, dimension of heroic will, dimension of compassion and universal love, and dimension of competence, chiseled skill and untiring labour. A well-developed character is integrated character; it is able to sharpen in-born capacities and potentialities towards their own highest values. A developed character is a developed personality that harmonises the demands of physical education, vital education, emotional education, of rational education, aesthetic education, ethical and spiritual education.

In our present system of education, all that we have conceived here to be relevant to the development of character is sadly missing. We are too preoccupied with mental development, and even in the field of mental development, we give a preponderant importance to those qualities which are relevant to our present examination system. We are thus not giving so much importance to the development of power of understanding as to the power of memory.

Our education is limited to the imparting of information; we hardly aim at imparting knowledge; and development of wisdom is entirely out of the court. We do not emphasise the learning of *facts*. We do not give importance to the pursuit of truth; we propose only the pursuit of piece-meal assemblage of topics and subjects which are prescribed in our syllabus. It is only recently that some place is being given to physical education and aesthetic education. But the situation is entirely unsatisfactory when we come to the domain of character development. Even our thinking on the subject of values which are central to character development is beset with confusions and doubts. Our first necessity is to explore the basic ideas in regard to values, to determine what they mean and what place they can be given and in what way they can be implemented in our system of education.

Let us dwell a little upon the word "value". This word, as understood in the context of educational philosophy, refers to those desirable ideals and goals which are intrinsic in themselves and which, when achieved or attempted to be achieved, evoke a deep sense of fulfilment to one or many or all parts of what we consider to be the highest elements of our nature. In a sense, it may be urged that the word "value" is basically undefinable, since it denotes a fundamental category and it is itself the highest genus of that category. At the same time, there is a common understanding in regard to truth, beauty and goodness which can be conceived as the supreme values of life.

They are intrinsic in character, and they are ends-in-themselves. Even if there are wide differences as to what is meant by these three terms, there is an agreement that they are most desirable ideals and mere orientation towards them inspires development of those states of our being and becoming in which we can hope to find some kind of ultimate fulfilment.

These three great ideals can guide us in developing all that we have spoken of as character and all that can be considered to be of highest value to integral personality. As a result, in the domain of physical education, we discover the values of health, grace and beauty. In the domain of emotional education, we arrive at the values of harmony and friendliness, of courage and heroism, of endurance and perseverance and of irresistible will to conquer the forces of ignorance, division and injustice. In the sphere of mental education, the values that emerge are those of utmost impartiality, dispassionate search after the Truth, widest possible synthesis, and calm and silence. The values pertaining to the aesthetic development would be those of the vision of Beauty and creative joy of the deepest possible aesthetic experience and expression.

When we come to the field of moral and spiritual values, the situation is rather difficult and complex. Is there, we may ask, any valid distinction between moral and spiritual values? In answer, it may be said that much depends upon what we intend in include in our definition of the word "morality" or in the word "spirituality". In Indian thought, the distinction between morality and spirituality has been clearly made and each one has its specific and distinguishing connotation.

The word "morality" connotes a pursuit of the control and mastery over impulses and desires under the guidance and supervening inspiration of a standard of conduct formulated in consideration of man's station and duties in the society or in consideration of any discovered or prescribed intrinsic law of an ideal. Morality is often conceived as a preparation for spirituality. Spirituality begins when one seeks whatever one conceives to be the ultimate and absolute, for its own sake unconditionally and without any reserve whatsoever. Moreover, while morality is often limited to the domain of duties, spirituality is fundamentally a search of the *knowledge* of the highest and the absolute by direct experience and manifestation of the search in every mode of living, thinking and acting.

Again, both the moral and the spiritual are to be distinguished from what is called "religious" when we speak of religious education. Religion, which can be called *sampradaya* has the following distinguishing features:

— A specific religious belief or creed or doctrine about the nature of Reality, scripture and traditional founder, prophet or incarnation;

— Every specific religion has, as its essential ingredient, certain prescribed acts, rituals and ceremonies;

— A religious authority to which religious matters are referred and the decision of which is final.

Both moral and spiritual values can be practised irrespective of whether one believes in one religion or another or whether one believes in no religion. Both morality and spirituality can be independent of rituals and ceremonies and of any acts specifically prescribed by any particular religion. And both of them are independent of any authority except that of one's own free judgement and direct spiritual experience.

It is also useful to distinguish religion from what in India is called "dharma". Dharma is not any religious creed or dogma and system of rituals but a deeper law of the harmonious and interdependent growth of the deepest aspirations of the collectivity and of the individuals that constitute the collectivity. Dharma can be regarded as an ordered system of moral and spiritual values.

Values that we seek in the moral and spiritual domain are those of sincerity, faithfulness, obedience to whatever one conceives to be the highest, gratitude, selflessness, freedom from egoism, equality in joy and suffering, in honour and dishonour, in success and failure, pursuit of the deepest and the highest, and of the absolute and the ultimate, and progressive expression of this pursuit in thought, feeling and action.

It must be observed that the pursuit of these values is not intrinsically related to any particular religion. These values are intrinsic and ends in themselves, irrespective of whether one holds any particular doctrine of ethics, religion or spirituality. Whether one belongs to one religion or the other, or to no religion, one can pursue these values devotedly and zealously.

Having clarified some of the important elements of education for character development, it is necessary to underline that this education should not be conceived as a training in certain Do's and Don'ts. It may be mentioned that Do's and Don'ts refer to outer actions; and outer actions derive their value only in relation to the inner motive and the inner consciousness from which they emerge. The given right state of consciousness may express itself in different forms of action, and each of these actions would be right, since behind each one of them there is a living vibration of the right state of consciousness. On the other hand, there are several actions which may apparently seem good and right in their outer forms, and yet if they are not spontaneous expressions of the right motive, they cease to have any value from the point of view of character.

It is also to be underlined that education for character development cannot be confined to a specific period in the total framework of a timetable. All occasions of daily life should be utilised to bring the student nearer to the realisation of the ideals of character development. There are occasions when children express wild impulses and passions, and often they are in revolt. Children have their own daily battles of loyalties and friendships, and there are moments of desperate depression and of violent enthusiasm. There are occasions when children can be vexed, become sulky and go on strike. All these occasions are occasions for education for character development. With patience and perseverance, the teacher can utilise all these occasions to show the truth and light and to awaken among the children the right sense and the right sense of true progress.

It is also to be underlined that in the process of education for character development, character of the teacher is of supreme importance. We are thus required to demand from the teachers a very exacting role. For the fulfilment of this role, teachers themselves must feel inspired to learn the lessons of self-control and to foster harmonious blending of wisdom, will, courage, compassion, harmony, and competences of various kinds that are directly relevant to the tasks of teaching learning process. The teacher should be able to involve his or her total being in the teaching-learning process.

The question here is not merely to deal with subjects and books but also with faculties and capacities, and particularly, with the powers of will and concentration that are indispensable in developing character. The teacher will need to have not only a high degree of proficiency in his or her own subject of discipline but he or she will also need to arrive, as rapidly as possible, at a considerable maturity of the growth of personality, and he or she will need to look upon the work of teaching as a part of the discipline required for the development of his or her own personality and character. Only a teacher of high character can generate students of high character.

Education for Character Development

At the outset, we need to examine the view that values cannot be taught and, therefore, character development cannot be a subject matter for teaching. It is argued that there is a valid distinction between pursuit of knowledge and pursuit of character development and that while knowledge can be taught, character development falls outside the purview of the teaching process. But when we examine this view more closely, we find that what is meant is that the methods which are valid and appropriate in the field of learning in regard to knowledge are not applicable to the field of learning in the field of values which are central in the process of development of character.

We may readily accept this contention, and we may insist on the necessity of recognising the fact that corresponding to each domain of learning there are valid and appropriate methods and that the effectivity of learning will depend upon an ever-vigilant discovery of more and more appropriate methods in each domain of learning. It is clear, for example, that while philosophy can be learned and be taught by a process of discussion, swimming cannot be learned and taught by discussion. In order to learn to swim, one has to plunge and swim. Similarly, the methods of learning music or painting have to be quite different from those by which we learn mathematics or physics.

And, indeed, when we come to the realm of character and values, we must recognise the necessity of a greater scruple in prescribing the methods which can be considered to be distinctively appropriate to this field.

One speciality of the domain of character is that it is centrally related to volition and affection rather than to cognition. According to some, education for character development should be exclusively or more or less exclusively limited to certain prescribed acts of volition and that the education for character development should be judged by what a learner *does* rather than what he *knows*. This view is, however, too simplistic and exclusive and we should avoid the rigidity that arises from this kind of gross exclusivism.

There is also an opposite view according to which learning is primarily a cognitive process and, therefore, all the learning processes connected with character development should largely or preponderantly be limited to those methods which are appropriate to cognition. This view, too, is a gross exclusivism which should be avoided. A synthesis of these two views would result in the recommendation that in the processes of education for character development, methods appropriate to volition and affection should be more preponderant but appropriate methods to cognition also should have a legitimate and even an indispensable place. This is reinforced by the fact that the striving towards values stirs up the totality of the being, and cognition no less than volition and affection is or can be stimulated to its highest maximum degrees, provided that the process of learning involved in character development is allowed its natural fullness.

In any sound process of teaching and learning, three instruments which are available to the teacher are: instruction, example and influence. However, in our present system of education, instruction plays an overwhelmingly important role and often when we think of teaching we think only of instruction. It is this illegitimate identification of all teaching with instruction that causes much confusion and avoidable controversies. If we examine the matter carefully, we shall find that in an ideal system of teaching, instruction should play a much less important role than example and influence of the teacher. It is true that in the domain of learning where cognitive activities play a more important part, instruction through lecture and discussion may have, under certain circumstances, a larger role,. But in this domain of learning, where volition and affective activities play a larger part, instruction through methods other than lectures and discussions should play a larger role.

Unfortunately, our present system of education, being what it is, there is such rigidity that example and influence can play very limited effective role. In the present rigid and mechanical structure, the centre of attention is not the child but the book, the teacher, syllabus and the examination. The methods which are most conducive to the development of the character of the child such as the methods of self-learning, exercise of free will, individualised pace of progress, etc., do not have even an elbow room. Indeed, if this is the system of education and if we are to remain content with this system of education, most important elements of learning will for ever remain outside the system, and we cannot confidently recommend any effective system of learning, much less any effective programme of character development.

We must, therefore, envisage that sooner rather than later, our system of education will change in the right direction and increasing number of educationists and teachers must come forward to break the rigidities of our educational system. At the same time, we should also institute the right type of training for teachers so that teachers are oriented towards education for character development.

The change that we should envisage must also propose a radical transformation of our present system of examination. Apart from a number of undesirable aspects of our examination system, the one which is particularly conducive to what may be called "anti-value" is the tendency which promotes the idea that passing of examinations and earning of degree is the aim of education. Radical measures should be adopted to combat this idea and to introduce such changes in our examination system whereby the educational process can remain unalterably fixed on the right aims of education, which must place development of character in centrality. A radical change in the examination system is a necessary condition of any meaningful education for character development.

It is sometimes argued that values can best be taught through the instrumentality of a number of subjects rather than through any specific or special subject, whether we may call it by the name of "moral education" or ethics" or "value-education". There is no doubt a great force behind this contention and we may readily agree that we must have a well-conceived programme of studies of various subjects which would naturally provide, both in their content and thrust, the requisite materials for character development.

The question, however, is whether our current programmes of studies have been or are being so carefully devised so as to emphasis those aspects which can rightly provide to teachers and students the required opportunities, conditions and materials for character development. A massive work remains to be done in this connection.

At the same time, it may be suggested that even if our programmes of studies of various subjects are revised, there will still remain the specific areas of values which should receive a special, although not exclusive, attention and treatment. In other words, there seems to be a good ground to recommend that there should be, in the totality of educational programmes, a *core* programme of value-education and character development.

This core programme should, however, be so carefully devised that various threads of this progrmme are woven into the complex totality of all the other programmes of studies. The point to be underlined is that the central theme of education for character development would not form a mere appendage of all other subjects but would stand out as the overarching and the supervening subject of basic importance.

It is sometimes suggested that education for character development or value-oriented education is relevant only to the primary and secondary stages, but not beyond. For, it is argued, children by the time they complete secondary education would have already formed their basic attitudes, their traits of personality and their character, and nothing more needs to be done specially in that direction at the higher levels of education. But this argument misses the point that the important element in the development of character is the development of free-will and of the learner's free and rational acceptance of the value system and directions of the growth of character and personality. And this development can rightly be done only at the higher levels of education, when the learner has developed a will of his own to some extent and when he has basic intellectual and moral and aesthetic sensibilities enabling him to examine the basic values and aims of life.

The fundamental aims of higher education include the pursuit of clarity of thought, search for perfection, irresistible will to realise "*summum bonum*" and higher humanistic, scientific and professional skills. These are also essential requisites of integral development of personality and character. It is this that necessitates us to recommend that education for character development should also form a central focus of higher education.

The secret of education for character development is the way in which the teacher can inspire and kindle the quest among the students by means of one's own example of character and mastery of knowledge that is relevant to the over-arching importance of character both in the individual life and in the collective life. It is only by embodying values within oneself that the teacher can really radiate values to students.

While laying a great emphasis on the role of the teacher in respect of education for character development, it must be emphasised that education is a sub-system of society, and, therefore, the role of the society in stimulating and supporting aims of character development must be underlined. In this connection, two social actions may be suggested. Firstly, society must place the child in the centre of its attention and declare the sovereignty of the child. It must resolve to bestow upon the child the supreme care that it needs. It will organise all activities and also special activities in such a way that they become vehicles of character development of the child. And, secondly, just as the child always looks to the future, the society, too, will constantly strive to build the paths of the future. Just as child will grow increasingly into the vigorous and dynamic youth, the society also must continue to learn and to mature so as to manifest unfailing youthfulness. The society should recommend to all members to continue to learn and to grow so as to actualise a learning society.

The task of the teacher who aims at the character development of the child is to put the child upon the right road to its own perfection and to encourage it to follow that road, watching, suggesting, helping, but not imposing or interfering. The best method of suggestion is by personal example, daily conversation and books read from day-to-day. These books should contain, for the younger students, the lofty examples of the past, given not as moral lessons but as things of supreme human interest, and for the older students, great thoughts of great souls, passages of literature, which set fire to the highest emotions and prompt the highest ideals and aspirations, records of history and biographies which exemplify the living of those great thoughts, noble emotions and inspiring ideals.

Opportunities should be given to the students by embodying in actions the deeper and nobler impulses which rise within them.

An informal but profound study of the following questions would prove to be of immense value:

— What is action? How does it operate normally? Can action be controlled and guided? How can one achieve the maximum effectivity and larger scope of action?

— To whom should I belong? What is the meaning of allegiance? What is the highest to which my highest allegiance should be given?

— What is the purpose of the human body? What are the means by which the perfection of the body can be achieved?

— What are the highest means of knowledge? Is there something which being known, everything can be known?

— What is the nature of the mind? How does it operate in (a) scientific thinking, (b) mathematical thinking, and (c) philosophical thinking? It is possible to attain to a total state of concentration and even to arrive at total silence?

— How can we arrive at an artistic and creative experience? What is the essence of music? What is the essence of art? What is the essence of literature?

— What is the indispensable utility of technology in the human life and its perfection?

— What is the meaning of story? Is history an interesting and meaningful story? Is there an aim in history? What are lessons of history?

— What am I? And what is my own specific role in the world? How can I train myself to fulfil this role?

One can formulate many more questions but care should be taken to see that these questions and topics do not get compressed within a rigid framework of a formal study and examination. These are all living questions and the only thing that can be done is to see that they arise spontaneously during the educational process, and the courses of study regarding them develop in an evolutionary way, developing with inner growth of the students. It is best when these questions arise in the context of the living experience of the students.

The handling of these questions and topics should be informal and the following methods can be suggested:

— Each student should be suggested to choose from a list of questions, and he should be free to choose any one of them in accordance with his needs of a deep inquiry;

— students should study these questions individually with a possibility of consultation with their teachers when needed;

— to enable individual study, the teachers should suggest relevant materials or books, or else he should prepare special worksheets;

— informal talks on these questions can be arranged, but they should not take the form of any moral or religious preaching; the temper of these studies should be scientific, interesting and profound;

— there should be a room of Silence in every school and college, and students should be free to go to that room, whenever they wish to have an inner reflection, meditation or quiet study;

— seminars on the relevant questions and topics should be held periodically in the school and colleges and the students and teachers should be encouraged to participate in them;

— debates, too, can be organised relating to these questions and topics, but an attempt should be made at the end of every debate to synthesize various points of view; an idea must develop that behind every point of view there is some truth, and we should grow into a comprehensive vision in which all truths can be reconciled and synthesized, and in which all conflicting views can be transcended;

— artistic books and sculptural pieces relating to these questions and topics should be displayed prominently not only in schools and colleges, but everywhere in towns, villages, etc.;

— other media of communication should also be widely used for this purpose. In particular, society should produce films relating to these subjects and they should be made available to students and teachers;

— informality in instruction, joy in learning, utter dedication and strictness in training, and wide comprehension in student-teacher relationship – these will, in brief, govern the methods of learning.

There are aspects of the mental, vital and physical education which contribute to the development of character. The methods in regard to these that have emerged through various experimentations can be suggested as follows:

— In its natural state, the human mind is always limited in its vision, narrow in its understanding, rigid in its conceptions and a special effort is need to enlarge it, make it supple and deep. Hence, it is very necessary to develop in the child the inclination and capacity to consider everything from as many points of view as possible. There is an exercise in this connection which gives greater suppleness and elevation to thought. It is as follows. A clearly formulated thesis is set; against it is opposed the anti-thesis, formulated with the same precision. Then by careful reflection the problem must be widened or transcended so that a synthesis is found which unites the two contraries in a larger, higher and more comprehensive idea.

— Another exercise is to control the mind from judging things and people. For true knowledge belongs to a region much higher than that of the human mind, even beyond that of pure ideas. The mind has got to be made silent and attentive in order to receive knowledge from above and manifest it.

— Still another exercise: whenever there is a disagreement on any matter, as a decision, as a decision to take, or an action to accomplish, one must not stick to one's own conception or point of view. On the contrary, one must try to understand the other person's point of view, put oneself in his place and, instead of quarrelling or even fighting, find out a solution which can reasonably satisfy both parties; there is always one for people of good will.

— A wide, subtle, rich, complex, attentive and quiet and silent mind is an asset not only for the discovery of the deeper ethical, aesthetic, psychic and spiritual realities, but also for manifesting their truths and powers.

— The vital being in us is the seat of impulses and desires, of enthusiasm and violence, of dynamic energy and desperate depression, of passions and revolt. The vital is a good worker, but most often it seeks its own satisfaction. If that is refused totally or even partially, it gets vexed, sulky and goes on strike.

— An exercise at these moments is to remain quiet and refuse to act. For it is important to realise that at such times one does stupid things and in a few minutes can destroy or spoil what one has gained in months of regular effort, losing thus all the progress made.

— Another exercise is to deal with the vital as one deals with a child in revolt, with patience perseverance showing it the truth and light, endeavoring to convince it and awaken in it the goodwill which for a moment was veiled.

— A wide, strong, clam but dynamic vital capable of right emotion, right decision, and right execution by force and energy, is an invaluable aid to the psychic and spiritual realisation.

— The body by its nature is a docile and faithful instrument. But it is very often misused by the mind with its dogmas, its rigid and arbitrary principles, and by the vital with its passions, its excesses and dissipations. It is these which are the cause of bodily fatigue, exhaustion and disease. The body must therefore be free from the tyranny of the mind and of the vital; and this can be done by training the body to feel and sense the psychic presence within and to learn to obey its governance. The emphasis on the development of strength, suppleness, calm, quiet, poise, grace and beauty in physical education, whether done by *Yogic Asanas* or by other methods of physical culture, such as games and sports, or Japanese Judo and similar exercise will ensure the contact of the body with the psychic centre and the body will learn to put forth at every minute the effort that is demanded of it; for it will have learnt to find rest in action, to replace through contact with universal forces the energies it spends consciously and usefully. Bu this sound and balanced life, a new harmony will manifest in the body, reflecting the harmony of the regions which will give it the perfect proportions and the ideal beauty of form. It will then be in a constant process of transformation, and it will be possible for it to escape the necessity of disintegration and destruction.

The role that physical education can play in the development of character has not been sufficiently understood. In our country, physical education has been neglected almost completely and this neglect is one of the causes of the low morale of the people. It is, therefore, necessary to bring forth the value of physical education not only in regard to the fitness of the body but also for the great contribution it makes for the intellectual, moral and spiritual development of character and personality.

It has been found necessary by recent research in yogic education that students should develop a high sense of physical culture and a bodily need of daily physical exercise. Our programme in schools and colleges should be so organised that everyday a student is able to devote at least one hour for physical education, either in the form of *Yogic Asanas* and allied exercise or in the form of gymnastics, athletics, aquatics or games.

There are many sports which help to form and necessitate the qualities of courage, hardihood, energetic action and initiative for skill, steadiness of will or rapid decision and action, the perception of what is to be done in an emergency and dexterity in doing it. Another invaluable result of these activities is the growth of the sporting spirit. That includes good humour and tolerance and consideration for all, a right attitude and friendliness to competitors and rivals, self-control and scrupulous observance of the laws of the games, fair play and avoidance of the use of foul means, an equal acceptance of victory or defeat without bad humour, resentment or ill-will towards successful competitors, loyal acceptance of the decisions of the appointed judge, umpire or referee. More important still is the custom of discipline, obedience, order, habit of team work, which certain games necessitate.

In the words of Sri Aurobindo :

> "If they (the above qualities) could be made more common not only in the life of the individual but in the national life and in the international where at the present day the opposite tendencies have become too rampant, existence in this troubled world of ours would be smoother and might open to a greater chance of concord and amity of which it

> stands very much in need...The nation which possesses them in the highest degree is likely to be strongest for victory, success and greatness, but also for the contribution it can make towards the bringing about of unity and more harmonious world order towards which we look as our hope for humanity's future."

At higher levels of education, it may be suggested that a critical study of values is itself an essential part of value-education. Exploration of all that mankind has thought on this subject should suitably be presented to the students, so that they have before them a wide spectrum of ideas which they can explore and experiment with. Topics such as man in the universe, aim of human life, concept of progress, definition of values, and ideals of liberty, equality and fraternity could be recommended as a necessary part of a special programme of character development.

Since values are those desirable ideals and goals which are intrinsic in themselves, and which, when achieved, or attempted to be achieved, have a deep sense of fulfilment of one or many or all parts and faculties of personality, it is necessary that the programme of character development should include a study of faculties and capacities that constitute our personality and the correlation of each faculty with its corresponding values.

Science and values should also be an important part of character development. Pursuit of the value of truth through science and self-knowledge as also the correlation of science and values with the theme of progress and welfare of human mind should be an important part of the progrmme.

13

Aurobindo Educational Centres

Sri Aurobindo Institute of Vocational Training

Sri Aurobindo Institute of Vocational Training offers to the youth in the age group of fifteen to thirty-five a six-month basic training in one of the 8 different trades, with special stress on practical work. Keeping in view our commitment to National Integration, the participants were selected from several states. Care was taken to choose boys and girls from economically weaker strata of society.

During the year under report, 93 youths completed the training course in two batches. In addition to the training in their respective trades the trainees attended a 10-day first aid course, basic training in computers and English and Hindi classes regularly and participated in the daily meditation. They also did one hour of cooperative manual labour (shramdan) every day and had one hour of physical education every evening-including 'keep-fit' exercises and vigorous games for which we have extensive facilities.

They were taken for picnics and sightseeing. They witnessed the various cultural and educational activities on the Ashram campus. The 6-month all-round training and living and interacting in the uplifting Ashram ambience provides the trainees an opportunity for integral personality growth. The trainees were advised about career options.

Sponorships for Miscellancous Academic and Other Coures

Mountaineering and sports

Rs. 6,991/- were paid to 2 parents for training in Basic Water Sport course and Rs. 2,161 to 2 persons for mountaineering course.

IGNOU/Open school/miscellaneous

A sum of Rs.87,346/- was awarded as scholarships to 16 students who are pursuing academics in various fields. Details are as under:

— IGNOU: 4 candidates appeared for various exams under IGNOU.

— Open School: 1 candidate under Open School.

— Other Courses: 1 candidate for Library Science course at Annamalai University, 1 candidate for naturopathy, 1 candidate for call centre training, 1 candidate for HDENSM, 1 candidate for computer and English course, 1 candidate for course at British School of Language, 2 candidates for other courses.

— New Delhi Schools/Colleges : 2 candidates were granted scholarships.

— Other Schools : 1 candidate was granted scholarship.

Music

A sum of Rs.13,000/- was awarded by the Sri Aurobindo Education Society as Scholarships to students for continuing with training in their chosen fields (instrumental, vocal, dance). Three (3) students benefited from this scholarship.

Computers

Computers were arranged for distribution to needy village schools.

Scholarships to Teacher-Trainees

Rs.1,06,000 was the total amount spent on scholarships to 20 teacher-trainees by the Sri Aurobindo Education Society which runs a 3-year Teacher Training Institute. For teachers who are in the 1st, 2nd and 3rd year of training the monthly scholarships ranged from Rs.400/- to Rs.700/-. The Society also takes care of their board and lodging.

Scholarships for Vocational Training

A sum of Rs.1,76,400/- was the amount incurred on boarding & lodging and stipend (Rs.300/- per month) paid to 98 students of the Sri Aurobindo Institute of Vocational Training who underwent basic training in various 6-month courses.

Free Distribution of Clothes, Books, Toys

During the year under report, many of our well-wishers donated sweaters and blankets which were distributed to the needy. Substantial quantity of old/new clothes, books and toys were also collected and sent to needy village schools.

Computer Distribution

Computers were donated to us by our well-wishers. Some had parts that were not working. So all the working parts of different computers were integrated together to form working sets (set of CPU, monitor, keyboard, mouse) of computers. Two such working computers were given to a Madhya Pradesh school.

THE MOTHER'S INTERNATIONAL SCHOOL

School Result (2005-2006 Session)

The secondary school results in the Mother's International School were outstanding this year as well. A total of 180 students appeared for the class X Board exams and as many as 60 students scored above 90% marks in the aggregate, the highest being 96.80% scored by Mukta Nag. The results were cent per cent as usual. Barring 2 students who were placed in the 2nd division, the rest scored first division and above. Five students scored cent per cent marks in Mathematics and 4 students had cent per cent in Science. There was one cent per cent in Social Studies as well. The total number of distinctions in different subjects was 811. The average percentage in different subjects was : English 85.50%, Maths 87.31%, Science 88.21%, Social Studies 88.36%, Hindi 79.07%, Sanskrit 88.84%, French 83%.

In class XII, we sent 153 students for the Board exams. The results were 100%. There was only one second division. The highest aggregate in the Science Stream was 93.80%, in the Commerce Stream 93.40% and in the Humanities Stream 91.20%. Shivani Saxena topped in the Science Stream, Gypsa Srivastava in the Commerce Stream and Gautam Khazanchi in the Humanities Stream. In Physics as many as 18 students scored 95% marks. In Mathematics three students had cent per cent marks.

Talent festival (April 2005)

The entire school participated in a talent festival. There were a number of items to choose from. It was a joyous day since each child got a chance to express himself and realize his potential. Certificates of merit were given.

MIS participation in the Inter-school Events (July-Sept. 2005)

Chinmaya Youth Festival organised by Chinmaya Mission:

Niharika Sehgal of class X got the 1st position in the Art competition and MIS secured the 1st position in dance competition.

Students' Science Seminar organised by the Directorate of Education held at Science Centre: Paarth Gupta of class X secured second position for his project.

8th Shri Surendra Nath Jauhar 'Faquir' Memorial Invitational Football Tournament 2005 16 schools participated in the tournament.

— Winners were the Modern School (Barakhamba Road)

— Runners up were the Mother's International School

Carmel Convent Inter-school Quiz Competition: Shreyas K. Reddy, Nabankur Deb and Rohan Ghosh of class XII got the 1st prize. MIS won the Overall Trophy.

Junior Sri Debate organised by the Shri Ram School, D.L.F. Paartha Sarathi of class VII won the award for the Best Speaker. MIS won the Best School Trophy.

Outlook Debate Contest organised by the Outlook magazine, held at Tagore International School. Stuti Rawat of class XII of our school participated and secured the Second position; she also qualified for zonals.

Fundamental Quiz organized by The Times of India, held at Siri Fort Auditorium MIS secured the third position.

BOSCO PSI-PHI 2005 organised by Don Bosco School, Alaknanda. MIS won the Overall Trophy.

Drug Abuse Awareness Symposium organised by Modern School, Barakhamba Road: MIS bagged the 1st Prize, for the second consecutive year.

Social Science Quiz organized by Vasant Valley School:. MIS secured the 1st position.

National Mathematics Talent Search organised by Manav Sthali School: Nikhil Kumar of class VIII and Paarth Gupta of class IX won the First position. Pankaj Choudhary of class VII, Shraya Agarwal and Jyoti Gupta of class VIII, Anindita Pal and Aman Goel of class X won the Second position.

E-Spice organised by DPS, Noida:

— *Zarquon Test:* Sarvagya Sharma and Akshay Verma of class X won the 1st position.

— *Quiz & Cross Word:* Sarvagya Sharma and Akshay Verma won the 2nd position.

— *Programming:* Milind Ganjoo of class X and Pranav Gupta of class XII won the 1st position.

— *Group Discussion:* Milind Ganjoo won the 2nd position.

HT Pace Inquizitive held at Talkatora Stadium. Shreyas Reddy and Nabankur Deb of class XII won the 1st position in Delhi and also won the Overall Trophy at the National Level.

Connect 2005 organised by Springdales School, Pusa Road:

— *Quiz:* Sarvagya Sharma and Akshay Verma won the 1st position.

— *Gaming:* Raag Yadava won the 2nd position

— *Surprise Event:* Akshay Verma won the 1st position.

MIS won the Overall Best School Trophy.

Economics Festival 'ECONOMITE' organised by Modern School, Vasant Vihar:

— *Panel Discussion:* Utathya Chattopadhyaya won the 1st position

— *Symposium:* Aditi Oberoi and Ashish Virmani won the 2nd position.

Economics Festival 'ECONORM' organised by D.P.S., R.K. Puram:

— *Symposium:* Aditi Oberoi won the 2nd Best Speaker position.

— *Quiz :* Ashish Virmani and Shreyas Reddy won the 1st position.

Inter-school Literacy Festival organised by Springdales School, Dhaula Kuan. Gayatri Nair won the 1st position in Declamation. Sadhvi Takyar secured the 2nd position in Recitation and Tarini Bandhu and Vibhuti Verma secured the 2nd position in Story Writing.

Modem 2005 organised by Modern School, Vasant Vihar.

— *Quiz :* Akshay Verma of class X and Sarvagya Sharma of class XII won the 1st position.

— *Programming :* Milind Ganjoo and Pranav Gupta of class X won the 3rd position.

MIS won the Overall Trophy.

Participation of MIS students in Inter-school Events (Oct. 2005 to March 2006)

Computer

In Dynamix hosted by Ramjas School, R.K. Puram, MIS secured the Overall Winners Trophy. In Code Wars computer festival hosted by D.P.S. Vasant Kunj, MIS won the Overall Winners Trophy. In Force Fest organized by A.P.J. School, Sheikh Sarai, MIS won Overall 2nd position.

English

English Forensics Competition in Original Oratory held at America School: MIS stood First and won the Best Speaker award.

Science

In the Anveshika Inter-school Science Festival organised by Sardar Patel Vidyalaya, MIS won the Best Overall School Trophy. Kritika Adhikary got the First Prize and Rs. 30,000 in Green Olympiad organised by TERI. In the Science and Technology week organised by Gyan Bharati School, MIS won the Best Overall School Trophy.

— *Quiz:* Our school stood First in the Japan Quiz 2005 held by the Japanese Cultural Information Centre, Embassy of Japan. In the TERRA Environment Quiz, MIS reached the semifinal round

— *Theatre:* In the Theatre Festival held at Sanskriti School, MIS won the Runners-up Trophy and the Best Actor award.

— *Sanskrit:* The school won the Overall Trophy in the Shloka Recitation Competition held at D.P.S. Mathura Road, our students getting First positions in different categories.

Annual Events

The Accolades Day was celebrated on 12 November 2005. The Annual Day celebration "Piercing the Veils of Darkness" took place on 10 December 2005, in which vignettes of the contribution of great philosophers and great teachers to the evolution of mankind were presented through beautiful tableaux-a vedic gurukula 'The Rishi and the Brahmacharis', battlefield of Kurkshetra 'The Divine Teacher and the Human Disiciple', Buddha's teaching 'The Seeker and the Teacher'. There were, too, presentations on Socrates, Sufi wisdom, Shantiniketan, Maria Montessori, the modern classics The Little Prince & Jonathan Livingstone Seagull and the Integral Education of Sri Aurobindo & the Mother. The celebration concluded with 'Raag Symphony' by the school orchestra including presentations based on Indian classical music & compositions by Pandit Ravi Shankar and Rabindranath Tagore.

Ms Cherie Booth (Blair) visits the MIS

The Mother's International School took great pride in hosting the visit of Ms Cherie Booth, QC, wife of the British Prime Minister Mr Tony Blair on 8 August 2005. The VVIP was offered a glimpse of the quintessential Indian culture through a presentation of yoga and a Rajasthani folk dance, each of them exhibiting the perfect synchronicity and splendid harmony that is the hallmark of the composite culture of India. In her speech she expressed her sincere appreciation of these performances and also of the efforts taken by the Mother's International School towards a proper realization of the Indo-UK Exchange Programme 'Dreams+Teams' conceived and organized by the British Council. In her entry into the Visitor's Book Ms Booth thanked the School profusely for "a display of excellence in every way-spiritual, cultural, physical and mental".

Bharat Ratna Pandit Ravi Shankar visits the M.I.S. (7th March 2006)

It was a very special day for the M.I.S. The famous Pandit Ravi Shankar, who was the pioneer in making Indian Classical music popular in the West, and thus bringing the East & the West closer to each other, visited our campus on 7 March 2006. He was received at the gate, and after a visit to the Shrine he attended a Special Assembly at the M.I.S. where Pandit Barunkumar Pal, one of his senior disciples, conducted a beautiful orchestra: a large group of students participated-playing various melodies on violin, sitar, Hawaiian guitar, flute and other instruments with perfect harmony. It was nice to hear the great sitar maestro say that he was overwhelmed by the superb presentation. He spent most of the afternoon here and was shown round the campus.

Tours

The following students tours were arranged during the year :

1. Class IV Jaipur
2. Class V Aurovalley, Haridwar, Rishikesh, Dehradun, Rajaji National Park
3. Class VI Madhuban, Talla Ramgarh
4. Class VII Aurangabad, Ajanta and Ellora
5. Class VIII Nainital (Rock-climbing, trekking)
6. Class IX Pondicherry and Auroville
7. Class X /XI Dalhousie

Scholarships to Mis Students

Given by the MIS

36 Sri Aurobindo Merit Scholarships were awarded to deserving students of The Mother's International School for their excellent academic performance. Scholarships ranging from Rs.2,400/- to Rs. 6,000/- were awarded as 1st, 2nd, 3rd prizes to these students. A sum of Rs.1,46,400/- was given away as scholarships to these children. 34 other scholarships were given to students for there achievements in various fields from other funds. Rs.13,415 were spent on other scholarships/prizes. An additional amount of Rs. 1,12,080 was given as freeships to 8 children of volunteers.

Given by the SAES

Rs. 54,200/- were paid to 4 needy students.

Mirambika School

Mirambika school and the teacher training activity has completed 25 years this year. The progress made over these 25 years has borne fruit in that there have been several occasions when Integral Education has been discussed, practised, and the approach has seen many children qualify and enter the world of work. Last year Mirambika had the opportunity to hold meetings to orient parents on Integral Education in which Partho, Mathhijs, Neeltje and Anuradha participated as resource persons. The outcome of the meetings had a far-reaching impact on creating a awareness and conviction about the implicit worth of the approach and methods.

The children took part in several activities related to sports, and a physical demonstration was held. There were tours to Ramgarh, Dalhousie and Aurovalley. As a part of the learning process, the children also went to Agra, visited several biodiversity projects in Delhi and participated in the Mathematics Olympiad. There were seminars in which our teachers presented papers on mental, vital, and physical development and shared their experiences gained through action research.

Our teachers also held teacher orientation camps in Kechla, Angul in Orissa in which teachers from Integral Schools in Orissa participated. Community service camps in Ramgarh were also held.

10 teacher-trainees completed their 3-year course and have found jobs in several schools in India. Our volunteers also contributed to developing and using the Free Progress education principles to construct curriculum in science, mathematics and social science teaching. Mirambika's experience was also documented in an NCERT supported study on Teacher Education: 'The Role of the Reflective Teacher and Innovative Teacher Education Curriculum'.

This year 16 children completed their 10-year schooling in Mirambika and joined the Mother's International School and other schools in Delhi to finish their High School. 20 new children joined the school at the Red and Blue Group level.

The Mirambika team has worked specially during this 25th year to introspect and gain from their experience to envisage new directions of growth in the future.

The annual function 'Thanksgiving 2006' was held on 24 March 2006. Besides the items presented by the students of different Groups, the teacher-trainees performed a delightful Western folk dance.

Matri Karuna Vidyalaya

Another glorious action-packed year for MKV has left its mark on this much-loved and tenderly nurtured institution. An over-all improvement in academic standard and behaviour of the MKV students is noteworthy. The dedicated and skilful service of the Principal and the teachers continue to work wonders.

Eight children from class V said goodbye to MKV. Six of them were absorbed by local Govt. schools after successfully clearing their entrance tests, one even made it to a Public School and another happily moved to the boarding school in Ratlam.

The new academic session saw 14 toddlers comfortably settled in the Nursery Section. A few conditional offers made to the parents to fulfil the family planning requirement, were realised in mid-session, bringing the total to 20 pupils. A few vacant places were filled with new admission to Prep, I, II and III.

As usual, MKV remained open during school vacations. The Summer School was managed by MIS students of class XII. In spite of sizzling heat and dust, the enthusiastic force of 200 youngsters worked out innovative and enjoyable teaching activities based on the school syllabus.

For a unique music workshop held under Guru-Shishya-Parampara, children from classes III, IV and V were given a chance to stay on the Ashram premises along with pupils from Ushagram, Madhya Pradesh, Dehradun and the MIS. Each child armed with his/her own musical instrument, spent productive hours playing with the diverse group. The enriching experience of activity-filled days augmented children's self-confidence and communication skills. Each participant underwent a rare experience of blending in with people from diverse social and cultural backgrounds.

Students of classes III, IV and V worked under Mohini Anand and Mitu's supervision. Activity-based learning took place with the help of Mr Sharma (a fabulous retired Maths teacher) and Shubha (MIS parent). Almost all the children are making an effort to converse in English. Chandra, a hardworking trainee, kept them busy at the Handmade Paper Unit.

Premshila, a teacher-trainee, took care of dance, music and drama. The children also tried their hands at clay modelling and wood work. Twelve students participated in HUDCO Painting Competition.

Jatin, the budding artist, who learns at Matri Kala Mandir, has been awarded Avantika, Khshitij and several other certificates of merit. The Sports Day held on the Children's Day went off very well.

All the national and religious festivals were celebrated by MKV. Trainees spent hours researching and planning the activities. As a result each occasion was complemented with interesting displays of art work, creative writing as well as activities like storytelling, drama, music and dance. MKV orchestra performed for Matri Kala Mandir to pay homage to Sri Aurobindo and the Mother, sang devotional songs, recited Durga Stotra and performed a dance based on Durga Stuti on 21 February 2006.

There was an exhibition with a difference on the Annual Day. Each class worked on a separate topic. This resulted in an amazing display of hand-crafted exhibits done in clay, paper and wood. Children also indulged in a fair amount of creative writing.

Thankfully the generous donors continue to help in making the children look well- groomed, well-nourished and happy. Books and excursions, including a wonderful day at the District Park, are taken care of by the donors' generosity.

Parents' meetings have been well-attended and appreciated, mostly by mothers. In some of the gatherings trainees performed skits based on values required for harmonious community living. Swami Ranjit's talks on self-discipline, cleanliness, water harvesting and tree planting were well received.

Quite a few illiterate parents came forward to learn through a software prepared by Tata Consultancy Services. These classes were held twice a week.

MKV appears to be functioning well as a training ground for teacher-trainees. Arrival of three new trainees was a great help.

Matri Kala Mandir

Matri Kala Mandir, which offers training in fine arts, performing arts, etc., has witnessed an increasing inflow of learners in all the courses-enough proof of acceptance of Indian classical music and dance forms by the younger generation even in this era of Westernization of Indian society. Moreover, the stress and strain of modern days drags the elder ones too to take shelter in Indian classical music-be it vocal or instrumental. Hence we are having more elderly learners in vocal music.

At present we have 573 students on our rolls. In fact, the number is limited by room facilities. Besides the music, dance and painting classes, MKM conducted gymnastics, Tae kwon do, table tennis and yoga classes too.

Classes for students of MIS, Mirambika and Matri Karuna Vidyalaya were also held after school hours. Two programmes were held during the year-one on 20 August 2005 and the other on 16 February 2006-in which a large number of students displayed their talents in painting, various Indian dance forms, Hindustani & Carnatic vocal music and Indian classical and Western music on instruments.

Constructions

The construction of the new auditorium building of M.I.S. was started.

Publications

Four issues of the quarterly magazine The Call Beyond and a Souvenir were brought out this year.

Koraput Unit, Orissa

Value Education

Sri Aurobindo Education Society has been regularly conducting Value Education programmes for teachers, teacher-trainees and students in Delhi, Orissa and Uttaranchal.

We have developed our own module. We begin the day with yogasanas and pranayam. We then have interactive sessions. At the end of the three days each participant gets a set of books.

In the recent past we have shifted our focus from urban to rural participants so as to reach into the interiors of our vast country, bringing in awareness in the youth of rural India.

Teacher Programmes

Workshops for Teachers at Kechla, district Koraput, Orissa

We conducted 2 workshops for teachers from Integral Schools of Orissa at Kechla, district Koraput, Orissa as follows:

1. There were 21 participants and 6 resource persons in the workshop held from 22 to 24 May 2005.
2. There were 41 participants and 6 resource persons in the workshop conducted from 27 to 24 May 2005.

We organised one workshop at Dera, district Angul, in which we had 50 participants and 4 resource persons.

Programme Objectives:

(a) Sensitivity towards environment.

(b) Awareness of using waste materials in teaching-learning process.

(c) Dignity of labour.

(d) Self-awareness and consciousness through meditation, introspection, 'question-answer' sessions.

(e) Integration of values in subject teaching-courage, confidence, etc.

Activities, included demonstration of how to teach creatively, how to develop values in students, how to involve and educate parents, meditation, drama & role play, environmental awareness through campus cleaning and avoiding use of polythene, arts & crafts, singing rhymes, etc.

Katni Unit, M.P.

Sponsorships

During the year we had 18 children under our sponsorship. 9 children were sponsored in a school in Rewa, M.P. and the other 9 in a school in Ratlam, M.P. The amount spent on the sponsorship of these 18 children during the year was Rs.1,60,000/-.

Scholarships

Two children benefited from the scholarships given by the Society. A sum of Rs.17,000/- was incurred on these scholarships.

Report of the Nainital Unit, Uttaranchal

Value Education Workshops for Teachers/ Teacher-Training and Student

Sri Aurobindo Education Society has been regularly conducting Value Education programmes for teachers, teacher-trainees and students in Delhi, Orissa and Uttaranchal.

We have developed our own module. We begin the day with yogasanas and pranayam. We then have interactive sessions. At the end of the three days each participant gets a set of books. In the recent past we have shifted our focus from urban to rural participants so as to reach into the interiors of our vast country, bringing in awareness in the youth of rural India.

Student Programmes

Workshop for Students at Talla Ramgarh, district Nainital, Uttaranchal

Two 3-day workshops on Value Education and Leadership training were organised from 17 to 19 May

2005 and 20, 21 & 23 May 2005 at Madhuban Ashram, Talla Ramgarh. There were 55 students from classes 9th and 11th from Shri Narayan Swami Inter College, village Talla Ramgarh and 45 students of class 8th from Saraswati Shishu Mandir, Sunrise School, Talla Ramgarh and Rajkiya Uchchatar Madhyamik Vidyalaya, village Pichaltaana, district Nainital.

These workshops were meant to create self-awareness and build one's relationship with others, nature and surroundings. The students were made conscious of the influx of commercialisation and the web it creates in society, their role in the development of their society, their village and the country.

The programme consisted of : yogasanas, health awareness sessions and medical check-up by Dr Pradhan, ex-Professor of Physiology, MAMC and Dr Ishwaran, a medical practitioner working extensively on integral health; sessions on value education were conducted by Ms Vijay Bharti, educator of value-based education and Ms Smita Gupta, trained counsellor and social worker who has worked as a school counsellor.

The day started with a practical session of yogasanas. Students were made aware of the beneficial effects of yoga. Later, sessions were taken on value education using the methodology of stories, group discussions, individual introspection, role plays, games and activities.

The students filled in an integral health questionnaire specially designed for these workshops. The concept of integral health was introduced which includes spiritual, mental, physical and social health. The questionnaire helped them in understanding the importance of a balanced diet, the relationship one has with family members, one's contribution to the home, to the surroundings, one's religious values, thoughts, attitudes and belief system, etc. This was followed by detailed discussions individually and in groups on dental hygiene and care, common eye ailments is and how to take care of eyes, importance of good sleep and drinking 8 glasses of water daily. A special session was taken with the girls on changes during puberty, the importance of personal hygiene and cleanliness and special care during menstruation.

The sessions were planned to bring out awareness of the physical & mental capacities and emotional responses of the students. They were made aware of their potential, weaknesses, fears and aspirations. Through stories and situation analysis we took them through a journey of their values and the value crisis that exists within oneself and in society at large. They were made to see the inner dynamics which plays a major role in their behaviour. A lot of emphasis was placed on building up confidence in them and encouraging public speaking. Social issues like cheating in exams, consumption and addiction of tobacco and gutka, early marriage of girls, gender differentiation, environmental degradation and conservation, etc. were discussed after having asked them to prepare role plays and skits on these topics. They were made aware of their responses and their responsibility, and of the harmful effects of using polythene. They were taught how to make paper bags from old newspapers.

As part of the programme on health-awareness, the concept of integral health was introduced and discussed. A specially designed questionnaire was given to the students on the basis of which individual counselling and a complete health check-up was done by the team of doctors.

Music can be a very important source of stimulating patriotism and uplifting human consciousness. Keeping this aim in mind, music sessions were organised where songs of different languages were taught.

All the students were given a set of books.

The workshop was well appreciated as could be seen from the feedback received from the students.

Abstract of Value Education Workshops

A Total of three workshops were conducted for Students as follows :

Date	Place of Workshop	No. of Participants
17-19 May 2005	Talla Ramgarh, Uttaranchal	55
20-13 May 2005	Talla Ramgarh, Uttaranchal	45
	Total	100

Scholarships for Miscellaneous Academic and Other Courses

Academic Scholarships

School	No. of Children	Amount (Rs.)
At Nainital	2	12,000/-
At Madhuban	20	1,05,394/-
Total	22	1,17,394/-

Mountaineering and Sports

Two persons were granted scholarship for training in Basic water sport course amounting to Rs. 6,991/- and an amount of Rs. 2,161/- was spent on 2 candidates for Mountaineering Course. Total amount spent was Rs. 9,152/-.

Camps at Van Niwas, Nainital

Adventure (Youth) Camps

Adventure (Youth) Camps during Summer

Ten 8-day Adventure (Youth) Camps were organised from April to June 2005 in which 1,045 youth (mostly students) took part. They were mostly students from

Heritage School, Sawan Public School, Mehta Vidyalaya of Bharatiya Vidya Bhavan & M.I.S., Sri Aurobindo Youth Council, Baroda, Pilani, Udavi School, Auroville, Birla Balika Vidyapeeth & Birla Public School, Sri Aurobindo Integral School, K.V.O. & Udayachal High School, Mumbai, K.V.O. & Shri Kutchi Mitra Mandal, Hyderabad, Sri Aurobindo Society Centre Surat, Bangalore, B.Y. Bhavan's Mehta Vidyalaya, Chennai, M.P., The Mother's Academy, Patna, Hariharanand Public School, Haridwar, Amar Nath Vidya Ashram, Mathura, Heritage School, Ramgarh.

The campers enjoyed a 5-day course in rock-climbing which was packed with fun and adventure. On the first day, they learnt the elementary climbing techniques during a scrambling tour over rocky terrain. The next two days they climbed rock-faces with the help of ropes. The fourth day had rappelling-the spectacular leaping down a rock-face using ropes. On the last day, the trainees did river-crossing. Apart from the thrill and adventure, one gets a practical lesson in courage, endurance, alertness, discipline and co-operation, through this training.

Adventure (Youth) Camps during Autumn

Two Youth Camps were conducted from 9 to 26 October 2005 for 160 participants from DAV Centenary Public School, Community Develeopoment & Health Project, St. Stephens Hospital, Haryana, Amar Nath Vidya Ashram, Mathura.

Sri Aurobindo National Integration Camps

Two 8-day Sri Aurobindo National Integration Camps were held from 11 June 2005 with similar activities. There were 244 participants who came from 19 states. In addition to national integration activities like group singing of patriotic songs in several Indian languages the campers did rock-climbing, river-crossing and trekking.

The campers learnt to live a spiritually oriented and harmonious collective life.

The morning 'keep-fit' session followed by shramdan, trekking, games, the eating and living together-all helped in bringing the campers close to each other in a healthy and meaningful way.

The participants got an opportunity to develop higher life values through meditation and satsang, through cultural exchange, interaction with ashramites and other campers, through the benign influence of the ordered and creative life, through a communion with nature and through the spiritually charged atmosphere of the place. They learnt to channelise their energies along positive, constructive and creative lines.

Treks started with the shortest one to Land's End and covered several interesting places, including the 15 km trek to Kainchi temple, and ended with the trek to Naina Peak. The treks also provided ideal conditions for integration, as friendships are formed during the course of the trek when the campers begin to interact amongst themselves as they go through the scenic forest routes.

At 7 p.m. every day, the participants collected in the meditation hall to meditate and listen to lectures on subjects like 'self-awareness', 'national integration', 'integration within', or any other spiritual topic.

Another SANIC was conducted specially for teachers from 21 June 2005-with similar activities. A valedictory function was held on 28 June which was graced by Mahamahim Rajyapal of Uttaranchal, His Excellency Sudarshan Agarwal who gave away certificates to the participants. He emphasised the importance of such National Integration Camps in a country like India which is like a bouquet of various religions & races.

Bibliography

Banerjee, S.P., *Philosophy of Sri Aurobindo,* Aavishkar Publishers and Distributors, Jaipur, 2004

Purani A. B., The Life of Sri Aurobindo, 1981.

Ghose, Aurobindo, *Secret of the Veda,* New U.S. Edition, Lotus Press (WI), January 1995.

Pandit, Sri M. P., *Bases of Sadhana,* 1981.

_______________ ., *Bases of Tantra Sadhana,* 1981

_______________ ., *Commentaries on Sri Aurobindo's Thought Vol. I.,* 1981

_______________ ., *Commentaries on the Mother's Min Vol. I.,* 1981.

_______________ ., *Dhyana (meditation),* 1981

_______________ ., *Gems from the Tantras (Kularnava) Vol. 1.,* 1981

_______________ ., *Gems from the Tantras Vol. 2.,* 1981

_______________ ., *Heart of Sadhana,* 1981

_______________ ., *How Do I Begin?,* 1981

_______________ ., *How Do I Proceed?,* 1981

_______________ ., *Japa (mantra yoga),* 1981

_______________ ., *Kundalini Yoga,* 1981

_______________ ., *Legends in The Life Divine,* 1981

_______________ ., *Life Beautiful,* 1981

_______________ ., *Lights on the Tantra,* 1981

_______________ ., *A Peep into His Past,* 1981

_______________ ., *Mystic Approach to the Veda & the Upanishad,* 1981

_______________ ., *Occult Lines Behind Life,* 1981

_______________ ., *Pandit in America,* 1981

_______________ ., *Pitfalls in Sadhana,* 1981

________________., *Selected Works of M.P. Pandit Vol. 2: The Mother*, 1981

________________., *Selected Works of M.P. Pandit Vol. 3: Yoga*, 1981

________________., *Selected Works of M.P. Pandit Vol. 4: Traditions*, 1981

________________., *Selected Works of M.P. Pandit Vol. 5: The World*, 1981

Index